Be the Best You Can Be

Chicken Soup for the Soul: Be the Best You Can Be
Inspiring True Stories about Goals & Values for Kids & Preteens
Amy Newmark, Dr. Milton Boniuk. Foreword by David Leebron.

Published by CSS Boniuk, an imprint of Chicken Soup for the Soul Publishing, LLC
www.chickensoup.com. Copyright © 2015 by Chicken Soup for the Soul Publishing, LLC.
All Rights Reserved.

The publisher gratefully acknowledges the many publishers and individuals who granted
Chicken Soup for the Soul permission to reprint the cited material.

Front cover photo courtesy of iStockPhoto.com/renplett (© renplett).
Back cover and interior photo courtesy of iStockPhoto.com/Lazarev (© Lazarev).
Photo of Amy Newmark courtesy of Susan Morrow at SwickPix.

Cover and Interior Design & Layout by Brian Taylor

Distributed to the booktrade by Simon & Schuster. SAN: 200-2442

Publisher's Cataloging-In-Publication Data
(Prepared by The Donohue Group, Inc.)

Chicken soup for the soul : be the best you can be : inspiring true
  stories about goals & values for kids & preteens / [compiled by] Amy
  Newmark [and] Dr. Milton Boniuk ; foreword by David Leebron, President
  of Rice University.

   pages ; cm

   Summary: A collection of inspirational stories about kids making good decisions, doing
the right thing, and being kind.
   Interest age level: 007-013.
   ISBN: 978-1-942649-00-7

   1. Self-actualization (Psychology) in children--Literary collections--Juvenile literature. 2.
Self-actualization (Psychology) in children--Anecdotes--Juvenile literature. 3. Children--
Conduct of life--Literary collections--Juvenile literature. 4. Children--Conduct of life--Anec-
dotes--Juvenile literature. 5. Self-actualization (Psychology) in children--Literary collections.
6. Self-actualization (Psychology) in children--Anecdotes. 7. Children--Conduct of life--
Literary collections. 8. Children--Conduct of life--Anecdotes. 9. Anecdotes. I. Newmark,
Amy. II. Boniuk, Milton. III. Leebron, David W. IV. Title: Be the best you can be : inspiring
true stories about goals & values for kids & preteens

BF637.S4 C45 2015
158.1/083   2015931355

PRINTED IN THE UNITED STATES OF AMERICA
on acid∞free paper

25 24 23 22 21 20 19 18 17 16 15   01 02 03 04 05 06 07 08 09 10 11

Be the Best You Can Be

Inspiring True Stories
about Goals & Values for
Kids & Preteens

Amy Newmark & Dr. Milton Boniuk
Foreword by David W. Leebron

Chicken Soup for the Soul Publishing, LLC
Cos Cob, CT

The Boniuk Foundation
www.theboniukfoundation.org

Changing lives one story at a time™
www.chickensoup.com

Contents

❶

~Making Your Best Effort~

❷

~Doing the Right Thing~

❸
~Accepting Differences~

❹
~Appreciating Your Family~

❺
~Handling Bullies~

❻

~Having Confidence in Yourself~

❼

~Being Generous~

❽
~Making True Friends~

❾
~Accepting Responsibility~

❿
~Being Kind~

⑪

~Being Grateful~

⑫

~Getting Through Tough Times~

Foreword

We undertake the education of our children in many ways and for many purposes. We educate our children to give them knowledge, to impart skills, to inculcate values, and to develop character. We use many different means to educate our children, from the examples we set to traditional classroom instruction to the use of the newest digital technologies. But from the beginning of human history, one of the most common ways we educate our children is through stories.

Such stories can teach us and inspire us along many dimensions. They can teach us to be strong and confident in the face of adversity. They can teach us to be kind, generous and forgiving to others, and to be grateful for those who seek to help us. They can inspire us to be bold enough to change what is wrong in our lives, or wrong in the world we see.

The stories in this volume were selected by Dr. Milton Boniuk and the team listed in his introduction, and published with the support of The Boniuk Foundation. Dr. Boniuk and his wife Laurie are two of the most remarkable people I have met. They have generously devoted substantial resources to fostering religious tolerance in particular, but also improving the education of our children to instill broad values of tolerance and appreciation for diversity of all kinds. They believe that the education of our children is the foundation of a better society.

This work takes place not only as in this publication through the efforts of the Boniuk Foundation, but also through an allied endeavor at Rice University, The Boniuk Institute for the Study and Advancement of Religious Tolerance. The mission of the institute, founded in 2013, is "to understand and promote religious tolerance by using innovative methods to" undertake research, produce educational programming, and foster dialogue. It identifies religious *intolerance* as one of the root causes of war, discrimination, and violence in our world, and is committed to undertake those educational and research activities that will begin to eliminate such intolerance. (You can find more information at www.boniuk.rice.edu.)

While the goal of this volume is considerably broader, and it addresses many of the values and behaviors we seek to instill in our children, almost all of them also affect the degree to which we practice and foster tolerant and indeed welcoming attitudes toward the differences we see in others. The Boniuks sincerely hope, as do so many of us, that through such efforts we can raise new generations that will end the hatred and violence that has ruined so many lives. This volume of brief stories celebrates the very best in the human spirit, and is worth reading both to our children and to ourselves.

~David W. Leebron
President, Rice University

Introduction

O ver a decade ago, I concluded that my primary philanthropic goal should be to promote religious tolerance, and I decided to start at the university level. In November 2003 I met with Malcom Gillis, then president of Rice University, and proposed making a pledge to endow a program to promote religious tolerance at Rice University. Six months later, in April 2004, The Boniuk Center at Rice was established.

The Center did good work, and hosted a variety of excellent programs, but it did not take long for me to realize that the goal of universal tolerance would be very difficult to achieve, and that a greater effort would be required. Historically, our world has been one where religious differences, and the desire for wealth and power over others, have been the primary reasons for most major conflicts.

During 2012 and 2013, after a series of discussions with the current Rice President David Leebron, my wife Laurie and I decided to make a further commitment to tolerance, and a mutual decision was made to expand The Boniuk Center into The Boniuk Institute for the Study and Advancement of Religious Tolerance. Part of this new commitment was to support new projects that we felt would be helpful in changing our society for the better. Hundreds of organizations worldwide have tried to eliminate hate speech, and to promote interfaith relations and diversity. In spite of all those efforts, the world has actually become less tolerant, especially in the area of religious tolerance.

As a member of the Houston Holocaust Museum board since its founding, I have witnessed the wonderful efforts that education programs for students and teachers can have, but I have felt that many students, who were positively affected initially by the programs, frequently went home to prejudiced parents who countered the positive effects of these educational programs. In addition, the abuse of our constitutional right to freedom of speech, and the spread of the Internet and social media, has resulted in the promotion of hatred and intolerance.

We recognized a need for new approaches. At The Boniuk Center in 2010, I came up with the idea of sponsoring symposia on intra-faith conflicts starting with the Abrahamic religions, and The Boniuk Center hosted symposia on Judaism, Christianity, and Islam. A survey on the religious background and tolerance attitudes of students at Rice University occurred in January of 2015. We hope this survey will be replicated at other universities throughout the country. We hope the survey program will help us determine what students and others feel are the changes necessary within themselves, their religions, and society to promote universal tolerance and peace.

We are also working on projects to foster better understanding of different approaches taken within major religions toward their religious texts. One of these projects is the Quran project, which is primarily educational, and is scheduled to begin soon under the direction of Emran El-Badawi, PhD, Program Director and Assistant Professor of Arab Studies at the University of Houston. This project will entail the publication of two volumes. The first volume will be an original Arabic edition of the Quran with an accepted English translation. The second volume will contain a brief history of Islam, a list with description of the seventy-three potential sects, and a discussion of controversial areas by representatives of the major Islamic sects.

Still, it is not enough. We need to start with a younger audience. We need to supplement our existing worldwide programs with educational programs that start with preschool children and continue throughout the entire scholastic experience. In conjunction with education, it is important to try to transform our religions, many of which have a long history of violence and intolerance, toward a more tolerant viewpoint, not only toward other religions, but also within branches or sects of some major religious groups.

I have long been a fan of the Chicken Soup for the Soul books, and I realized that this type of book could be of great help in reaching the younger demographic audience that I wanted to reach. I decided to pursue that possibility. I reached out to Chicken Soup for the Soul, and I was answered with enthusiasm. I was given the opportunity to meet with Bill Rouhana and Amy Newmark, the CEO and Publisher, respectively, of Chicken Soup for the Soul since they led a group that acquired it in 2008. Bill and Amy hosted me for an all-day meeting at their offices in Connecticut in late September 2014. Subsequent to that meeting, we entered into an agreement to publish three books utilizing stories that I, and my helpers, would select from their library of more than 20,000 stories that had appeared in more than 250 books. Chicken Soup for the Soul has sold hundreds of millions of copies of its books worldwide and they have been translated into more than forty languages.

Part of the agreement with Bill and Amy was a plan to provide a set of books for students and teachers for each classroom in Harris County, Texas (more than 900,000 students) and to promote a program to be used by teachers in public, private, and charter schools throughout the county. We also agreed to support a thirty-minute TV program for families to be shown on Saturday mornings on a major TV network, which we expect to reach millions of viewers. This program is expected to start in October of 2015, and will promote integrity, good choices, respect, compassion, and tolerance.

This book, the first of three to be published this year, is for children and preteens. We hope that parents and teachers will also read these stories, and we hope that they will provide a forum for discussion and feedback.

In our discussions with President David Leebron about the formation of The Boniuk Institute, he suggested that my wife and I form The Boniuk Foundation, as a separate 501c(3) nonprofit organization, for any nonacademic programs or potential legislative advocacy activity we wished to pursue. It is for this reason that our "Chicken Soup for the Soul" program is sponsored and funded by The Boniuk Foundation, which will also devote most of its efforts to the problem of religious tolerance.

I would like to acknowledge the assistance of the following individuals who helped select the stories for inclusion in this book: my wife Laurie, my son David Boniuk, Yan Digilov, Mike Pardee, Dr. Sylvia Orengo-Nania and her daughter Julia Nania, her nieces Anna Hanel and Marisa Rao, Dr. Ron and Wendy Pelton and their son Lee Pelton, a freshman at Rice University. I would also like to thank David Leebron, president of Rice University, Malcom Gillis, former president of Rice, Bill Barnett and James Crownover, former chairmen of the board at Rice, and Charlie Landgraf, member of the board of trustees and current chairman of the advisory board of The Boniuk Institute at Rice University, for their support.

~Dr. Milton Boniuk

Be the Best You Can Be

Making Your Best Effort

On Top
of the World

With innovation and technology,
seems we have forgotten to cherish the true beauty the world has to offer.
~A.C. Van Cherub

This past summer I joined my family for their annual Adirondack vacation. Every July my sister and her family rent a cottage on a lake, the same place my family has stayed since I was a little kid. They always take my parents along. And every few years I join them too.

There are plenty of activities to keep everyone busy: swimming, fishing, canoeing and sand castle building on the beach.

Every evening at dusk, everyone gathers on the beach for a bonfire and s'mores and, at least once during the week, a pair of melted flip-flops when someone gets their chilly feet too close to the fire.

Anyway, by the third day of the vacation, I had noticed that my ten-year-old niece had spent most of her time watching cable TV, playing pinball at the arcade and browsing through the gift shops in town. Not exactly the wilderness experience I remembered from my youth.

So that night at the bonfire I told my niece I thought this was the year she and I should hike to the top of the mountain across the lake. The mountain is called Rocky Point because the peak is bare and rock-covered. It is considered one of the smaller mountains in the

Adirondacks. Since nothing was planned for the following morning, we could hike it the next day.

"Well," replied my niece. "Tomorrow there are some shows I want to watch on the Disney Channel, so I'm going to be pretty busy."

"When your mother and I used to come here when we were your age, the cottage didn't have a television," I informed her.

My niece looked incredulous for a moment, and then asked: "So you had to watch all your TV shows on your laptop?"

I closed my eyes for a moment and rubbed my temples.

"We didn't have laptops either. We just didn't watch TV," I said. "We were too busy swimming and canoeing and hiking up mountains."

"Sounds more like punishment than a vacation." My niece shrugged her shoulders. "Besides, I don't think I can walk that far."

"Your mother and I hiked it every year when we were kids," I said. "It only takes a half-hour of steady walking to get to the top."

"Fine, I'll go," my niece grumbled. I knew she was agreeing just to shut me up, but I would take anything I could get. "If you and Mom could do it, then I can too, I guess."

The next morning was a perfect day for a hike, with sunshine, clear skies, and the temperature in the low seventies. I got up early and made some sandwiches and filled a couple of water bottles, which I tucked into my backpack along with the bug spray and the camera.

My niece came shuffling downstairs and announced in a very unenthusiastic, robot-like voice. "I'm ready to go hiking, Uncle David." Then she turned to her mother and asked: "Can I take my $10 spending money?"

"Why are you bringing your money hiking?" her mother asked.

"In case I see something I want to buy at the gift shop on top of the mountain," she replied.

"There are no shops," I said

"What's at the top?" my niece asked.

"Rocks mostly," I answered, "and an incredible view of the lake. You can even see this cottage from up there."

There was a moment of silence. "That's it?" she said. "You mean there's not even a restaurant or an ice cream shop?"

I shook my head. "It's a mountain, not a mall. It'll still be a fun trip," I insisted.

My niece sighed dramatically and rolled her eyes, but we climbed into my car and drove to the trailhead about ten minutes away.

"I'm still not sure this is a good idea," my niece said as she stood at the edge of the gravel parking lot and looked down the shaded trail that led into the woods. "But if you and Mom could do it, I can too, I guess."

For the moment she was determined to start our journey.

About 200 yards into the forest, the trail began to climb a steep slope. I pointed out birch bark trees and a natural spring that bubbled out of the ground and a flowering plant called trillium, which I explained was an endangered species. My niece didn't share my enthusiasm.

She was thirsty.

She was tired.

She was sweaty.

She was bored.

I handed her the water bottle as she sat on a fallen log and took a break. "You know, I think we're almost to the top," I told her.

"You already said that three times," she replied. "And we're not there yet."

She grumbled another complaint as we continued on. She might not have been happy, but at least I was proud that she had the determination not to quit before we reached the top.

A while later we did make it to the top. First, my niece looked up, noticing we were no longer under the trees. "Where are we?" she asked.

She stopped, looked around and saw where we were.

Her jaw dropped, her eyes opened wide and she shouted: "Oh my gosh, I don't believe it. We're on top of the world. It's awesome!" It had taken us almost an hour to make the climb, but it was worth it.

A refreshing breeze brushed the mountaintop, not a cloud was in the sky and miles and miles of trees and lakes spread out below us.

We sat on a large boulder and took in the view, while eating our peanut butter and jelly sandwiches and pointing out islands and roads and, of course, the cottage where we were staying.

"This is the best, Uncle David. Can we come up here another day before we go back home? It's so cool."

No stores, no restaurants, not even an ice cream shop, but she had learned it was cool to climb to the top of a mountain.

And if I had given in to her complaining we never would have attempted it at all; which is a good reminder that sometimes a little determination is all you need to get to the top of the world.

~David Hull

There's No "I" in Team

I am a member of a team, and I rely on the team, I defer to it and sacrifice for it, because the team, not the individual, is the ultimate champion.
~Mia Hamm

I love hockey. I mean I r-e-a-l-l-y love hockey. I love hockey more than snow days, summer, or even Halloween candy! I love hockey so much that I wanted to play after my brother's funeral because I knew it would make me feel happy. I wanted to score a goal for him. I ended up scoring four.

I play center forward and I love the feeling when I get a breakaway skating in and out of players and trying to "top shelf" the puck. I love taking the risk to skate and score even if I miss.

At the end of the year we had a banquet where the coaches handed out awards. I was pretty sure I was going to get one because I was one of the lead scorers on our team. They handed out five awards and when the last one was announced, and it was not for me, I was devastated. It took everything within me not to cry. I bit my cheek and tried really hard to smile and be happy for my teammates who did get one. When we got into the parking lot I was choking back the tears. I couldn't wait to get into the car and really let it all out. When we got home I had a long talk with my mom and told her how I felt before bed. I fell asleep with a crying headache.

When I woke up in the morning there was a card waiting for me on the kitchen table.

Dearest Aedyn:

I just wanted to write you a note of encouragement because I know you felt disappointed about not getting an award tonight. Do you remember how I told you that everything happens for a reason? And, how most of the time, when we are in the moment of what we might think is unfair, we don't have the full picture? We only have the small square of the GPS screen like in Dad's car, not the whole "life map." In the end, it is best to say "It is what it is" and choose joy and happiness anyway. No one can ever take away your choice to choose to be happy regardless of what's going on around you.

Dad and I were talking tonight — exchanging stories about how beautiful you are, how smart you are, how athletic, kind, and funny you are. And I was crying so much because you are just the whole package — "it" — everything! And what I realized and we hope you do too, is that you don't need an award to tell you how great you are. You are strong enough and smart enough to just know it and feel it in your soul.

Close your eyes. Put your hand on your heart. Breathe deeply until you feel your beautiful spirit floating up. When you do, love that moment. You only need to know in your heart. We know it.

Love you so, so, so, much.
Mom and Dad

P.S. I hope you love this card. We bought it in Ireland. If you read the back you'll learn about dreaming. Don't ever stop dreaming or believing that dreams come true, because they do! Just not always with the timing we think they should!

Love you more than words can say.

This year at our tournament when I was coming out of the change room, my coach grabbed my arm and told me that he doesn't measure our games by the goals that are scored. He told me that he appreciated that I could play defensively and set up plays and that's what hockey is all about.

When I thought about what he said later on, I realized that he was right. I realized last year I was focused on scoring and keeping the puck to myself, but that this year I had given a lot of effort to passing and working as a team player.

In that moment, I knew why I hadn't earned a trophy, but more than that, I realized that there is no "I" in team.

I'm so grateful that I learned that life lesson.

~Aedyn MacKenzie, 14

1,000 Makes a Day

The dictionary is the only place that success comes before work.
Work is the key to success, and hard work can help you accomplish anything.
~Vince Lombardi

t was 1995 and my sophomore year in high school in Claflin, Kansas. We were in the middle of our third game of the season in Ellsworth, Kansas, when I went up for a routine lay-up and was undercut by an opposing player. I took a hard fall on my right wrist and hand. Unfortunately, that just happened to be my shooting hand. After being taken out of the game, I could hardly stay still as the pain was as severe as I had ever felt in my life, and soon my wrist was swollen like a balloon.

My coach, Clint Kinnamon, immediately checked on me. Despite my pleas to simply tape me up and send me back into the game, Coach Kinnamon immediately motioned to my mom in the gymnasium stands, and then instructed her to take me to an emergency room as soon as possible.

My mom is a nurse, and thankfully she had some Tylenol with her to help relieve the pain during the trip to the hospital. Unfortunately, the attending physician spoke with broken English, and neither of us fully understood his diagnosis. However, it was clear from him that X-rays revealed I had not broken my wrist, but instead suffered a severe sprain. Despite the pain, I was relieved to hear him report that I should be back on the floor in two weeks.

We quickly returned to the Ellsworth gym in time for me to ride the bus home with my teammates. I was telling everyone that my wrist was fine and not broken, even waving it around throughout the ride home for all to see. Unfortunately, it was after I got home and the pain medication wore off that I began experiencing the most excruciating pain of my life. I spent the night screaming in pain… a night that is forever etched in my mind.

The next morning, my parents took me to a specialist, who quickly revealed through an X-ray that I had indeed a major break in my radius, as well as a chip in my ulna. Although devastating news, I was somewhat relieved to learn that the bone had stayed in place, and it appeared as though I would not need surgery. Only time would heal this wound. The physician informed me that I would be required to wear a hard cast on my right wrist for four weeks, followed by a soft cast for another four weeks.

It was at this time that I realized I could turn this devastating event into something positive, and I dedicated myself to doing just that. Almost immediately, due to the limitations with my shooting hand, I dedicated myself to learning to shoot left-handed. It was a daily struggle, but I was committed to using this time to improve and come back even stronger than before. Yes, I was limited in many ways, but the opportunity was before me. As the old saying goes, "It's not what you do; it's what you do next that really counts."

After four weeks, I was cleared to play with a soft cast on my right wrist, and I was forced to shoot left-handed for the next four weeks. Despite the fact I was happy to be back in uniform, it was not until our team had reached the regional tournament that my soft cast was removed. It was obvious from the start of the playoffs that my right hand and wrist had become very weak from the eight weeks of inactivity and that my muscles had atrophied. My previous shooting accuracy suffered greatly.

Like many high school athletes, I had committed myself to one simple dream… to win a state championship. My dream was close to reality as we were playing in the semi-finals of the state tournament… just one more win and the Claflin Wildcats would play the next day for the state championship.

The most anticipated game in my young career soon turned into one of the most disappointing events in my life. To put it mildly, my shooting performance was awful. I still remember the statistics: four for twenty-one from the field, and we ultimately lost the game by just a few points. I knew I had let down my team, my school and my entire community. I was devastated and completely humiliated by the defeat. If only I had made a couple of those baskets, we would have likely won the state championship.

I had worked so hard throughout my childhood, and when I was needed the most, I couldn't perform to the level I wanted and my team needed. I had worked so hard and overcome the adversity of a serious injury. I was at such a low point during that time that I could have easily and totally given up the game of basketball and never looked back. I was simply that low.

Throughout life, the choices you make as you experience challenges and adversity will shape you and ultimately be the determining factor in your ability to reach your goals and succeed. I had two choices. I could quit, or I could dedicate myself to being the best I could be. Of course, I chose the latter.

I committed myself to a simple and clear goal: to make 1,000 shots a day. I wanted to not just return to my pre-injury ability, but I was committed to returning that next season as an even better shooter.

A thousand shots a day is a major commitment, but I am proud to say I kept that commitment and made 1,000 shots a day until my freshman year in college.

I ultimately achieved some major goals in high school. No, we never won that coveted state championship (something that still haunts me today), but I was fortunate to break several Kansas high school records, including the career scoring leader for girls' basketball. I was selected as an all-state player and eventually named to the *USA Today* top five team and was named to the Kodak All-American high school team, being named as the Most Valuable Player in that game. I was honored to be selected as a member of the junior world championship team, as well.

I was highly recruited and eventually selected South West Missouri State over Kansas State and national powerhouse Connecticut. It was perhaps the best decision I've ever made in my life, as I was able to play on a great team with some terrific talent, and we literally changed the face of Springfield, Missouri, in the process.

My college coach (Cheryl Burnett) challenged my 1,000 shots a day routine, suggesting it would hamper my ability to have the "legs left" to survive the rigorous college schedule. I developed another practice regimen that focused on quality shooting practice versus quantity of shots made.

My college career was truly a dream come true for me. Not only did our team reach the Final Four, but I was showered with individual honors and trophies beyond my wildest dreams. I was a two-time all-American, recipient of the Wade Trophy and Broderick Cup, and ultimately broke the individual career scoring record for women's college basketball—a record that still stands today.

Eventually, I was drafted by the Portland Fire of the WNBA and named WNBA Rookie of the Year in 2001. After more than a dozen injuries and follow-up surgeries, my pro career was cut short.

While I never sought individual fame or glory, I was both honored and humbled by the recognition. As I look back, I know that all of the success I have enjoyed throughout my life was a result of many things: great teammates, great coaches, a supportive and encouraging family, and yes, those 1,000 shots a day.

Basketball literally opened up a world for me that I never dreamed possible. In retrospect, being injured early in my career played a huge role in my development as a player. I made a choice to overcome the adversity and my life and career were forever changed.

Adversity presents opportunities. Never ever stop believing in yourself and pursue your goals. Yes, dreams do come true—even for a girl from a small town in rural Kansas—and I'm living proof of that. It all started with 1,000 shots a day.

~Jackie Stiles, former high school, collegiate, and WNBA star

Going to the Dogs

If we did all the things we are capable of doing,
we would literally astound ourselves.
~Thomas Edison

One day my mom and I were sitting in her office looking at a magazine called *Humane Society News*. We read a very sad story about a New Jersey police dog named Solo that had been sent into a building to catch an armed suspect. The last thing Solo did before entering the building was to lick his owner's face. A few minutes later, Solo was shot and killed in the line of duty. I knew how sad that officer must have felt because my own dog, Kela, had recently died. I felt like my world had ended when I lost Kela. She had been my best friend since I could remember.

The article went on to tell about a fund-raiser that was going on in New Jersey to help buy bulletproof vests for the police dogs there. I thought, *Every police dog should be protected just like the police. I may be a kid, but why can't I do a fund-raiser to help save the dogs in our area?*

Then I found out that a bulletproof vest for a police dog costs $475. My mom thought it was a lot of money for an eleven-year-old girl to raise, but she told me to go ahead and try anyway.

We called our local Oceanside Police Department and found out that their dogs needed bulletproof vests. At that point, I realized that

I needed a name for the fund-raiser and thought since I was trying to protect just one dog's life, I would call my program Vest A Dog.

I decided that veterinarian offices and pet stores would be really good places to go with donation boxes and Vest A Dog flyers. I used little green Chinese take-out boxes, decorated with a picture of Tiko, the dog I chose to vest, and me. I wrote on each box "Help protect the life of a police dog by donating a dollar."

One afternoon, after all the boxes had been distributed throughout our community, I got a call from a local newspaper reporter who had seen one of my fliers. The reporter decided to do an article about Vest A Dog. *That ought to spread the word*, I thought. I asked K9 Officer Jim Wall, who is Tiko's partner, if they would have their picture taken with me for the article and they did.

After the article came out, I waited for a few days before checking to see if there were any donations. I was really nervous when I finally went to collect the money. *Would there be anything in the boxes?* I wondered. I really wasn't sure that I could raise enough to buy the vest. But when I collected the first box, I couldn't believe my eyes. I realized that there are many generous animal lovers out there. The box was practically overflowing with dollar bills! I kept checking back to collect the donations every few days. After about three weeks, I counted the money from all of the boxes. It totaled over three thousand dollars! I was so excited and totally amazed at the amount of money that I had raised. Not only was there enough money to buy Tiko's vest, but Vest A Dog had raised enough to buy vests for the other five unprotected dogs on the Oceanside Police Department. I couldn't believe it!

When the officers from the K9 unit found out that they were going to be able to protect all six of their dogs, they couldn't stop thanking me. They decided to put together a presentation ceremony where I would give the six vests I was donating to the department's dogs. That's where I got to meet all of the other police dogs and their handlers. I was actually a little scared of them, but the officers assured me that the dogs were very friendly. I learned that these were not just police dogs, but also the officers' family pet. Again, I thought of my dog Kela and also about Solo. I wanted even more to make sure that these police dogs didn't die while trying to protect people.

Once I began presenting the vests at the ceremony, I kept seeing television reporters come in and set up cameras. I never expected to see so many news stations there! I was excited to talk with them about what I was doing. When they asked me if I was going to continue my Vest A Dog program to help protect the other fifty dogs in San Diego County, where we live, I replied, "Yes! We need to protect these dogs because they protect us every day."

Soon the phone was ringing off the hook! Each day, reporters from newspapers and television stations called with interview requests. They wanted more information about my Vest A Dog program and also wanted to know where donations could be made. The media is so powerful! People began to mail donations to Vest A Dog!

Looking back, the success of Vest A Dog totally surprised me at first. Then I realized that it wasn't unusual that a lot of other people felt the same way I did about these dogs. They just didn't know how to help before Vest A Dog got started.

So far, Vest A Dog has raised more than twenty-five thousand dollars and has supplied *all* of the law enforcement dogs within San Diego County with a protective vest! Then, just when I had achieved what I thought was my highest goal, people from all over the country began to call me to find out how to raise funds to vest dogs in their areas. So now my fund-raiser is continuing nationwide, and I have a Web page to tell other people how to organize a fund-raiser like the one that I did.

Knowing that more and more dogs are being protected is really rewarding. It has made all my efforts more than worth it.

Then, one day after school, my mom told me that the Society for the Prevention of Cruelty to Animals (SPCA) wanted to honor me for the work that I had done to protect police dogs. They invited my mom and me to New York so that I could receive an award and a check for five thousand dollars! That vested another ten dogs!

I'm so proud and happy that the money I have raised is all going to the dogs. I'm still amazed that I have vested so many dogs when I really wasn't sure if I could vest even one. Even though some days I was tired from schoolwork, I knew it was important to continue fundraising to help save these special dogs. It was a lot of hard work but I learned that if you just keep going, you can accomplish anything. Don't think that just because you are a kid that you can't make a difference. Even if you think something is impossible, it can be done.

~Stephanie Taylor, 11

Two Tickets
to the Big Game

I discovered I always have choices,
and sometimes it's only a choice of attitude.
~Judith M. Knowlton

Two tickets. Only two tickets to the big quarterfinals basketball game.

Three pairs of eyes all focused on the tickets in Dad's outstretched hand. Marcus, the oldest, spoke the question running through everyone's mind: "Only two tickets? But, Dad, which of us gets to go with you?"

"Yeah, Daddy, who gets to go?" repeated Caleb, the youngest.

"Dad, can't you get any more tickets?" I asked. I might be the in-between sister, but I was just as eager as my basketball-crazy brothers were for a night out with Dad.

"I'm afraid not," Dad answered. "Mr. Williams only has two season tickets. He was thoughtful enough to offer the tickets to Saturday's game to me when he found out he'd be out of town this weekend."

Dad scratched his head. "Caleb, don't you think you're a little young to enjoy a professional basketball game...?"

"Am not! Am not!" Caleb insisted. "I know all the best shooters! I know the team's record! I know..."

"All right, all right," Dad finally had to agree. He shifted his focus and tried again. "Jill, since you're a girl…"

Before I could respond, Mom came to my defense. "Don't you dare say 'because you're a girl,'" she said to Dad. "Jill's out there practicing at the hoop with Marcus and all of his friends, and she's better than quite a few of them, too!"

"Okay, okay," Dad held up his hands in a "time-out" signal. "I guess I'll have to figure out a fair way of choosing between the three of you by tomorrow morning. I'll have to decide who deserves it most. Let me sleep on it—okay, guys… and girls?" he added quickly before Mom and I could correct him.

The next morning, Marcus hurried into the kitchen and plopped down at the breakfast table. "Where's Dad?" he asked as he reached for a box of cereal.

"And 'good morning' to you, too," I responded in between sips of orange juice.

"Sorry, but you can guess what I was dreaming about all last night," Marcus explained. "So—where is he?"

"He and Mom went to pick up some books from the library," Caleb answered, digging his spoon into a mound of cereal.

"And he said we should all get started on our Saturday chores as soon as we finish breakfast," I added.

"Chores! He's got to be kidding," Marcus said as he set down his glass of milk with a thud. "How can we concentrate on chores when the big game is a mere eleven hours away?"

"Parents! They just don't understand!" I agreed, popping the last piece of English muffin into my mouth.

"I'm going for the morning newspaper," Marcus announced. "There's probably a preview of tonight's game in the sports section."

"Wait for me!" Caleb added, slurping the last of his milk and dashing after his brother.

The back door snapped shut as the two boys trotted down the driveway. I looked at the breakfast table in front of me: tiny puddles of milk, bits of soggy cereal here and there, a small glob of grape jelly melting in the morning sunlight. *Well,* I thought to myself as I pushed my chair away from the table, *looks like Saturday morning chores start right here.*

A few minutes later, as I was washing off the kitchen countertops, I heard the familiar "thump… thump… thump" of the basketball bouncing off of the driveway. I glanced out of the kitchen window and saw Marcus practicing his hook shot while Caleb cheered him on. Frustrated, I knocked on the window three times. When the boys looked up, I meaningfully held up a kitchen sponge and dishtowel.

Marcus casually nodded to me and held up five fingers. Taking his cue from his older brother, Caleb did the same.

Sure, five more minutes! I thought to myself. *I'll just bet.* I opened the lower cabinet and tossed an empty muffin package into the almost-full wastebasket. I reached for a twister to tie up the plastic liner bag and carted it out to the garbage container outside the back door.

"He dribbles… he shoots! If I make this next shot, I get the tickets to tonight's game," Marcus teased as he shot for the hoop. "Hooray! Two points! And I get the ticket!"

"Do not!" Caleb shouted.

"You guys, Mom and Dad will be back any minute," I reminded them as I lifted the lid on the garbage container and placed the full plastic bag inside.

"Okay, we're coming in to help," Marcus said, dribbling the basketball around and around Caleb, who tried again and again to steal it. "Just one more minute."

"Yeah, just one more minute," Caleb added as he finally managed to tip the ball out of his brother's grasp.

I shook my head from side to side as I began to replace the lid on the garbage container. Then a flash of white on the inside of the heavy black plastic lid caught my attention. A white envelope… it must have stuck to the lid by accident. But then I noticed that the envelope was actually taped to the inside of the lid, and someone had written the word "Congratulations!" on the front of the envelope, too.

I lifted the flap on the envelope and pulled out a folded piece of paper. "To the one who deserves to go," the paper read, and inside of it was a ticket to the basketball game! *I don't believe it,* I thought. *I'm the one that gets to go! But how did Dad know?*

Then I thought back to Dad's comment last night: "I'll have to decide who deserves it most." I smiled. Leave it to Dad to figure out who the most deserving kid really was.

By now, Marcus and Caleb had worn themselves out. They shuffled toward the back door. "Come on, little brother, we'd better get started on our chores if we want to have a chance at getting that ticket to the game."

I turned in their direction and held up the ticket, the note and the envelope. "It might be a little too late for that," I said with a sly grin.

Marcus and Caleb looked at each other with question marks in their eyes, as Mom and Dad's car pulled into the driveway.

That evening turned out to be as special as I'd imagined: Two seats at center court, and a dad and his daughter cheering their team to victory. It was a long-remembered lesson in responsibility from a dad who let his kids make their own choices and earn their own rewards.

~J. Styron Madsen

The Power of the Pen

Woman must not accept; she must challenge.
She must not be awed by that which has been built up around her;
she must reverence that within her which struggles for expression.
~Margaret Sanger

The very first speech I ever had to write changed my life more than I could ever have imagined. I was a third-grader when I chose Susan B. Anthony to be the topic.

When I got the assignment, I went to the library and began researching the Women's Fight for the Right to Vote. I learned that Susan B. Anthony led the fight to give women a say in our society. She overcame a lot of obstacles in order to do that. I never really thought about a time when women had no voting rights and that their opinions didn't count.

It was sad that Susan fought so hard for women's rights and never got to vote. She died fourteen years before the passage of the 19th Amendment that gave women the right to vote. But she knew that her goal would be achieved. She said that "failure is impossible," and she was right.

About a week after giving my school speech, my mom read a newspaper article about "The Group Portrait Monument," a statue honoring Susan B. Anthony and other early women's rights leaders. The problem was that few people ever got to see the statue. It was dedicated in the U.S. Capitol Rotunda in 1921, but within twenty-four hours it was taken down to the Capitol basement and stored where it had remained for nearly eighty years.

When I read that article, I was furious! This statue belonged in a place of honor. I felt that it should be in the Rotunda, along with the statues of Abraham Lincoln, Martin Luther King Jr. and George Washington. Do you know that there are *no* statues of women there?

The article asked for donations because it would take $74,000 to move the thirteen-ton statue out of the basement. I decided to write a letter with a self-addressed envelope asking my relatives and friends to send a Susan B. Anthony coin or a $1 bill to me to contribute to the Women's Suffrage Statue Campaign. I really wanted to help get that statue moved out of the basement.

Every day I ran to the mailbox after school. Every night, after my homework, I wrote more letters at the kitchen table. Pretty soon the whole family got involved in the project. My seven-year-old brother, David, licked stamps and envelopes. My mother and grandmother found addresses for people I wanted to contact and my dad drove me around and gave me tons of encouragement when I spoke to big groups. I passed around a piggy bank for donations at the end of each speech. I sent more than $500 to the fund in the first three months. Pretty soon, I had raised $2,000. I began visualizing that statue up in the Rotunda next to the greatest Americans in history.

I was discouraged when I heard that four other times, in 1928, 1932, 1950 and 1995, people had tried to get the statue out of the basement and had failed. I learned that the House and Senate would have to vote on relocating the statue. More determined than before, I spent three weeks writing to every representative and senator in the United States, urging them to vote yes on the bill to relocate the statue. This was not about politics. It was about respect and responsibility. Susan B. Anthony fought for my rights, and now I was fighting for hers!

The Senate unanimously voted to restore the statue to the Rotunda, but Newt Gingrich, the Speaker of the House, didn't want to use any tax money to pay for the cost of relocating the statue. Even if we raised enough money, the statue couldn't be relocated without a unanimous vote in the House.

There was only one thing to do… write more letters! I wrote a letter to Mr. Gingrich *every other week for an entire year!* Boy, did that try my patience! I sent about twenty-five letters to him before I got a reply. He finally wrote a letter saying that a committee would study the issue.

At that point, I figured that I had better write to every member of the House again. By now I had mailed more than 2,000 letters!

My grandmother helped with postage costs by getting her friends and church groups to donate rolls of stamps to help me with the battle. I got writer's cramp from writing letters and discovered that it takes a lot of work to bring about change. But if you believe in something, it's worth the hard work.

My biggest boost came when I was interviewed on radio and TV shows. Then, a bunch of newspaper and magazine articles came out telling thousands more people about what I was trying to do. As a result of all that attention, I was invited to speak at a fund-raising event for the Woman's Suffrage Statue Campaign in Washington, D.C., in July of 1996. I had never flown in an airplane. My whole family got to go and my brother had a great time. He thought that was a pretty good reward for licking all those stamps!

But the best part was getting to see the statue, even if it was in the smelly old basement. I thought it looked really beautiful. I've heard people say that they think that the statue is ugly. To that I say—it was an ugly time! The three women in the statue have their arms pinned in marble because they were trapped by "slavery!"

I spoke from my heart when I talked to all those people and received a standing ovation for my speech!

After I got home, I continued to write letters. I wouldn't give up! It took women seventy-two years to win the right to vote, but they didn't give up until they reached their goal… and neither would I!

On September 27, 1996, House Resolution 216, the bill to get the statue moved, passed unanimously. My mom and I jumped up and down in our living room when we heard the news. We just kept screaming, "We won!"

The statue stayed in the Rotunda for a year and then was moved to another place of honor in Washington, where everyone can see it. It will never go back to that awful basement again!

I've learned a lot from this experience… mostly about respecting people who fought for rights that too many people take for granted. I've learned to have more patience. If there is a problem, don't say "someone else will fix it." You have to do it yourself.

I'll turn eighteen in a few years and will be able to vote in the year 2005. When I vote, I'll silently thank Susan B. Anthony for her fight and for helping me discover the power of the pen.

~Arlys Angelique Endres, 13, as told by Carol Osman Brown

Believing in My Strength

*What lies behind us and what lies ahead of us
are tiny matters compared to what lies within us.*
~Oliver Wendell Holmes

I am different from a lot of other kids. I have cerebral palsy, which happened to me before I was born. I was born really early, and I had an injury to my brain; because of this I am not able to use some of the muscles in my body in a normal way. Kids like me who have CP may not be able to walk, talk, eat or play the same way as most other kids do.

One of my legs is shorter and smaller than my other leg. I don't have very much control over that leg and foot; for example, I can hardly bend my toes. When I try to move that foot, I get a tingly kind of pins-and-needles sensation, like it has fallen asleep. I have to wear a brace on my leg to keep it from curling up, and that makes it hard for me to balance. I bump into things a lot. You may think it is no big deal to have a weak leg and to come in last in all of the races you compete in… but it is. When you are growing up, you don't want to be the one who always lags behind.

Because I walk differently and wear a brace, kids call me "retard" and other names. People even imitate the way I run. You honestly don't know how cruel kids can be unless you experience it. I try to rise above it, but sometimes I just have to cry my feelings out. Sometimes I come home with my eyes red from crying. It's not fun to be made fun of over something that I can't control.

CP is not an illness or a disease. It isn't contagious. It will never go away. I will never grow out of it; I will have CP for my whole life. Over the years, I have learned to rise above the people who don't understand my situation. I have learned to look for my strong points and not be pulled down by my weaker ones. One of my strong points is singing, and I try to focus on that. I try especially hard at whatever I do. I think that is something that keeps me going every day.

If you have some kind of disability, I encourage you to start today to do something that makes you happy. You can do whatever you believe you can. Talk to someone who may struggle with the same thing that you do, because it may help you a lot.

I hope my story inspires you to take a better look at life and to let you know there are kids just like you who have a hard time, too. Just don't let your hard times take the place of your dreams, and keep reaching for the stars.

~Kelsey Peters, 10

EDITORS' NOTE: For information on cerebral palsy, go to www.cdc.gov/ncbddd.

A Silent Voice

The situation seemed hopeless.

From the first day he entered my junior-high classroom, Willard P. Franklin existed in his own world, shutting out his classmates and me, his teacher. My attempts at establishing a friendly relationship with him were met with complete indifference. Even a "Good morning, Willard" received only an inaudible grunt. I could see that his classmates fared no better. Willard was strictly a loner who seemed to have no desire or need to break his barrier of silence.

Shortly after the Thanksgiving holiday, we received word of the annual Christmas collection of money for the less fortunate people in our school district.

"Christmas is a season of giving," I told my students. "There are a few students in the school who might not have a happy holiday season. By contributing to our Christmas collection, you will help buy food, clothing and toys for these needy people. We start the collection tomorrow."

When I called for the contributions the next day, I discovered that almost everyone had forgotten. Except for Willard P. Franklin. The boy dug deep into his pants pockets as he strolled up to my desk. Carefully, he dropped two quarters into the small container.

"I don't need no milk for lunch," he mumbled. For a moment, just a moment, he smiled. Then he turned and walked back to his desk.

That night, after school, I took our meager contribution to the school principal. I couldn't help sharing the incident that had taken place.

"I may be wrong, but I believe Willard might be getting ready to become a part of the world around him," I told the principal.

"Yes, I believe it sounds hopeful," he nodded. "And I have a hunch we might do well to have him share a bit of his world with us. I just received a list of the poor families in our school who most need help through the Christmas collection. Here, take a look at it."

As I gazed down to read, I discovered Willard P. Franklin and his family were the top names on the list.

~David R. Collins

The Last Runner

The difference between perseverance and obstinacy
is that one comes from a strong will,
and the other from a strong won't.
~Henry Ward Beecher

The annual marathon in my town usually occurs during a heat wave. My job was to follow behind the runners in an ambulance in case any of them needed medical attention. The driver and I were in an air-conditioned ambulance behind approximately one hundred athletes waiting to hear the sharp crack of the starting gun.

"We're supposed to stay behind the last runner, so take it slowly," I said to the driver, Doug, as we began to creep forward.

"Let's just hope the last runner is fast!" He laughed.

As they began to pace themselves, the front runners started to disappear. It was then that my eyes were drawn to the woman in blue silk running shorts and a baggy white T-shirt.

"Doug, look!"

We knew we were already watching our "last runner." Her feet were turned in, yet her left knee was turned out. Her legs were so crippled and bent that it seemed impossible for her to be able to walk, let alone run a marathon.

Doug and I watched in silence as she slowly moved forward. We didn't say a thing. We would move forward a little bit, then stop and wait for her to gain some distance. Then we'd slowly move forward a little bit more.

As I watched her struggle to put one foot in front of the other, I found myself breathing for her and urging her forward. I wanted her to stop, and at the same time, I prayed that she wouldn't.

Finally, she was the only runner left in sight. Tears streamed down my face as I sat on the edge of my seat and watched with awe, amazement and even reverence as she pushed forward with sheer determination through the last miles.

When the finish line came into sight, trash lay everywhere and the cheering crowds had long gone home. Yet, standing straight and ever so proud waited a lone man. He was holding one end of a ribbon of crepe paper tied to a post. She slowly crossed through, leaving both ends of the paper fluttering behind her.

I do not know this woman's name, but that day she became a part of my life—a part I often depend on. For her, it wasn't about beating the other runners or winning a trophy, it was about finishing what she had set out to do, no matter what. When I think things are too difficult or too time-consuming, or I get those "I-just-can't-do-its," I think of the last runner. Then I realize how easy the task before me really is.

~Lisa Beach

Conversation Starters

1. In the story "Going to the Dogs," which starts on page 20, Stephanie starts a fundraiser. What did she call it and why?

2. On page 13, the title of the story is "There's no 'I' in Team." What does this phrase mean?

3. "Two Tickets to the Big Game" begins on page 24. In this story, there is only one ticket available for three children. How would you decide who gets the ticket to the game?

Chapter
2

Be the Best You Can Be

Doing the Right Thing

Standing in Solidarity

Even if a unity of faith is not possible, a unity of love is.
~Hans Urs von Balthasar

Five miles from our home in LaVerne, California, are two Muslim schools that I did not realize were there until the days following the terrorist attacks in September. Then came that day, September 11, 2001, that changed every American's life in some way.

It became a time to watch the unbelievable scenes on the television news. Later, a question came to my mind. What could I ever do to help ease the pain in this tough situation? One answer came very unexpectedly.

My husband, Chuck, a pastor in the Church of the Brethren, was invited by a Muslim acquaintance to an interfaith meeting on the Friday following the attacks. There, one idea presented was to give support to the Muslim schools, which had closed upon hearing the news of the terrorist attacks.

A few days later, a phone call came asking us to go stand in front of these schools when they reopened. All we were expected to do was to be a "presence" there, to show our support for the Muslims as human beings and fellow Americans, not as terrorists. It sounded simple enough.

With some uncertainty, I arrived at the gated school the morning it reopened, September 19. Several other Brethren, as well as people from other denominations came. Our waving, smiling and greetings began to be returned to us immediately by the parents and teachers as they drove into the drop-off area. Many expressed their appreciation for us being there. As days passed, we were given donuts, flowers, letters of thanks from the students, a breakfast and a thank-you luncheon where plaques were presented to the LaVerne and Pomona Fellowship Churches of the Brethren. These plaques state that we are united under the same God.

We have become acquainted with these dear Muslims who are more like us than I could have imagined. Never have they tried to convert us or terrify us. They have been very accepting of who we are. In fact, it was an amazing moment when one Muslim stated that some of them wanted to come to our worship service in LaVerne. Her faith encouraged learning about other faiths, she reported. The date of October 14 was set for their visit, and thirty of these new Muslim friends were warmly greeted by our congregation.

The following Monday, we heard that their attendance at our church had been a meaningful time for them. They sent a note of gratitude to the LaVerne congregation.

For us, a relationship with the Muslim community is just beginning. We have been invited to attend their worship service. We have scheduled a planning session to determine how we can work together. Out of tragedy has emerged a Christian-Muslim relationship that is exciting and fulfilling. Little did I dream of what blessings were in store for us from being just a "presence" at the Muslim City of Knowledge School, and little did I know how much our presence would mean to the teachers and students. A thank-you note from a fifth-grader said it all:

> Dear People,
> You make me feel safe. Without you, I wouldn't feel safe. I like how polite you are. With you I won't feel suspicious. This is a thanks from my best friends and me.
> Love,
> Hassan

~Shirley Boyer

The Coolest Friend Ever

Courage is what it takes to stand up and speak;
courage is also what it takes to sit down and listen.
~Winston Churchill

When I turned twelve, I hung out with a kid named Raymond Sproat. We became friends and classmates in the eighth grade. Raymond was willowy and dark-skinned, and had eyes the color of cinnamon toast. He was the coolest kid I had ever known. He used foul language, smoked cigarettes, and could hit a baseball farther than anyone I'd ever seen. He would do the wildest things and take the craziest chances. Raymond cheated on exams, cut classes, and picked fights with kids twice his size. He had a scar on his chin from where he dove from a bridge and hit the bottom of the river.

We hung around a lot together that year, even though we weren't very much alike. Neither of us had other friends. I think we had an unspoken respect for one another.

I admired and envied Raymond. He was fearless, confident. He never backed away from trouble. I wanted to be more like Raymond because I was tired of being picked on. I was sick of bullies hawking snot on my shirt and then howling like monkeys when I tried to wipe it off. I had had enough of being taunted with nicknames like Dork Face whenever I walked past them.

My faith in Raymond was boundless. I remember riding down the steepest streets in town on the handlebars of his rusty old bicycle. We flew down those streets. If we had hit a rock or a pothole I would have been ground into the pavement, probably splitting open my head in the process. But I wasn't worried. He led me into danger many times, but he always led me out again.

Raymond and I did some wild things together. Sometimes we would hop aboard a lumber train headed south and ride it for several miles, with the poison heat of the diesel exhaust sweeping back into our faces. I always went along with whatever he said. I never questioned Raymond's judgment.

That is, until one day just before the start of school.

It was the first week of September. The weather was unseasonably cold and damp. A drab cloak of low clouds had swallowed the town and sunk down against the earth itself. I woke early, tugged on my jeans and T-shirt and headed for Raymond's house. I knocked and he came out.

"Let's get out of here," he whispered, letting the door close softly.

"Where are we going?" I asked, but he didn't answer. With Raymond leading we headed east, toward the edge of town. By then I knew where we were going.

Our clubhouse was located deep in a forest of second growth redwood. The woods were thick there, branches coming to within four feet of the ground in many places. There was no path leading to the place. It was well concealed, hidden away in the thicket. The clubhouse was little more than a few planks nailed together to keep out the weather, but it was ours. We walked along without speaking, pushing our way through a tangle of salal and blackberry vines.

At one point Raymond stopped and pointed to his jacket: "Check this out," he said. The metal tip of a flat bottle protruded from a side pocket.

"What is it?" I asked. Raymond laughed.

"What do you think?" He pulled out the bottle and held it up for me to see. "It's whiskey. I stole it from my old man."

"What are we gonna do with it?"

Raymond laughed again. "We're gonna drink it."

I must have made a face because Raymond looked at me and said,

"You're not chicken, are you?" I nodded. I never thought of lying to him. He cuffed me on the shoulder lightly. "Don't be scared. Booze can't hurt you."

I nodded again, satisfied. Raymond smiled and took off, climbing the hill with me in hot pursuit.

Halfway up the ridge it began to rain. Thunder whacked and cracked. Lightning flashed so close that I could smell it, and not far away there was a splintering, rending sound as a tree fell.

We reached the clubhouse and crawled in through the entrance. It was damp and dark inside, and laced with a myriad of spider webs that clung to my face. With a wave of my hand I brushed them aside, shuddering at the thought of a spider making tracks along my neck.

Raymond removed the bottle from his jacket, unscrewed the cap and took a long drink. He handed the bottle to me.

"Try it," he said. "You never tasted anything like it in your life. Tastes like fire." Bravely, feeling privileged and adult, I took the bottle and raised it to my mouth. Then I stopped.

"No, thanks," I told him. "I don't want any."

He looked shocked. "What do you mean?"

"Just what I said."

I realized that my refusal to drink with Raymond was testing the limits of our friendship. That he might not want to pal around with me any longer. But I also knew that a true friend wouldn't force you to do things you didn't want to. I had already seen what liquor did to adults, how it brought out the worst in them and made them act irresponsibly. I wanted no part of that.

Raymond sat there for a moment, just staring at me. Then he shrugged and said, "That's okay, Tim. I understand."

It was the coolest thing I'd ever heard my friend say....

~Timothy Martin

Call Me

Reputation is what other people know about you. Honor is what you know about yourself.
~Lois McMaster Bujold

"I know it's here somewhere."

I dropped my book bag to dig through my coat pockets. When I dumped my purse out onto the table, everyone waiting in line behind me groaned. I glanced up at the lunchroom clock. Only three minutes until the bell, and it was the last day to order a class memory book if you wanted your name printed on the front. I did, but for some reason, I couldn't find my wallet. The line began to move around me.

"Come on, Cindy!" Darcy might as well have stamped her foot, she sounded so impatient. "We'll be late for class."

"Darcy, please!" I snapped back. Even though we were best friends, Darcy and I often frustrated each other. We were just so different. Darcy had "budgeted" for her memory book and ordered it the first day of school, while I had almost forgotten... again.

"Darcy, my wallet's gone." I threw my things back into my purse. "My memory book money was in it."

"Someone took it." Darcy, as usual, was quick to point away from the bright side of things.

"Oh, I'm sure I just misplaced it," I hoped.

We rushed into class just before the second bell. Darcy took center stage to my problem and happily spread the news about the theft. By last period in gym class, I was tired of being stopped and having to say over and over again, "I'm sure I just left it at home." Rushing late into the locker room, I changed then ran to catch up with my soccer team.

The game was a close one, and our team was the last one back into the locker room. Darcy was waiting for me as impatiently as always. She brushed past the new girl, Juanita, to hurry me along.

I turned my back on her to open my locker. "Darcy, I know, I know, we have to go."

There was a gasp behind me, and when I looked back at Darcy, her face was white with shock. There, at her feet, was my wallet.

"It fell out of her locker!" Darcy pointed at Juanita. "She stole it."

Everyone took up the accusation at once.

"That new girl stole it."

"Darcy caught her red-handed."

"I knew there was something about her."

"Report her!"

I looked over at Juanita. I had never really noticed her before, beyond her "new girl" label. Juanita picked up the wallet and held it out to me. Her hands were trembling. "I found it in the parking lot. I was going to give it to you before gym, but you were late."

Darcy practically spit the words "I'm so sure!" at her.

"Really, it's true." Juanita's eyes began to fill with tears.

I reached for my wallet. I didn't know what to think, but when I looked over at Darcy, her smugness made me feel sick inside. I looked at Juanita. She was scared but looked sincere. I knew I held her reputation in my hands.

"I am so glad you found it," I smiled. "Thanks, Juanita."

The tension around us broke.

"Good thing she found it," everyone but Darcy agreed.

I changed quickly. "Come on, Darcy, there's just enough time to order my book."

"If there is any money left in your wallet."

"Not now, Darcy!"

"You are so naïve!"

It wasn't until we were standing in line that I opened my wallet.

"It's all here." I couldn't help but feel relieved. A folded piece of paper fluttered from my wallet. Darcy bent down to pick it up and handed it to me. I opened it to see what it was.

"She just didn't have time to empty it yet," Darcy scoffed. "I know her type. I had her number the first day she came."

"You had her number, all right. Well, I have it now, too."

"It's about time," Darcy huffed.

"Maybe that's the problem, Darcy. Maybe you spend too much time numbering people."

Darcy grabbed the note, read it and threw it back at me.

"Whatever!" she said and stomped off. I knew that something had broken between us.

I read the note again.

Cindy,
I found your wallet in the parking lot. Hope nothing is missing.

Juanita

P.S. My phone number is 555-3218. Maybe you could call me sometime.

And I did.

~Cynthia M. Hamond

Growing a Spine

A lot of people are afraid to tell the truth, to say no. That's where toughness comes into play. Toughness is not being a bully. It's having backbone.
~Robert Kiyosaki

I don't remember important things from middle school: student council elections, school dances, most of algebra... but I'll always remember the little things, like a single bench in the gym locker room, because that's where I started the slow process of growing a spine.

It was seventh grade, and it was supposed to be the turning point of my middle school career.

Sixth grade had been awful. I hadn't wanted to go to optional sixth grade at a middle school at all—I'd wanted to stay in sixth grade at my elementary school with my best friend in the universe, Jesse. But Mom insisted, and so I went forth to the middle school along with the more "mature" students from my elementary, girls who cared more about nail polish and gossip than reading and pretend. In elementary school, Jesse and I had scorned those girls as being shallow and unoriginal. In sixth grade I found myself trying to fit in with those same girls.

I gossiped and schemed my way into a small group. There were four of us: Tina, Ashley, Katie, and me. Tina was the ringleader, our Queen of Hearts. We spent most of our time trying to get on her good side, and neurotically worrying that she was talking about us behind our backs. And we were right to stress. Not unlike the Queen of Hearts,

Tina's whims were subject to change, and she chose a different group member to ostracize every month. (Only instead of "Off with her head!" it was more like "Off of our exclusive lunch table!")

You might ask, "Why would you want to stay friends with someone like that?" I often asked myself the same question. What it came down to was fear. I was a spineless little wuss who avoided confrontation whenever possible and had relied on Jesse for protection throughout my entire childhood. The group offered me the same protection— a place to sit at lunch, someone to walk with between classes. Being friends with Tina was better than being confronted by her. Plus, I told myself, it would only last a year. In seventh grade, Jesse would come to my school, and everything would go back to normal.

And that day had finally arrived. I sought Jesse out and knowledgably led her to our homeroom.

While we waited for our new class assignments, Jesse introduced me to her friend Alice, an unsure-looking, fast-talking girl who she'd met in sixth grade. I greeted her enthusiastically, telling her, "Maybe you'll be in the same class as Jesse and me." Jesse was the smartest girl I knew, and I had no doubt that she'd get into the accelerated class with me. If Alice was smart too, we'd almost be enough to have a group of our own!

Papers were passed out that held our schedules and class assignments. "7X," I recited my class name proudly.

"7X," Alice read.

"7Y," said Jesse, crestfallen.

I swear, for a moment my heart stopped beating. "That can't be right," I said. "Look in the upper right hand corner. It should say 7X."

She shook her head, and I grabbed the paper from her. Sure enough, she was in a different class with a different schedule. I would be stuck in Cliqueland without an ally for two more years.

We ranted angrily for the rest of the class—Jesse and I for obvious reasons, Alice because she would not know anyone in the accelerated class. "Don't worry," said Jesse confidently. "Val's my best friend. She'll take care of you."

At that point, I probably gulped.

You see, our first class was Art, a room with huge double desks. In our group, we had an arrangement. Whenever the class had to pick partners, I was always with Katie, leaving Tina free to sit with the marginally cooler Ashley. So I found myself hovering in the back of the Art room, staring at two empty chairs. Would I abandon Katie and risk Tina's possessive wrath or would I sit with Alice, who I didn't even know?

I took a deep breath and sat beside Alice.

I power-walked into the hallway when that first class ended, but Tina caught up with me anyway. "So are you, like, dumping Katie now?" she asked.

"Of course not!" I said. "I can be friends with both of them."

That was easier said than done.

Alice threw off the number of girls in our class from eight to an uneven nine, and so the partner issue came up over and over. When history projects were assigned, Katie moved her desk expectantly toward mine. "Maybe we can ask Mr. P if we could have a third person," I said.

"He said only two people," said Katie, with an air of "there's nothing we can do." So, being my typical spineless self, we left Alice alone.

After a few weeks of trying to bounce between Alice and the group, Tina decided that it was time to be more forceful. "Why are you hanging out with Alice, anyway?" she demanded, as we walked to gym class. "She doesn't even like you. She's just using you because she has no friends."

I walked on to the locker room, to the gym bench where our group always changed clothes, fear clenching up my stomach, my heart pounding. Nothing would ever change. I asked myself why I even bothered to help someone like Alice, who I hadn't really bonded with. We probably, I rationalized, had nothing in common.

Then Alice dumped her gym bag on our bench and Tina said, "There isn't really room for you."

I stood silently, watching Alice pull her gym bag off the bench and leave, the words "She'll protect you" repeating insistently in my head. I listened to Tina laugh, watched Katie smirk, and it hit me — it didn't matter if Alice and I never got close. The girls in my group were not the type of people I wanted to be.

I wish I could tell you that I confronted Tina then and there, that I called her all kinds of deliciously vicious names and declared my alliance to Alice, once and for all. But I don't think people go from being completely spineless to speaking their mind in a matter of minutes. A transition like that takes time. But I can tell you that I never chose the group over Alice again.

The funny part is: once Tina saw that I wouldn't back down, she abruptly decided Alice was cool. We were a group of five for the two months before Tina moved (oh happy day!) to Pennsylvania.

A few weeks after the gym bench incident, Alice called me with a homework question. We somehow got onto the topic of books, and realized we loved all the same authors. We talked for hours.

Ten years later, we're still friends.

~Valerie Howlett

The Rescue

We must reach out our hand in friendship and dignity both to those who would befriend us and those who would be our enemy.
~Arthur Ashe

t was a cold fall day. The wind gusted under a cloudy gray sky. My children, who were seldom deterred by the weather, were outside playing. Suddenly there was a commotion on the front porch. I opened the door to find my young daughter shivering as she held her damp jacket against her.

Cheeks red from the weather, she stood on the porch and looked up at me. In her eyes I could see both defiance and tears. I pulled her inside and asked what had happened. "What are you doing with your jacket off?" She just looked down and said nothing. Her jacket moved slightly. I pushed aside the folds of the jacket to find a pitiful wet kitten. The kitten shivered and mewed in protest.

"They were throwing the kitten into the swimming pool," she sobbed. "I begged them to stop, but they just kept doing it." She hugged the bundled kitten close. I waited patiently for her to continue. "I grabbed it and ran." Once again, defiance dominated her small face. My daughter had championed this kitten and she did not care about the consequences.

I hugged her and took the kitten from her. Ordering her to immediately change into dry clothes, I found a soft hand towel and set about drying off the unhappy kitten. The kitten wiggled with my efforts to dry him, but soon a fluffy little yellow creature began to emerge. The kitten looked to be about half grown.

Her clothes changed, my daughter hugged the kitten close as I warmed up some milk for him to drink. She placed him lovingly on the floor so he could lap it up.

"Momma, it was awful," she said. "Why would they do that?"

She explained that a couple of neighborhood boys kept tossing the kitten into one of those small children's pools that had filled with rainwater from the night before. One of boys was the owner of the kitten.

"I don't know," I said soothingly, "but I'm proud that you had the courage to put a stop to it."

"I'm not in trouble?" she asked in a surprised voice. "I just ran off with the kitten," she said, as if she did not believe that she was not in trouble.

"No sweetie," I said, tears now in my eyes for my brave little hero. "I am very proud of you." I held her close and tenderly, just as she had held the kitten.

Now warm and full of milk, the kitten began to meow again. "I think he's confused and a little scared," I told my daughter. She picked him up and cuddled him in her lap, stroking him softly until he fell asleep.

"We need to call his family," I said. "They need to know what happened and where their cat is."

My daughter's eyes widened. "No! They'll hurt him again."

I was uncertain about what to do. I knew I needed to make the call, but I also knew that the boy was likely to mistreat the kitten again. I began to pray about it as I got up to make us some lunch.

In his usual fashion, our son burst through the door. Slow and easy were terms that he was unfamiliar with. He stopped when he saw his sister sitting with the kitten in her lap. "Are you in trouble for stealing that kitten?" he asked her.

"She didn't steal the kitten," I said. "She rescued it. I'm going to call the family in a few minutes and let them know what happened."

He shrugged his shoulders and headed for his room. I headed for the telephone. I spoke with the mom and told her what had happened. She was disappointed in her son, but not surprised. This son was born after her other children were in high school. Shortly after his birth, her husband had died from a heart attack. She was left on her own to raise her son and provide for her children. Life was difficult for them. She had hoped he would consider the kitten a nice companion.

"Well, he's young," I said. "Sometimes children don't realize how harmful it is to play roughly with animals." She agreed to walk over to get the kitten after supper.

Coming home from work, my husband was surprised to see our children, on the floor, giggling and playing with the little ball of fur. He looked over at me with a question on his face. "No, I did not bring home a kitten. It's not ours."

"She rescued it," my son said, pointing at his sister. "It was awesome." We explained to my husband what had occurred that day. While we ate, we discussed the fate of the kitten, trying to reassure my daughter that everything would be okay. We said the boys had just gotten carried away and did not see how much they were harming the kitten, although we were not entirely sure that was true.

After we had eaten and were settled in our favorite seats, watching TV, we heard the knock at the door. My daughter, once again, had a panicked look on her face.

"Don't worry," I said. "It will work out. Just wait and see." I prayed very hard that I was right about that.

My husband answered the door and asked the mom to come in. Behind her, his head hanging low, was her son. He shuffled behind her as my husband led them into the den and offered them seats. My daughter was on the other side of the room, protectively holding the kitten.

The mother explained how she had spoken with her son and thought he now understood that what he had done was dangerous and that the kitten could have died. Then she spoke to her son. "Is there something you would like to say?"

For the first time, he looked up and we could see that his eyes were red as if he had been crying. He looked directly at our daughter.

"I'm sorry," he said. "I just thought it was funny. I didn't think about the kitten getting hurt." He looked at the kitten and then hung his head again.

Again, his mother spoke. "We have agreed that maybe a kitten was not a good choice for him."

The boy looked up, his face more animated. "I'm going to get a dog!"

"Yes," his mother said. She looked at us. "We are going to the animal shelter to pick out a dog. We want a full grown dog, not a puppy. I want a dog my son can roll around and play with."

"The kitten is going to my sister," she continued. "She doesn't have young children, so he will have a good home." She reached for the kitten. Satisfied, my daughter laid him in her arms.

The boy got his dog and it was just what he needed. He was lively and fun and followed him everywhere he went. All of the neighborhood children loved him, including my little hero.

~Debbie Acklin

Being True to Myself

Between two evils, choose neither; between two goods, choose both.
~Tryon Edwards

My parents and I had been planning my brother's birthday party since the beginning of March. Johnny would be six years old in two days. My mom was going to bake her special chocolate cake with white icing. As I watched her, I thought, *Gee, I wonder what I can do to make my brother's birthday special.*

I decided to empty my coin jar and see how much money I had saved. I was disappointed to find much less than I had imagined. "Oh, no, I only have about three dollars," I muttered to myself. I knew my parents had already bought a present for me to give to Johnny, but I wanted to buy him something I had chosen myself and with the money I had saved. I wanted to buy him the paint-by-number kit I had seen at the store, but the set cost more than I had saved.

Disappointed, I went into my parents' bedroom where my dad kept loose change on top of the dresser. I stood on my tiptoes and saw some dimes, nickels, and a few quarters. I carefully counted out what I needed to make up the difference. *I'm sure Dad won't mind just this once,* I thought. However, I was soon overcome by guilt. Even though there was no one else in the bedroom, I felt like I was being watched. Mom was always telling us about the importance of honesty. She had even made up a short poem for us:

Always be honest in everything you say and do,
Because God is always watching over you.
When there seems to be no one else around,
That's where God is always found.

Maybe my plan wasn't such a great idea after all, I thought. My dad would be home in another hour, and my mom was busy in the kitchen preparing dinner. I jingled the change around in my pocket while wondering what to do.

I grabbed my jacket from the closet and headed toward the door.

"Where are you going, honey?" Mom asked.

"Oh, just up to the corner store," I replied.

"Well, don't stay out too long. Daddy will be home soon."

"Okay, Mom."

Once I got to the store, I took the paint-by-number kit from the shelf.

"Can I help you, young lady?" the salesclerk asked.

"No… I'm just looking, thank you," I said.

"That's a really nice paint kit. We sell a lot of them and, as you can see, that's the last one," she said.

I nodded my head in agreement, but finally decided to do what was right.

I placed the paint-by-number kit back on the shelf and headed home.

Luckily, once I got home, Mom was busy talking on the phone, so I was able to slip past the kitchen without being noticed. I went to my parents' room to return the coins I had taken. I arranged them into a neat stack—just like they were before—and sighed with relief, knowing I had done the right thing.

I knew the paint kit would have been the perfect present for my brother. I would just have to wait until I saved the extra money I needed. I figured I could earn it by doing odd jobs around the house. Mrs. Davis, the salesclerk, had even agreed that she would hold the paint set behind the counter for me until I had enough money to pay for it.

I wasn't able to buy the paint kit until two weeks later, but it seemed extra special when I was finally able to lay *my* money on the counter. I smiled as I raced home knowing I had made the right decision.

~Terri Meehan

Just Do It

No one is useless in this world who lightens the burdens of another.
~Charles Dickens

As a preteen, I was pretty lazy when it came to "doing" for my family. I worked hard at school, did tons of homework, practiced for piano lessons, and sometimes babysat my younger sister. Still, I found myself regularly resisting the urge to help out at home with even the simplest things.

If my mother or father asked me to do something, I would do it: not a problem. But the fact that I always needed to be asked or told to do things—things I could plainly see needed doing—undoubtedly bugged my parents. What Mom and Dad didn't realize, though, was that by age ten my resistance to chipping in even bugged me!

For a long time, I wasn't bothered enough to actually do anything about it. But my guilty conscience—knowing I could and should do more for my folks, and not just when asked—led me to feel pretty bad about myself.

Every Wednesday afternoon, for example, my mother drove me to another town for a piano lesson. During my half-hour lesson, she'd rush to the nearby grocery store and buy a week's worth of groceries. Given the fact that my mom had just driven me twelve miles there, twelve miles back, paid for my lesson, and bought me a candy bar, you'd think I'd be grateful and gracious enough to help her bring the groceries into the house without being asked. But I wasn't.

I knew I should help her. But with homework weighing heavily on my mind—and with "me" still the center of my universe—I generally just brought in an armload and left the rest for Mom as I ran to my room, shut the door, and started studying.

Don't get me wrong: being conscientious about school is a good thing, and I know my parents appreciated my hard work and good grades. But the thing is, even holed up in my room, I still felt guilty about not helping my mother more. Sure, I had work to do—but she'd worked all day, too! And after hauling in those bags, and putting the food away, Mom still had to whip up a tasty dinner for the five of us. Small wonder I felt guilty.

A similar situation occurred on summer weekends as my family headed north to our rustic lakeside cabin. Each of us kids was expected to pack our own basket of clothes and toys, carry it to the car and, later, bring it inside the camp. But besides our individual baskets, that station wagon was always jam-packed with coolers, camp gear, and bags of food. Once again—if asked—I'd help carry in everything else. But if left to my own devices, I was much more apt to dump my basket inside, then head outdoors to explore the woods. Exploring trumped helping every time.

Exploring is a good thing, sure, and it turned me into a lifelong naturalist. But my "not helping" was gradually becoming a bigger and bigger problem for me because in my heart and my head I knew I was skirting responsibility—not to mention, it obviously made my parents cranky to have to continually ask for my help.

Deep down I wanted to change my ways. But I also realized that once I did change, there'd be no going back. Once I took on more responsibilities, my parents would start expecting more of me. At age ten, I sensed that this one small change would mark the start of something far bigger: my personal transition from a cared-for, semi-spoiled child to a more mature, responsible, caring and giving young person.

I'll never forget the Wednesday I made a conscious decision to jump in and see what happened. Returning home from my lesson, I disappeared into my room, as usual. But once inside, I felt that deep and burning shame. Dumping my schoolbooks and music on the bed, I abruptly opened my door and headed back to the garage to help my mother.

I'm sure Mom thanked me that day, but her thanks are not what I remember. What I remember most is the incredible sense of peace and satisfaction I felt after helping her. Working hard at school always made me feel good. But what surprised me that day was how happy I felt just helping my mom—all on my own.

At the time, I imagine Mom wondered: "Is this a one-time deal or will Wendy help me again next week?"

Unknown to her, I'd already vowed to pitch in every single Wednesday—and from that day on, I did. It was such a small action. Yet what a nice little difference it made in my mom's life! And what a huge difference it made in mine. The selfishness and guilt I'd struggled with for so long suddenly vanished, replaced by a warm glow of pride.

As for those summer treks to the lake, ditto! Instead of just carrying my own stuff, I began returning to the car for more loads—even when my father was in a really grouchy "long week at work" mood. The first time I did it, Dad probably wondered the same thing as Mom: "Is this a one-time deal?"

But over time, I showed my sincerity by continuing to help out with the loading and unloading. The neat thing was, the more I helped out, the better I felt about myself and my place within my family. As Mom and Dad realized they could count on me more, our trips became far less stressful, too. In short, it was a win-win situation for everyone.

Sometimes the little things we put off doing the longest turn out to be the simplest things to accomplish. Helping out more—and offering to help rather than waiting to be asked—made my parents and me a lot happier. And feeling happy trumps feeling guilty any day.

~Wendy Hobday Haugh

The Sweetest Thing

No legacy is so rich as honesty.
~William Shakespeare

I had been following my mom and her shopping cart around our small-town grocery store for what felt like forever, at least six aisles and the bakery department. At ten years old, I was obsessed with candy and got permission to head up front to the checkout aisle. Once there, I ran my fingers over the rows and rows of goodies trying to settle on a favorite and dreaming of what it would be like to devour the entire rack full. I smelled large shiny brown wrappers and shook palm-sized purple boxes. I loved almost all of the treats, but chocolate was always my first choice. Skittles and Starbursts were okay, too, especially the yellows and reds.

As I was pondering all things sweet, I noticed a man a few feet away pushing buttons on the ATM machine. Most people I knew didn't use that magic cash machine. My parents still preferred to drive to the bank to get money. This man, though, looked younger than my parents. He was dressed in a suit, had dark hair, and seemed to be late for something, anxiously waiting for his cash to appear. The machine made a grinding noise, and he immediately grabbed a stack of bills and headed out. Bored with the candy, I wandered over to the ATM, where I started pushing the buttons as if looking for some secret combination. Eventually, I peered into the bottom of the machine and saw it: a beautiful, crisp $20 bill. Though I wanted to believe my magic had made the cash appear, I knew the man in the suit must have left it behind.

I held the money in my hand, staring at the number "20" and feeling richer than I ever had. The bill was so smooth, without a crease on it, so perfect that I wondered if maybe it had been printed inside that machine. I thought about slipping the money into my pocket. No one would know, but it didn't feel right. I knew it wasn't mine. I hadn't earned it. I saw how hard my dad worked to make money. I watched him come home from work exhausted each evening. Sadly, this $20 didn't belong to me. I needed to find its owner, but first I had to find my mom.

I started running through the market frantically, when I finally found my mom wandering the produce aisle. "Mom!" I panted wildly.

She whirled around, clearly concerned. "What's wrong?" she asked.

"There was this guy using the money machine, and he left $20 in it. We have to find him and give it back!"

She paused a moment, then pushed her full cart to the side and took my hand. "He might be gone already," she said kindly, trying to lessen the potential disappointment that always followed when I had my mind set on something that didn't or couldn't happen, like receiving a perfect score on a test or that coveted solo in choir.

"But we'll look for him," she said reassuringly.

"I think he was walking to his car," I said.

We scurried out the automatic doors, only to see several men in the parking lot. "That's him," I cried, as I pointed my finger toward the man in the suit. "I think…" He was stepping into his car.

"Are you sure?" my mom asked, looking at me nervously.

"Pretty sure," I replied.

"Excuse me, sir," my mom asked as she approached the young man. "Were you just at the cash machine?"

"Yes," he said tentatively, wondering what was coming next.

"Well, my daughter found money in there and thinks it may belong it you." She pointed to me and he smiled.

"Let me check," he said, as he pulled out his brown leather wallet and multiple bills. "Twenty, forty, sixty, eighty... I think I got it all."

"Okay," my mom said, as she turned away.

"Mom, that's him," I insisted in a whisper.

"Oh wait," he said with surprise. "You're right! I'm missing a $20 bill."

"Here you go," I said, beaming with pride. "Twenty dollars," I proclaimed, as if I was a detective who had solved a major mystery.

"Thank you so much," he said in an official tone. "That was so nice of you," he said, bending down and shaking my hand as he would an adult. My heart swelled. I felt important. I felt special. "Thank you," he repeated.

"You're welcome," I said.

"You must be so proud," the man said, turning to my mother.

"I am," she smiled.

"Can I get your address?" he asked. "I want to send your daughter a thank you card. What's your name, honey?" he said, turning back to me.

"Felice," I answered. My mom gave him my dad's work address, and we said goodbye.

When my mom and I returned to the store, my mind was racing. Twenty dollars. What could I have done with that $20? I bet I could have bought a puppy or every single candy bar in town! But now none of that would happen. I knew I had done the right thing. My parents had always taught me to be a good citizen, but usually that just meant holding open doors or being polite to adults. I had never had to give up money before, especially not twenty whole dollars.

A few weeks later, my dad came home from work with a big brown box in his hands. "Felice!" he called, "I got a package for you!" I jumped up from the recliner I was sharing with my little sister and ran toward the front door. "Here" he said, as he put the box on the floor so I could get a good look at it. "Let's open it up." Within the box was a note and a smaller shoebox. I ripped it open to find dozens of packages of candy, Applets & Cottlets, a Pacific Northwest powered-sugar treat.

"Oh my gosh!" I screamed as my dad handed me the card. "Dear Felice, Thank you very much for returning my $20. You are a great girl, and I appreciate your honesty. I hope you enjoy this candy. Best Wishes, Tom." Tom included his business card. Turns out he was vice-president for the candy company, which sounded like the coolest job ever. I had done the right thing and now I had been gifted with candy. And though it wasn't chocolate, I loved it, sharing with my family and eating one bar every night until it was gone. It tasted sweet, sugary, and also satisfying, each bite reminding me that what I had done mattered. That I made someone happy. That my honesty, although it wouldn't always be rewarded with candy, would make a difference to someone. And that was the sweetest part of all.

~Felice Keller Becker

The Slam Book

Often the right path is the one that may be hardest for you to follow. But the hard path is also the one that will make you grow as a human being.
~Karen Mueller Coombs

I stared at the page so hard I thought my eyes would pop out. There was my name, and scrawled right underneath it the words "The Mop." My heart pounded, my face and ears burned red hot. I wanted to run, hide, anything to get away from the destructive words of this cruel creation by some of my classmates. They called it the "Slam" book.

I couldn't imagine anything worse than being thirteen, living in a new town, going to a new school, trying to make new friends and then having some unknown person write this in a book for everybody to read.

I'd watched during math class as the black book circulated from desk to desk. Each time the teacher turned toward the blackboard, the book was swiftly passed to the next person and hidden until it could be opened, read and written in. When it landed on my desk, I opened it and saw the vicious anonymous comments scribbled across each page.

Who are these people? Why would someone say these things? "Barbara—The Mop." I'd only been at the school a month. I didn't even know them. My fragile confidence was shattered. I'd tried to make new friends, but it hadn't been easy. It was a small town, and they'd all known each other for years. I wondered, *Will I ever fit in?*

I turned the pages to other names. Amanda, "conceited, big lips, hairy eyebrows." I thought she was nice and even pretty. Courtney, "witch's pointed nose, thick glasses." I was just getting to know Courtney. She lived around the corner from me, and we walked to school some mornings. She was kind to me and had a good sense of humor.

I hated school for the next few days and did whatever I could to not be noticed. But that didn't last long. It couldn't. The vicious book kept circulating and gathering more anonymous slander. Somehow I knew the cycle had to be stopped—but how? Determining right from wrong is usually not all that difficult. The scary part is doing it, and I had to dig deep to muster my courage. I wasn't all that brave.

I didn't tell the teachers or rant and rave at the students, although I wanted to scream at a few. Instead, I did the only thing I could do—I refused to participate.

"No," I stammered, pulse racing. "I won't read it, and I won't write in it," I said the next time the book came my way. The boys mocked anyone, especially a newcomer, who refused to participate. Standing alone against them took all the courage I had, at a time when I needed friends.

Suddenly, I noticed other girls saying no, and one even ripped out the page with her name on it. Finally, when all the girls refused and there wasn't an audience, the book faded away into oblivion. The old saying, "If you extinguish the reward, you extinguish the behavior" proved true. We eliminated the reward.

There was, however, another lesson I learned from this experience—one that proved more valuable than just affirming right from wrong. I learned to make up my own mind about people. I learned to understand and welcome their differences, to not accept someone else's shallow criticisms or petty observations, but to see people for who they really are.

Amanda was proud of her full mouth, thick dark eyebrows and olive skin, all of which were beautiful attributes of her Italian heritage.

Courtney's poor vision didn't diminish her wit and intelligence. She made me laugh, and eventually we became best friends.

And as for me; I learned to laugh when "The Mop" stayed with me as a nickname. I looked at my tangle of naturally curly hair that wanted to go its own way and eventually came to love it. It wasn't going to be tamed, and neither was I.

The "Slam" book showed up another year, but its history was short lived, and its impact minimal. The girls refused to be intimidated, refused to participate, and the reward was once again extinguished.

~Barbara J. Ragsdale

Conversation Starters

1. "Call Me" starts on page 48. In this story, who took Cindy's wallet and what was the reason?

2. On page 45, the story is titled "The Coolest Friend Ever." Do you think that Tim's friend Raymond was cool? What traits do you believe make a cool friend?

3. "Just Do It" begins on page 62. What is something you can do at home to make someone else happy?

Chapter 3

Be the Best You Can Be

Accepting Differences

Alone

Be yourself; everyone else is already taken.
~Oscar Wilde

"How was school today?" I asked my youngest daughter as she walked in the door.

The sad look on her face and in her eyes gave me the answer before she spoke these words: "Why doesn't anyone want to be my friend?"

After two years in our small town we had begun to know a few people. Yet even though Amee had already spent those years with the same group of students no one from her class chose to get to know her and become her friend. Amee walked to and from school alone. She played alone at recess and ate alone at lunch since no one in her class wanted her around. No one picked her to be on their team in gym class or for class projects. There were no after-school homework groups or fun times, no birthday party invitations, no sleepovers with the girls, no one to whisper secrets and dreams to. Her classmates simply excluded her.

She just wanted to be accepted, to belong to a group, to have some friends. In her loneliness she begged me to talk to the teacher. "Mom, help them understand why I need help. Tell them I just want to be friends. I try my best."

Thinking Amee had a great idea I talked to the teacher but her reply made us sad.

"No, we don't need to tell the students anything about her disabilities. You know how mean children can be. This will only single her out."

Then, some of the girls began yelling at her to quit staring at them. They didn't realize the staring indicated that Amee was having an absence spell seizure and not simply staring to be rude. Some of her classmates tried to push her aside so they could spend time with her teacher assistant. Occasionally some of the girls said mean things that hurt her feelings and once they even pushed her. Each day my daughter came home sad. She became so frustrated she did not want to go to school anymore. She begged me to talk to the teacher again. I did but the teacher refused to change her mind. No matter how sad and hurt Amee felt, she continued to treat her classmates kindly, even the ones who tormented her, hoping they would become her friends.

Finally school finished for the summer. The holiday meant visits to her older sisters, which she looked forward to. Summer holidays meant time with grandma and grandpa whom she loved very much. This summer meant being a junior attendant at her oldest sister's wedding. This summer meant time away from those who chose to exclude her, tease her and hurt her.

As summer drew to a close and the start of school drew closer Amee began to beg, "Mom, please talk to the new teacher. Maybe she'll let you talk to the kids. They'll all be the same. I don't know why they don't like me. Tell them why I sometimes stare. Tell them why I need help. If you help them understand maybe they'll be my friends this year."

It hurt to see her so fearful about the new school year. This year's teacher agreed to let me talk to both grade six classrooms during health class. I planned my presentation. I checked with Amee to see what she thought. She smiled, hoping this year would bring friendships and fun. She remained convinced that a talk to the class would change everything.

On the day of the presentation, Amee's lopsided ponytail bounced as she rushed to school with a smile on her face. Later that morning I gave my talk to the students. "Put the hand you use all the time on your desk." Once every student had one hand on the desk I continued. "Now put that hand in your lap or behind your back. You can't use it for the rest of the class no matter what you have to do."

They had fun trying to print and then write their names. I assigned the second task and stood back to watch the students problem-solve their way through tying shoelaces. Some students began working in pairs to have two hands available for the job. Some attempted it on their own and frustration soon showed on their faces and in their actions. Finally one boy put up his hand and said, "I can't do this with one hand. I need help."

The rest of his classmates nodded in agreement.

I began to simply explain brain injury, cerebral palsy and epilepsy to the class. I personalized all the information by sharing Amee's story. Cerebral palsy affected her right side especially her hand and arm. The hand and arm would not work the way their hands worked but her leg functioned well enough to allow her to run races with Special Olympics. I explained the small absence spell seizures that mimicked staring and how medication did not always work as well as it should. Brain damage due to the stroke she suffered at birth caused both these conditions, as well as learning disabilities, which meant she needed more time and lots of repetition and help to learn simple lessons.

I ended with an object lesson especially for the girls in the class. I asked them to put their hair in a ponytail with only one hand and then change their earrings. The girls looked at me and then at the very crooked ponytail Amee had accomplished on her own. One girl shouted, "So that's why her ponytail is always messy."

Another girl said, "That's not fair. She's had lots of practice. We've never tried that."

I smiled as I watched awareness show in the faces of her classmates. Maybe this new understanding would make a difference in attitudes and actions. Maybe Amee's idea would work.

Changes began to take place. Some of her classmates asked her to be in their group for class projects. Some included her at recess and noon hours. They quit yelling about her staring and began to acknowledge her need for a teacher assistant. They excitedly cheered for her when she ran her races with Special Olympics and helped celebrate her abilities.

Total change takes time. Amee still walked home alone after school. No birthday invitations or sleepover invitations arrived. But knowledge provided more understanding. Meanness and exclusion decreased during the school day. Amee started to feel like she belonged and enjoyed going to school. She remained convinced that friendships would follow.

~Carol Elaine Harrison

You'll Be Good for Him

Courage is not the absence of fear, but rather the judgement that something else is more important than fear.
~Ambrose Redmoon

heard the rhythmic clatter of metal crutches coming down the hallway. I looked up to see ten-year-old Brian smiling at me in the doorway, his blond hair tousled. Every day, Brian arrived at school cheerful and ready to work.

Brian had a great sense of humor and loved his own jokes. He was my first "handicapped" student. Everyone who worked with Brian told me, "You'll be good for him."

Brian worked with the adaptive physical education teacher and swam three mornings a week. He kept a busy school-day schedule. Everything he did required more effort than it did for the other students.

One day, Brian agreed to talk to the class about his handicap. The students liked Brian and wondered what he did after school. He told them that he watched a lot of TV, or played with his dog. Brian felt proud to be a Cub Scout and enjoyed being a member.

The students then asked him why he used different paper and a special magnifying lens and lamp when he read. Brian explained that he had a tracking problem, and that he could see better out of one eye than the other. "I'm going to have another eye operation," he said casually. "I'm used to it. I've already had six operations." He laughed nervously, adjusting his thick-lens glasses. Brian had already had two hip surgeries, two ankle surgeries and two eye surgeries.

Brian explained how he'd been trained to fall when he lost his balance, so that he wouldn't hurt himself. I felt badly when he fell, but he didn't fuss. I admired his fortitude.

He said he often felt left out, then somebody asked if people ever made fun of him. He replied that he'd been called every name you could think of, but that he usually tried to ignore it.

I asked Brian if he ever became discouraged.

"Well, to tell you the truth," he said, "I do. Sometimes I get really mad if I can't do something. Sometimes I even cry."

At this point I ended the discussion. I felt the important questions had been answered. The students applauded.

"Can you walk at all without your crutches?" one of the boys shouted.

"Yeah," he said shyly.

"Would you like to walk for us?" I asked him gently.

"Yeah! Come on, Brian. You can do it!" several students shouted.

"Well—I guess," he answered reluctantly.

Brian removed his crutches and balanced himself. He proceeded to walk awkwardly across the room. "I look like a drunk," he muttered. It wasn't smooth, but Brian walked on his own. Everyone clapped and shouted.

"That's great, Brian!" I placed my hand on his shoulder.

Brian laughed nervously while I had to hold back tears. His honesty and courage touched me. I then realized that maybe I wasn't as good for Brian as he was good for me—for all of us.

~Eugene Gagliano

Anyone Who's Anyone Knows the Horah

If we look at the path, we do not see the sky.
~Native American Saying

There was a point in my life when, almost every single weekend, I would pull out the nicest clothes that I owned, put on what little make-up I knew how to apply, and strap on a pair of not-so-high heels to dance the night away with all of my friends. That time, surprisingly, was seventh grade.

I hadn't realized how many of my friends were Jewish until they each started turning thirteen and having the inevitable Bar or Bat Mitzvah. I became accustomed to the routine: Go to the service. Try not to giggle when they recite their Torah portions, no matter how off-key. Throw gummy candy when the service is done. Bring $36 in an envelope to the party for whoever was becoming a man or woman. Dance the electric slide in tube socks. Repeat.

And repeat and repeat. Countless weeks of Bar and Bat Mitzvahs and I became an expert. I could do the horah flawlessly and anticipated the rhymes for the candle ceremony. Every time I went to a Bar Mitzvah with someone less experienced, I felt like the person at the movie who spoils the plot.

"This is the part where they march around and carry the Torah," I'd whisper to the new Bar Mitzvah-goer. "Don't touch it with your hands!"

Week after week, I took pictures with my friends that were turned into key chains and wore silly party favor sombreros. I anticipated the moment when my middle school boyfriend would ask me to dance, eyes on the floor and hands fidgeting. I made sure to remove my heels, towering over him even when barefoot. Then we would dance, arms straightened, with a good three feet separating our bodies.

Inevitably, I started to get jealous. Every week I watched a new friend, sometimes someone I barely knew, be doted on. I wanted my parents to stand on the bema in front of everyone and give a speech about how proud of me they were for having accomplished all the work that went into a Bat Mitzvah. Instead, my mom, a professional chef, was cooking every day for people who weren't me, and my dad was working long hours in New York City and living with his new wife. I envied the kids whose happily married parents were planning elaborate ceremonies and parties for their kids as they entered adulthood.

I started to consider the possibility of having my own Bat Mitzvah. Although my Dad was Catholic and I was currently enrolled in Sunday school, my mom was a non-practicing Jew. If my friends, whose grades were surely worse than mine, could learn Hebrew, why couldn't I? It was an obsession. I imagined what my Bat Mitzvah dress would look like, who I would invite to the party, and I envisioned all those smiling faces in the synagogue, staring up at me as I did my haftorah portion.

What I like to call the "Bar Mitzvah" phase of my life came and passed, as we all started to turn fourteen and enter eighth grade. My desire to have my own Bat Mitzvah decreased when I realized how much work and dedication it would take for me to pioneer my own religious education, ceremony, and party. But a big part of my realization was seeing why, exactly, I even wanted one in the first place.

I was looking for faith, for family, and for appreciation. I wanted to feel part of a religious community for the first time in my life, and

I wanted my whole family to congregate because of my hard work. I found other ways to get those things.

I joined the church choir a few years later. Singing had always been my passion, and it helped me feel the spirituality I was seeking. In high school, I managed great grades and tried out for every musical I possibly could. I had found a way to get that attention I craved—I could be on stage.

But every now and then, when a big, white envelope with calligraphic lettering arrives in the mail from some family friend turning thirteen, I smile and think of all the outfits I wore, the boys I danced with, and the chicken tenders I scooped onto my plate from the buffet line. Bar Mitzvahs were awkward and loud and completely over the top. But most of all, they were fun.

~Madeline Clapps

A Different Sister

I choose not to place "DIS" in my ability.
~Robert M. Hensel

I was standing in the park on the other side of our street watching the old Henderson place. My best friend Sam and his little brother TJ were with me.

"They're monsters, Richard," Sam said. "Someone told us at bowling. There are two sisters and they're monsters."

Sam was talking about the new family that had moved into the house. We'd seen the parents. They looked ordinary, but we had never seen the two girls. And there had never been any monsters living on our street before, so we wanted to find out all about them.

"How big are they?" TJ stretched his hands up high over his head. He knew about T. Rex and other dinosaurs.

"As big as full grown bears," Sam said with a nod to me. "And they hate little boys."

TJ moved behind his brother, but kept his eyes on the house.

That's when the garage door opened. We expected to see someone drive out but two girls walked out instead. They were pushing bicycles.

The girl in front was very pretty. She had curly blond hair and pink clothes. She was about as old as me.

"She looks all right," I said. "She's not a monster."

"Look at the other one!" TJ's voice was more squeaky than usual, as he pointed at the second girl coming down the driveway. She was bigger than the first one, and she had a crooked face. She swayed from side to side as she walked.

The girls pushed their bikes across the road toward us. That's when I noticed the big girl's tongue seemed to be blocking her mouth.

TJ became very brave. He jumped out from behind Sam and pointed and laughed at them. "Monsters! Monsters!" he yelled.

The two girls took no notice. The pretty girl was helping the other girl put on her helmet. TJ bent down, picked up a stick and threw it at them. The stick didn't even go close.

"TJ!" Sam and I both shouted at him at the same time, and he stepped back and looked very guilty.

I wanted to find out what the pretty girl's name was. She looked nice. And she didn't seem to be frightened of the other girl.

"Come on, Sam. Let's go and talk to them," I said.

TJ wanted to go home. He was almost crying and kept dragging on Sam's hand, so I went by myself.

"Hi, my name's Richard," I said.

"I'm Holly. This is my big sister Claire." Holly finished tightening both helmets while I looked closely at Claire. Her eyes were bulgy and she stared at the ground beside me.

"Hi," I said to her.

She didn't answer. She just stood and stared.

"Can she talk?" I asked Holly.

"I can talk!" Claire shouted. "And I can ride a bike. Can you ride a bike?"

"Yes, I can," I said. "I didn't mean to be rude. Don't be angry."

"She's not angry." Holly looked straight at me and smiled. "That's how she talks."

Holly had the best smile in the world. It was like it was a special smile just for me. And I couldn't help smiling back.

Then Claire got on her bike and nearly ran me down as she started off along the track.

"Sorry," Holly said, as she rode after Claire.

By this time Sam and TJ were almost out of sight. I ran home to get my bike so I could ride with the girls. When I got back to the park they were still going slowly around the track. I rode next to Holly with Claire riding ahead.

"What happened to her?" I said.

"What do you mean?" Holly said.

"Why does she look so strange and talk so loud?"

"Nothing happened to her," Holly said. "She's always been like that."

"Don't you mind going out with her, when kids point and laugh?"

"They soon stop when they get to know her," Holly said. "She says some funny things you know."

After a while the girls propped up their bikes and sat down to have the cookies and drinks they'd brought with them. I sat next to Holly and looked at Claire. She hadn't said anything funny since I'd been with them. In fact she hadn't said anything at all. She sure looked strange, but not scary-strange like she did at first.

"Do you eat cookies?" Claire shouted at me. She was holding out a cookie for me. I took it and she smiled for the first time. It was a lopsided smile and her tongue got in the way, but that was all right.

The next day I rode with them to the library. Claire waited outside to mind the bikes while Holly and I went in to find some books.

We'd only been in the library a few minutes, but when we came out the police were there. One of them was trying to talk to Claire, and the other one was talking to a woman next to her car. The side window of the car had been smashed and glass was on the ground.

"Did you see anything?" the policeman said to Claire.

"Yes," she shouted back at him.

The policeman waited a while and then said, "Well? What did you see?"

"Two men."

"Which way did they go?" the policeman asked.

"Nowhere," Claire shouted.

"They must have gone somewhere." The policeman seemed to be getting impatient with Claire.

"No. They're over there." Claire pointed at two men watching from behind a blue truck. They saw her point and they scrambled to get in the truck. But the police were too quick. They had their guns out and the men gave up.

The police found the woman's bag in the truck and lots of other things as well.

The woman came over to speak to Claire.

"Thank you," she said. "You're a very clever young lady."

"I know," shouted Claire. "They said I was stupid. They didn't care if I saw them smash your window."

"Well, here's a $20 reward for being such a good witness." The woman held out the bill to Claire. But she wouldn't take it.

"I don't have money," she shouted. "Holly has money."

"Thank you," Holly said as she accepted the bill. "I'll buy her something nice."

On the way home, Holly had to ride in front because Claire didn't know the way.

As I rode beside Claire I realized I had become used to her already. There wasn't anything scary about her at all. She might look unusual, but she was really a very nice person—just different.

~Richard Brookton

The Normal Girl in a Not-So-Normal Chair

The hardest struggle of all is to be something different
from what the average man is.
~Charles M. Schwab

As a twelve-and-a-half-year-old American girl, I like doing girly things. But many people aren't aware of that because they only see a twelve-and-a-half-year-old disabled girl who sits in a wheelchair. When I was in second grade, I was a speaker at an after-school program for children my age. In the beginning, the children were curious about my tubing and alarms. By the end of the program, when it was time for questions, they didn't know what to say to me. I guess they felt embarrassed. Instead of trying to talk to me, they ended up walking away and ignoring me. Unfortunately, this is a typical occurrence. Often, people would rather act like I am not there.

I use a wheelchair that has tubing to control my breathing and alarms to signal for assistance. To explain why I use this chair, with all of these devices, I need to explain my diagnosis. Before I was born, I had a stroke that affected my brain stem. It's as if my brain is a computer, and the circuit board shorted out. My muscles don't always do what I want them to, and most definitely not in a timely manner. I can breathe but not enough to stay alive, so I use a ventilator. I can stand, but I cannot control my muscles so I would wobble around or fall over. With a ventilator I am unable to use my voice to speak, so instead I blink yes or no with my eyes. To say yes, I blink twice, and once to say no. My mom also helps me by holding my hand while I type, which takes a very long time. My alarms notify my moms that my devices are having a problem. There are different sounds for different alarms, and sometimes they can be noisy. Now you understand what it is like to be in my chair.

As a preteen girl, I enjoy putting on make-up, dressing trendy, reading about anything I can, and being outside in nature. I need a ventilator to breathe and a wheelchair to move, but I have the same interests as any other preteen girl. People seem to forget this when they see me.

Often, when I go into a store with my family, people will stare and then avert their eyes. They don't think that I see them, but they are wrong. I am aware of a lot more than they think. People are afraid to be out of their comfort zone. They feel threatened by someone like me because they don't know what to say or do. What they don't realize is that not saying anything at all is more hurtful than anything they could have said. I want people to know that handicapped people have feelings too. If you walked into a place and everyone walked away from you, would it hurt your feelings? Well, that is how it feels for me.

By saying a simple "Hello" or asking my name, a stranger can brighten my day. This simple gesture makes me feel welcomed. I want people to know that being a preteen is hard enough, but sad stares from strangers makes it even harder. Don't feel sorry for me — my life is great! The next time you see a person in a wheelchair remember that a simple hello can go a long way. After all, a wheelchair doesn't make a person — what's in the chair is what's important.

~Dani P. d'Spirit

A Lesson in Ugly

Beauty is not in the face; beauty is a light in the heart.
~Kahlil Gibran

One of my earliest memories is being all dressed up to have my picture taken. I remember Mother bathing me, putting lotion on my hair and curling it around her finger as she blew on it. I twisted and squirmed and she patiently told me a story as she worked on my hair.

"This will make you pretty," she explained. "You're going to have your picture taken and you want to look pretty, don't you?"

I was a child in the late 40s and early 50s, and that was the time when ladies wore hats and gloves and nylon hose. Men wore three-piece suits, hats, and carried handkerchiefs. Whether it was to church, shopping, or to a special event, everyone dressed their best. There was no jeans, sweatshirts, tennis shoes, or baggy anything.

We lived in an antebellum house in Palestine, Texas, on a large two-acre lot. For some reason, we attracted the discarded and homeless pets of the area. If it was a stray, it ended up in our yard. In the evening Grandpa would fill a half dozen tin pie plates with leftovers and some cheap cat food and take them out into the backyard. He would bang a couple of plates together, yell "kitty, kitty, kitty." After he went back into the house, a dozen feral cats would creep out from the bushes, the sheds, and the storage building and chow down. Sometimes there was even a stray dog or two. If they were tame, Grandpa would try and find homes for them.

It was 1950 and just after Christmas when I came in from school, changed clothes, and grabbed a sandwich before heading across the hall to see my grandparents. I was surprised to see my grandmother sitting alone sipping coffee.

"Where's Grandpa?" I asked.

"Oh, he's in the basement working on an old stray cat that snuck in the basement window. The cat is badly burned, but you know your grandpa, he's determined to doctor that old cat up."

I headed for the cellar. In the past we had sewn up an old hen that had been attacked in the hen house, bandaged dozens of cuts, scrapes, and injuries of assorted cats, dogs, pigs, horses, and even a cow or two. Grandpa could not stand by and let any creature suffer.

Grandpa's back was to me and I couldn't see the cat that Grandma had mentioned. I saw a bottle of salve and one of Grandma's aloe vera plants sitting on the table, along with two large rolls of gauze and some adhesive tape. I thought the cat had probably blistered a foot or maybe his tail and hurried over to see if I could help.

As I reached his side and got a good look at his patient, I felt all the air sucked from my lungs. My gasp was loud and my grandfather looked at me and smiled a sad smile.

"Not very pretty, is he?" he said softly.

I couldn't answer. I had never seen anything so horrible. One side of the cat's face was totally devoid of hair and skin, his right ear was completely burned off and one eye was seared shut. There were large burns along his side and back, and his tail was missing. His legs and feet were blistered and raw, and the cat just lay in my grandfather's arms trembling.

"Is he going to die?" I whispered.

"Not if I can help it," Grandpa said with tears in his eyes.

"How did this happen?" I asked.

"He must have gotten cold and tried to get into the cellar. I figured he slipped when he got through the window and fell behind the furnace.

I kept hearing this faint cry so I came down and found him. He had managed to climb out from behind the furnace."

"But, he is one of the wild ones, isn't he? How come he's letting you hold him?"

"He knows, my dear. He knows I wouldn't hurt him. He needs help. His pain is stronger than his fear."

"Grandpa, even if he lives, he's going to be so ugly," I commented as I looked at the damage the furnace had done.

"So what?" my grandpa said harshly. "Would you love me less if I were burned and ugly?"

"Of c-course not," I stammered.

"Are you sure?" he stared at me. He was smearing the burn cream from the jar over the cat's face and stubble of an ear. "You know, I was always told not to judge a book by the cover. Do you know what that means?"

I nodded. "It means sometimes a book is really good even if the cover isn't."

"That's right," he smiled. "It's important to look good because most people are too quick to judge by appearances. Still, it's even more important to take the time to get to know people and find out if the person is a good person, a kind person, and a person who might enrich your life. You mustn't associate with people who are mean, have no respect, and disregard the law, but those people usually have a reputation that is well known."

"Mother always wants me to look pretty," I argued. "All the most popular people at school are pretty."

"That's for now," he explained. "Now is what young people think about, but now isn't all there is to life. Animals don't care who's popular and who's not. All animals care about is staying warm in the winter, cool in the summer, food to keep them from being hungry, and friends to share their lives with. They don't ask for a lot and they only judge by actions, not looks."

Grandpa doctored the poor cat, smearing ointment on his burns, bandaging his wounds, and all the while murmuring soft comforting sounds. We spent an hour in the basement that day. We bandaged and wrapped and squeezed out the cooling sap of the aloe vera plant and applied it to the places that were the most severe.

Every day for the next month, Grandpa and I changed bandages, reapplied medication and hand-fed the injured cat. He did recover, but his injuries had taken their toll on his appearance. He lost the use of his right eye and it grew shut and his ear was little more than a bald stub. His fur never grew back over the burn scars on his face or his body.

What I discovered, what my grandfather had tried to tell me, was that the sparkle in his good eye, the soft purr from his scarred chest, and the gentle rub of his mangled head against my leg gave me a feeling that I had never experienced before. When I gathered Lucky, his new name, into my arms, I didn't see an ugly cat. I saw a cat full of love and appreciation, and happy to be alive.

It may sound fake, unbelievable, and mushy, but that cat changed my outlook. That cat, my grandfather, and the advice he gave me opened doors I didn't know existed. I started looking at my classmates differently. The beautiful people didn't stand out so much anymore and I discovered lots of new friends who made my years in school the best. I never made the most popular list, but I didn't care. I wasn't the prettiest, but that didn't matter. My friends, like Lucky, knew how to be friends, how to love, laugh, and appreciate life. None of them were ugly, nor beautiful, but I discovered that there is a fine line between the two and that fine line is deep inside.

I still like to look my best, but now I look deeper, beneath, inside. After all, that's where real beauty lies. Ugly is a word that defines a person's action, feelings, and lifestyle. As far as I'm concerned it had nothing to do with looks.

~Bobbie Shafer

The Need for Speed

The ideal attitude is to be physically loose and mentally tight.
~Arthur Ashe

Every year, our youth group takes a three-day ski trip to White Face Mountain in Lake Placid, New York. But 2006 was special because Rebekah was old enough to attend the trip.

At age twelve, Rebekah has lived more in a lifetime than most. Born prematurely and with cerebral palsy, she has survived many surgeries, and also a battle with leukemia that was finally vanquished by a bone-marrow transplant. Embodied within this child are a strong will and a positive attitude. Somewhere along the way, she captured my spirit.

I invited Rebekah to attend the ski trip.

At first, her parents refused permission. I cannot even begin to imagine the internal struggle for them. This would be the first time that their daughter would be so far away from them. Rebekah's care would be in the hands of other people. I assured them that I would be there. I researched and talked to the adaptive ski program administrators at White Face Mountain. I arranged for an accessible room. And, finally, seeing Rebekah's excitement and insistence, they gave in.

I didn't anticipate the battles that would arise from other sources. Other chaperones for the trip thought I was crazy for inviting her. Her parents were criticized for letting her go. Her grandparents had long discussions with me about all of her needs and how much work she can be. Underneath it all, I sensed a deep, pervasive fear from everyone around me. Her family feared letting her go. The rest feared caring for a child with a disability who used a wheelchair.

All I could see was a young girl, desperately wanting to do something adventurous and on her own. I felt anger and frustration. Why should Rebekah be limited by her body? Why should she be limited by others afraid to take care of her? Why couldn't anybody else see that she needed this?

Rebekah came anyway, and I knew her parents were walking on pins and needles back home, almost sick with worry.

I will never forget the look on Rebekah's face when Donald Dew, the adaptive ski instructor, first strapped her into a specially made bi-ski. She glowed with excitement and adventure! Donald was remarkably prepared. He had specially tailored lesson plans for skiers with cerebral palsy.

Rebekah took off! We all stood in amazement as Donald taught her how to manipulate the bi-ski. Later, he told me that she had accomplished in two hours what he had hoped she would accomplish in three days. She was a natural at skiing.

In the middle of the first lesson, Donald asked me to follow Rebekah by holding on to the back of the bi-ski.

Unbeknownst to me, she had been planning this moment all morning in her mind. She headed straight down the hill, accelerating to a breakneck speed, dragging me all the way. We were out of control! What if we hit a tree? What about all those promises I made to her grandparents to keep her safe? I started screaming, "Rebekah! Turn! Turn! TURN!"

With a giggle, she turned and halted our wild slide. "Mrs. Muzzey, I have a need for speed. They've been holding me back all morning. Now I finally got it!" By the time Donald got to us, we were both laughing, with tears rolling down our cheeks.

At the end of the lesson, Donald took her to his office and had her call her parents to inform them of her success. "Mom, Dad, I'm having the time of my life! And I think you need to get yourselves in gear and learn to ski, because I love this!" I later found out that this phone call made all the difference to her parents. They were finally able to relax and get rid of the pins and needles.

Every night of the trip, we had group devotions. On the first night, I couldn't keep quiet about how awesome it was to watch Rebekah ski, about how far she had progressed in one day, and about the crazy trip she had taken with me in tow. I was so proud of her.

The next day, different people wanted to ski with her. One of them was the speaker we had hired. He was trying to explain what happened during that day's lesson. Instead of someone holding the back of the bi-ski, she had a tether attached from Donald to her bi-ski. But he wasn't getting the words out in a way that made sense. Rebekah finally piped up to explain, "Look, people. It was like a dog leash. I was on a dog leash!" I know I was holding my gut with pain from laughing.

By the end of the ski trip, almost everyone from our group took some time to come and ski with Rebekah. Everyone was talking about her. In those three short days, that precious soul captured many more spirits with her attitude and wit. No one was afraid of the girl in the wheelchair anymore.

~Linda Muzzey

Adam's Apples

After all, there is but one race—humanity.
~George Moore

One afternoon, my son came home from school with a puzzled look on his face. After asking him what was on his mind he said, "Are all people the same even if their skin color is different?"

I thought for a moment, then I said, "I'll explain, if you can just wait until we make a quick stop at the grocery store. I have something interesting to show you."

At the grocery store, I told him that we needed to buy apples. We went to the produce section where we bought some red apples, green apples and yellow apples.

At home, while we were putting all the groceries away, I told Adam, "It's time to answer your question." I put one of each type of apple on the countertop: first a red apple, followed by a green apple and then a yellow apple. Then I looked at Adam, who was sitting on the other side of the counter.

"Adam, people are just like apples. They come in all different colors, shapes and sizes. See, some of the apples have been bumped around and are bruised. On the outside, they may not even look as delicious as the others." As I was talking, Adam was examining each one carefully.

Then, I took each of the apples and peeled them, placing them back on the countertop, but in a different place.

"Okay, Adam, tell me which one is the red apple, the green apple and the yellow apple."

He said, "I can't tell. They all look the same now."

"Take a bite of each one. See if that helps you figure out which one is which."

He took big bites, and then a huge smile came across his face. "People are just like apples! They are all different, but once you take off the outside, they're pretty much the same on the inside."

"Right," I agreed. "Just like how everyone has their own personality but are still basically the same."

He totally got it. I didn't need to say or do anything else.

Now, when I bite into an apple, it tastes a little sweeter than before. What perfect food for thought.

~Kim Aaron

Sisterly Love

Sisters are different flowers from the same garden.
~Author Unknown

S ince the time we were young children, my sister and I have never gotten along. She was born two years, three months, and thirteen days after me. I've always been the good daughter, and she has always been the one in trouble.

My sister isn't like other sisters. She has had a lot of problems since birth and has always been hard to handle. She had to have a gastronomy tube to eat, she had seizures, and she required a lot of attention from our single parent mom. We were constantly making trips to the children's hospital to see doctors, the dentist, and other specialists.

But that wasn't the half of it. As she got older, my sister was diagnosed with ADHD, ADD, bipolar disorder, and eventually with pervasive developmental disorder, which falls somewhere on the autism spectrum. She doesn't show her emotions, doesn't talk about things, and is very angry and self-focused. I can't hold a conversation with her, show my feelings toward her, or do anything normal with her. I walk on eggshells when I'm around her, because I never know what will set her off.

When we were younger, we would play with Barbies together. She would always throw a fit when I wanted to clean up and go do something else. It was hard being her sister. We always fought and I would usually lose. I became her punching bag somewhere in our growing up years. She would hit me, leaving red handprints, sometimes drawing blood with her fingernails. I also became her verbal target. I'd hear things like, "I wish you were dead!" "I hate you!" and "There's no excuse for you."

I don't know how many times she left me in tears after one of her rages. There were times I would hide in my room because I was so afraid of her anger. Everyone around me kept saying, "Oh, it's just sisterly love. She'll grow out of it." I really grew to hate that saying. It wasn't sisterly love, and she wasn't going to grow out of it. I kept waiting for her to, but she never did.

I was put into counseling when I was in middle school, and the focus quickly went from what I was in there for to what was going on at home. My "relationship" with my sister was one of our main focuses in counseling. It was always frustrating for me, because it seemed no one was on my side. My sister got away with so much. In counseling, my counselor would call me the instigator, saying that I spurred her on. I was so angry with my counselor, I began lying to her when she asked about how things were going with my sister. I was tired of having it blamed on me. It just wasn't fair.

Right before I went away to college, all I kept hearing was, "I can't wait until you leave! I hate you, and I hope you never come back." I know she said it in anger, but it still hurt. I was relieved when I left for school. Home was once my refuge from the torments at school, but my sister took that refuge away. On breaks from school, I would go home and things with my sister were the same. We still didn't get along, and I was still scared of her when she was in a rage.

I've always observed other sisters and have been jealous of their relationships. I want to be able to joke and tease with my sister and not make her angry. I want to hug her, cuddle with her, and show her my love for her. I want to be able to sit and have talks with her. I want to hear about what is going on in her life. But I know these things aren't possible.

So, I'm doing the best I can with what I have. I send her text messages that let her know I am proud of her and that I love her. I leave her notes that tell her she can talk to me about anything, and I promise her that I won't tell Mom. She never takes me up on these notes, nor responds to my text messages. I've come to realize that she doesn't really hate me. She's probably just as frustrated as I am in dealing with all that is going on with her.

I've always wished that I could be in her shoes for one day so I could try to understand how she thinks and feels. While this is impossible, and I still don't understand her, I am beginning to understand a few things. I understand that if I refuse to argue with her, things don't get loud and explosive. If I watch, I can tell when she is getting aggravated and will stop whatever I'm doing that is causing her aggravation. I've learned that I can have a good time with my sister if I'm careful.

I wish I could understand more. I wish I could understand her disorders so I know how to interact with her. But I know things are not my fault. I've had to accept and love her for who she is, and I've stopped wishing she could be someone else because, while things are tough sometimes, she is still my sister.

~Mandilyn T. Criline

Conversation Starters

1. "Adam's Apples" is the story on page 99. What does Adam's mom teach him about how people and apples are similar?

2. On page 96, "The Need for Speed" introduces us to Rebekah. How do Rebekah's feelings change from the beginning to the end of the story? How do you think her parents' feelings changed?

3. Turn to page 86. How does this story, "A Different Sister," teach us a lesson in accepting differences?

Be the
Best You
Can Be

Appreciating
Your Family

My Sister, My Hero

You cannot do a kindness too soon,
for you never know how soon it will be too late.
~Ralph Waldo Emerson

The first full choir rehearsal of the school year took place in the school auditorium. Each grade had been practicing the songs separately, but this was the first time all the grades joined together to sing. My sister was a year older than I was and I watched as her grade filed in and took their places next to us on the stage.

Off to my right and in back of me I could hear giggling. As I turned my head around to see what was going on, I saw older boys and girls pointing down at a girl a few rows below them. I'd never seen this girl before but a couple of kids away from this girl stood my sister. She turned and glared at the group that was now openly making fun of this girl, saying things like "diaper" and "pee your pants" at her.

The teachers were too busy discussing the order of the songs to notice the commotion. Finally, the rehearsal started. After each song, the teachers would discuss any problems and while they did that, the little group of bullies were pointing, laughing, and talking just loud enough so that the girl, whoever she was, could hear what they were saying. One of the girls in my class whispered in my ear, "Did you know she's wearing diapers?"

At home that evening, I asked my sister about the girl I'd seen. She said that her name was Theresa and that she was a very nice girl.

"Why were those kids being mean to her?" I asked.

"Because they're jerks, that's why," she snapped, turning and stomping out the door.

The scene was the same at each choir rehearsal but as time went on more kids joined in teasing poor Theresa.

The day before the program, I was walking home from school when I heard voices behind me. The closer they got, the more I realized they were talking about me.

"There's little idiot's sister — you know, the one who loves pee-pee pants. Does your sister pee her pants too?"

I walked a little faster and then I felt a pebble hit me in the back. "Knock it off, you jerk!" I stuttered in the bravest voice I could find. By this time I was almost running.

"I'll bet you pee your panties too, don't you?"

Just then, one of the neighbors came out of her house and I took off running for mine. When I got home I ran down to my sister's room and knocked on her door.

Jannelle opened her door and I pushed my way into her room, screaming at her. "Why do you have to stick up for that girl, Janelle? Now I'm being bullied because of you. Why do you have to be her friend? I don't see anyone else being nice to her."

Janelle yelled back, "Because she's a wonderful person and she's dying!"

I will remember those words for as long as I live. Theresa wet her pants because she had an illness, an illness that was killing her. My sister was the only one nice enough to be her friend and stick up for her.

The choir program was great and since there were parents in the audience it was the one time that no one tortured Theresa. When the program ended, I watched as she introduced my sister to her parents. Theresa's mother had tears in her eyes as she hugged my sister. Smiling, Janelle turned around and gave Theresa a big hug. I noticed a lot of looks coming from some of the bullies but this time instead of being embarrassed I felt proud that Janelle was my sister. A few months later, Theresa passed away.

On that night, so very long ago, my sister became my hero. Throughout the years I watched her, always making friends with everyone. It didn't matter if they were fat, thin, brilliant, not so brilliant, shy, or loud, she never left anyone feeling isolated or alone. We never talked about Theresa or the night I was mad at her for being Theresa's friend. All I know is because of that night, something inside me changed and I never looked at anyone in the same way again.

~Jill Burns

My Dad
Made the Difference

*All about me may be silence and darkness, yet within me, in the spirit,
is music and brightness, and color flashes through all my thoughts.*
~Helen Keller

"There's nothing I can do," the eye doctor told my parents. "Take your baby home. She's blind." Mom and Dad clung to each other and wept freely. "All I can do is give her a full, happy life," Dad vowed. "I don't know how else to treat her except as I would any other child."

As I grew, my parents realized I could see partially. The greatest gift Dad gave me was expecting me to meet my potential and to persevere, even with my sight limitation. One day after school, my dad came home from work early and saw me holding *Dick and Jane* close to my eyes, struggling to read the letters. "Dad, I can't do this. It's too hard," I told him.

"Honey, you're not a quitter. I'll help you."

My brother banged through the door and blurted, "The kids are saying my sister is stupid because she can't read. Is that true?"

My voice quavered. "My eyes are bad, Dad. Does that mean I'm stupid? Will I ever be able to read?"

Dad squeezed my hand. "You can't see well, but that doesn't mean you're stupid. We'll work together, and you will read."

Dad made me want to try. He took out markers and paper. While

I lay on my stomach, he painstakingly drew letters big enough for me to see. It took hours. I also have some hearing loss. He pronounced the phonics slowly and distinctly so I could hear them. I learned to read and proudly read *Dick and Jane* with the rest of my first-grade class. Because of my dad, I had confidence in myself as a reader—until middle school.

One afternoon at the end of class, the teacher stepped out of the room, and a student taunted me. "You blind bat. If you get your face any nearer to that page, your eyes will fall out of your head!" I ran out of the school, tears glistening on my cheeks.

Dad was home when I burst into the house. "I thought I was a good reader, but I guess I'm not. The kids are making fun of me." I told him what my classmate had said.

Dad hugged me. "I'm sorry, Pam. Kids can be cruel, but that doesn't change the truth. You can read, right?" I nodded, unable to speak. "You can read. Your classmate can't take that away from you."

The knot in my stomach went away after Dad's encouragement. I walked over to the picture window and looked out. I saw our old sycamore tree blowing in the breeze against the blue sky. I noticed the plush green grass, Dad's enormous red roses on the hedge by the house, and how the amber sun shimmered as it began to set in the distance. "Dad, I see—how can I be blind?"

"From what you've described, you see big items, not detail. Others don't know how much you can or can't see. It's up to you to show them how capable you are," Dad said. I had a chance to prove this to myself soon after. At a fast-food court, the waitress asked my dad, "What does she want to order?"

"Excuse me," I spoke up and smiled. "I can decide for myself what I want." Dad nudged me and said, "That's my girl."

I used the sight I had and knew I was independent even as a blind person. Dad advised, "Take your cane in places like the grocery store so people will know you're blind. It's okay to let someone assist you because you do all you can on your own."

Dad taught me to laugh at myself. He reminded me of the time I tried to pick up a sign that was painted to the floor. Another time, we ate in the deli, and I attempted to eat flowers off an empty plate.

When I was ten, I wanted to ride a two-wheeler bike. I heard Dad say to Mom, "I'm not going to hold Pam back from the adventures any kid has." On my first attempt, I said, "Dad, what if I fall off?" He replied, "You'll get on and try again."

I recall summers outdoors roaming with my friends. We crossed streets, played in the creek, and swung on a tire swing. In order to roller-skate, I used big landmarks: carport poles, garbage cans, a sidewalk contrasting with the grass, and the dark shadow of the house. Once, however, I smacked into a pole anyway. While the dentist capped my tooth, he objected, "Why are you letting her skate?"

"Don't sighted children smash into poles?" Dad asked.

The dentist seemed appalled. He left for a minute, and I remarked, "Dad, don't tell him yesterday I climbed a tree."

"I won't. It will be our secret."

In the car, I exclaimed, "Dad, why do people think I can't do stuff?"

"They can't comprehend how they would do it if they couldn't see."

Dad continued to mentor and sustain me until all seven of my children were grown, and I became a grandmother. The legacy he gave me—unconditional love and determination—lives on within me and through them. I wouldn't be who I am today if it weren't for my dad. He made the difference for me to believe in myself.

Though my dad has died, I still feel him spurring me on, like that day I went on a field trip to Astoria, Oregon, where a column overlooks the surrounding beach area. "You can't climb that tower. You'll get hurt," a teacher informed me.

"Watch me," I replied. "Nobody tells me I can't do something." I started toward the column.

"She's spunky. I like that," another teacher said, following me, cheering all the way, just as Dad would have.

~Pam Johnson

Proud to Be Your Sister

Sisters function as safety nets in a chaotic world
simply by being there for each other.
~Carol Saline

Dear Alex,

There was never a certain time in my life when I found out you had special needs. The fact was always there, even if I didn't understand what "special needs" meant. Somehow, I just knew that you were different. Back at age four, it didn't matter that you couldn't play with me or that you had so many doctors. I thought it was cool that you went to a school with so many "fun" things to do. I was jealous that you got to have OT and PT every week.

As I got older, I realized that your special school, doctors, and therapies weren't such an awesome thing. I began to understand that you weren't just special. You were a special needs child.

Brain damage. ADHD. Legal blindness. Epilepsy. This is how the doctors describe you. But I have always seen more. I saw you speak for the first time at three years old. I saw you being rushed away in an ambulance at five in the morning. I saw you trying a new food and spitting it out. I saw you smile at me and it was that moment that I realized what a great brother I had.

When we were little and shared a room I never slept in my own bed. Do you remember, how as soon as Mom and Dad would shut the door, I'd climb into bed with you? We'd stay up for hours, playing our silly little word games, and I'd teach you how to say new things. I cherish those nights when we became more than just two siblings. When you became my best friend.

It could be a coincidence that Anna and Maddy shared a room and you and I shared one. But it was the best coincidence that has ever happened to me.

You were always afraid of so many things. The birthday song, fire, cameras, juice, fruit, clapping... I could go on and on. You are still afraid, trapped in a world of blurry color and unfocused light. I wish I could pull you out... but I can't.

Now that I'm older, I hear people using words like "retarded," "cripple," and "moron," and it breaks my heart. It hurts that others do not understand how hurtful their words are, even if they don't say them directly to those with special needs. It makes me mad that, time and time again, people who have a loved one with special needs try to educate these clueless nimrods and these people go and say we're stupid. When I hear someone use these words, regardless of what they actually mean, I think of you. To them, you are a retard. And I cry. Because those people are cruel.

If my classmates could meet you, I know they would understand. I know it! But they can't meet you.

You can be annoying, sure. I mean, you break my stuff, shriek at the top of your lungs, and mess up the computer.

When you have seizures and have to go to the hospital, it scares me. I hate that you have to experience that, even though I know you're lucky you don't have them as often as some kids do.

What I'm trying to say, Alex, is that I'm so proud to be your sister. I'm proud of all you have accomplished, and what you will accomplish.

Thank you for being there for me, a constant confidant, when I couldn't tell anyone else. Thank you for your hugs, thank you for telling me you love me, thank you for all the morals you have taught me.

You're beautiful.
Love you forever, Like you for always,
Kathryn

~Kathryn Malnight

A Mental Cancer

People are like stained-glass windows. They sparkle and shine when the sun is out, but when the darkness sets in their true beauty is revealed only if there is light from within.
~Elisabeth Kübler-Ross

t was December of my sixth grade year, and Mom wanted Quinn and me to run in the "Reindeer Run"—a one-mile "fun run" for kids. Quinn was an athletic, gorgeous, golden-haired nine-year-old; I was her stumpy, awkward-footed older sister. While I was twenty months older, Quinn had always been skinnier, just as strong, and nearly as tall. It was a no-brainer who should be running in front.

Yet on this sunny December day, my sister found herself doubled over after a mere five minutes of jogging. Mom and I exchanged a glance—where was the girl who clambered up doorframes and ate sugar straight from the packet? Where was my energetic little sister? I didn't know it then, but this was the first sign that my family dynamic was about to change. In a month, my sister would be diagnosed with a brain tumor.

In my experience with my sister's illness, I don't know that I learned anything too different from anyone else—though I have my own story to tell. One lesson that I have had to repeatedly learn over the past six years is that, as it was put by B.C. Forbes, "Jealousy... is a mental cancer." Even though Quinn has had to endure six brain surgeries, memory loss, impaired vision, learning disabilities, and count-less other side effects, I have been jealous of her just as many times as she has been to the doctor. Relatives we had never met came out of the woodwork, sending money, gifts, and cards that were addressed to her nine times out of ten. People at church, school, people I babysat for, people I hardly even knew all seemed to have a newfound reason to talk to me—about my sister. When Quinn was home from school because of chemotherapy and wanted something, all she had to do was ask, and she received.

I knew deep down that she was suffering from things I would never know the magnitude of, yet jealousy swelled inside me. While I was in no way ignored by my friends and family during this time (all were very supportive), I wanted the attention Quinn got—minus the whole "head about to explode" thing. Yet at some point, when I was feeling sorry for myself, it dawned on me that no matter what people gave Quinn, no matter what material items she now possessed, no matter how focused the spotlight now was on her, she would have traded it all to have the one thing I still took for granted: my health. I realized that the jealousy I felt inside was unhealthy, both for my own sanity and for my relationship with my family.

While the jealousy never left me, and even lingers to this day, I have learned to fight this mental "cancer" by giving to my sister. Yes, giving her the very thing everyone else was giving her—attention—is what has helped me to overcome my jealousy, because it made me realize that she deserves what she is given. This is probably the most important advice I could have been given six years ago: "Yes, you will be jealous. No, life isn't fair, but that doesn't mean you can't overcome your jealousy to be there for your sister."

I learned that life isn't always going to be about me, and I am a better person for that. A few years ago, when Quinn was taking a chemotherapy drug that made her tired and nauseous, she, Mom, and I were on our way to one of my favorite places: The North Carolina Renaissance Festival. We were almost there when Mom and I heard a noise: Quinn was about to blow banana chunks all over the back-seat. We pulled over into someone's private drive, which featured, among other high-class things, a flock of chickens pecking about. Immediately after hurling, Quinn argued that we needed to go to the Festival because I really wanted to. I argued back, "No, you don't feel well!" In addition, Quinn had thoroughly banana-chunk-ified her jeans, so we were going to head back home for the day, but, for whatever reason, somebody wanted us to be at that Festival because Mom unearthed a pair of sweats from the back of her cluttered car. Quinn changed in the driveway while Mom stood in front of her. I stood guard against the scrappy chickens.

It ended up working out, but later that night, Quinn told me how much it meant to her that I was willing to give up my yearly smoked turkey leg because she didn't feel well. It was her appreciation for my actions that made me realize her guilt at being the reason I had to give things up, whereas I always felt guilty for being able to do things she couldn't. This was another important thing I realized during my sister's illness.

My sister is the kind of person I try to emulate, and I hope (one day) my children will, too. If I can instill in my kids one-tenth of the courage and love their Aunt Quinn has shown me, I will consider my life a success. This is how I hope to use what I have learned during this experience for the service of a better world—I aspire to be a living example of what my sister has taught me. I also think that because of my experience over the past six years, I have something a lot of adults wish they did—the ability to empathize with people who are going through difficult situations. After watching my family struggle through many tough times, I have realized that you don't need to know what to say—you just have to say something.

~Spencer Scarvey

The Treasure

Forgiveness is a funny thing. It warms the heart and cools the sting.
~William Arthur Ward

At six years old, I dreamed of becoming an artist. My mom knew this, and so she gave the perfect gift to a first-grade artist like me. My friends and I called them "Stampy Markers." They quickly became my treasure.

Unfortunately, my little sister thought they were amazing, too. For three days in a row, she would ask to play with my markers. Finally, she stopped asking, and I was able to leave them out in my room when I went to school, certain that she understood they were off-limits to her.

The first day that I didn't hide them, I got home from school and went upstairs to my room. Right away, I saw that my markers weren't where I had left them. My rainbow-colored treasures were gone!

Suspecting that my sister might have something to do with their disappearance, I searched the house for her. I found her in the basement and, sure enough, she was working on some rainbow drawing with my markers surrounding her.

I started yelling at her and grabbed the markers—at least the ones I could reach—and ran back up to my room, slamming the door behind me. I sat there for at least half an hour, but it seemed like much longer. Finally, I heard my sister's footsteps coming up the stairs.

I opened my mouth, about to demand that she give the rest of my markers back, when I noticed a folded piece of paper being pushed underneath the door.

Once it reached my side of the door, I picked it up. As I read the words written on the cover, my anger quickly fell away, and tears began to well up in my eyes. Then they began running down my cheeks. On the front of the paper in rainbow colors were the words "Best Sister." Inside was a picture she had drawn of herself offering me a late birthday gift.

How could I continue to be selfish and angry at her? How could I blame her for wanting to play with my markers? They were practically irresistible. And the fact that she used them to make something special for me made me realize that the greatest gift and treasure of all is the love you have for your family—and the love they have for you.

I opened the door, reached out to her, gave her a hug, and told her I forgave her.

As for the markers, they ended up running out of color or got lost; I'm not sure which. After all that happened, it didn't really matter. What matters is that I still have the best sister and the greatest treasure. After all, only love lasts forever, and that's the only treasure that everyone can share.

~Charlotte Uteg

Jonny and Me

When you look at your life, the greatest happinesses are
family happinesses.
~Joyce Brothers

My family sometimes talks about "Before Jonny" and "After Jonny." But I've never known life without my special brother.

Not that we're not all special—at least that's what my parents say. We are fifty-four weeks apart, which to some people means we're "Irish Twins." And in a way, we really were like twins when we were little.

Now we're pretty different. That's because Jonny has Down syndrome, or as my mom calls it, "A Little Extra"—an extra chromosome on his twenty-first pair. I finally understood this when we made DNA models with gumdrops and pretzel sticks at school.

Jonny isn't really all that different, but his differences are enough to make him stand out in a crowd. Over the years, I've seen a lot of different reactions from people in all sorts of situations. But while I've heard stories about kids giving disabled kids a rough time, I've never seen that in the places where we've lived. In fact, Jonny seems to bring out the best in the people he meets. Now, when he walks down the halls of our high school, he's greeted with tons of high fives and cries of "Hey, Jonny!"

For a while, in middle school, I even worried that Jonny was more popular than me. When I told my dad how I felt, he said that Jonny had a long road ahead of him—and that he needed all the confidence he could get in his early years. Someday, my dad said, those people high-fiving and "Hey Jonny-ing" him would be the same people who might give jobs to him and other people with disabilities. My dad told me that soon middle school would be over. He said that what I was feeling was normal for a girl with an older brother in the same school and, as he often liked to repeat, "This too shall pass." I used to hate it when my dad said that, but as I get older I start to see that he has a point.

And it did pass—my mixed feelings about Jonny's popularity. Now I'm happy for him. I'm happy we live in a town where he can have a lot of friends and I'm proud of our school where four years ago a senior girl with Down syndrome was voted Homecoming Queen.

While my mom and dad have had to work hard to help Jonny reach his potential, they've worked as hard to help me reach mine. Jonny and I share a love of Broadway musicals and both of us hope someday to work onstage.

Seeing Jonny's life unfold has helped me see that there's a plan for mine as well. Just like Jonny's Down syndrome, our love of music and acting are things that were present in us the day we were born.

My parents say having a baby is like getting a gift from God. As they grow up, that gift is slowly unwrapped until we see what's inside.

Jonny's little extra was obvious the minute he was born. Unwrapping my package may have taken a little longer, but if there's one thing Jonny has taught our family, it's that each of us is a little different. But what's most important are the ways in which we are the same.

~Madeleine Curtis

Fifty-Six Grandparents

You must give some time to your fellow men. Even if it's a little thing, do something for others—something for which you get no pay but the privilege of doing it.
~Albert Schweitzer

There was my mother, standing in a fuzzy pink bunny costume, holding a basket of eggs. *This can't be happening,* I thought to myself. Being ten was hard enough.

I had begged to stay home that day, complaining I'd caught some rare disease and needed to stay in bed. My mother, who's a nurse, looked me over and sent me to school anyway. It was the day our fourth-grade class was taking a field trip to sing to the residents of a nearby convalescent home.

When we got there, I stood at the front door with my entire fourth-grade class, secretly wishing for that rare disease. I'd fall to the ground, be rushed away, and spared the humiliation of anyone ever knowing that I spent every day after school there—me and my mother, the Easter Bunny.

"Hi, Shelly!" The residents waved and smiled as we entered.

"Do you know them?" Angela asked, disgusted.

"No!" I replied. "They're just old and confused. They probably think I'm someone else. Besides, my name's Machille, not Shelly," I reminded her sarcastically.

The men and women who lived in the convalescent home were lined up outside their rooms. Most of them sat in wheelchairs, some stood behind walkers, and some had been wheeled out in their beds.

My mother had explained to me many times that these were special people. Now that they were older and needed a nurse's care for different reasons, they lived here with each other. I thought of it more like a "grandparents' pound"—forgotten grandparents. I saw who had visitors and who didn't.

Our class started singing, and I studied my shoelaces. If I looked up, I might make eye contact with one of them. Everything was going well until Mrs. Deist, our teacher, handed me four tulips that we were supposed to give to the residents. I quickly went to the back of the line. My mother didn't say a word to me; she just went along her way—hopping.

Last year, she had made a red bunny costume for me and we hopped down the halls together, laughing and singing. It had been a lot of fun. *But I'm too old for that now,* I thought.

I shuffled behind my class and gave my tulips to other classmates. They didn't ask any questions, just took the flowers.

"What are you little brats doing here?" Hattie May barked out, snatching a tulip from Jacob's hand.

Hattie May had been here for years. She had a disease that made her forget things and sometimes made her grumpy. She always liked me, though. Sometimes she called me Susie, but I didn't mind. My mom told me her daughter's name is Susie. I've seen Susie before—she's my mom's age, but Hattie's disease doesn't understand time.

Jacob's face turned bright red. The class giggled and pointed. My teacher did her best to keep us moving, knowing that Hattie May didn't mean any harm. I heard someone whisper, "Crazy old lady." The sinking feeling in the pit of my stomach got worse. I smiled at Hattie May as we passed, and she smiled at me.

"Shelly, how about a game of Fish?" Lou grinned, grabbing my arm.

My class and teacher turned and stared. I pulled my arm away and whispered to Lou, "Later, okay?"

I didn't look up; I just waited for the feet in front of me to start moving again. But they didn't move. I studied the tile floor, thinking how cold the floor seemed with the bright lights reflecting off of it. Now I felt like I was officially the "freak show."

"Machille, do you know these people?" Mrs. Deist asked me.

"Um… I… kinda… " I mumbled.

"Well, then, you should lead the way," she smiled and handed me a bunch of tulips.

Could it get any worse? I thought. As I moved to the front of the line, I could hear the rest of the class muttering under their breath. I know they were all talking about me, probably saying things like, "Well, she doesn't have any other friends; why shouldn't she hang out with a bunch of old people?"

I pulled up my chin and looked straight ahead. In front of me were rows of familiar and loving faces. They all smiled big, warm, real smiles. I couldn't help but smile back. I stepped forward and handed a tulip to Rose, a white-haired woman standing behind her walker.

"How's the hip feel today, Rose?" I asked with a grin.

"Okay, Shelly. Thanks for asking," Rose answered and squeezed my hand.

I suddenly forgot that the class was watching me. I continued down the hall, waved to Frank, and gave Mr. Blusso a high-five. When I was out of tulips, I turned back to Mrs. Deist, who handed me five more. Other kids had stopped and were talking with the patients. I saw Angela laughing as Frank showed her a card trick. Jacob was covering Mr. Blusso's legs with a blanket. Mrs. Deist put her arm around me and pulled me close.

"My mother was in a convalescent home for five years before she passed away. I wish she'd had someone like you to look in on her when I couldn't be there. You're very special, Machille," Mrs. Deist winked.

My mother picked that moment to hop over and thank us all for coming by. I proudly took her by the hand and introduced her to my class.

"This is my mom, Geneva. She works here, and every day she takes care of all these special people." I stood tall and straight as I delivered the information. The whole class began to clap.

"Wow. My mom would never put on a bunny costume. Your mom is cool," Tom said, slapping me on the back.

"Hey, do you think I could come by sometime with you after school? I really like that guy Lou, and he promised to teach me how to play gin rummy," Jacob asked.

"Me, too, Machille?" Angela chimed in.

My mother spoke before I could and explained about a program where kids can volunteer after school and on the weekends. The patients cheered at the idea, and my class seemed very excited, too.

That day, I realized how happy it made me to make other people smile and feel good. I should never be ashamed of that. I also learned how lucky I am. I have fifty-six grandparents.

~Machille Legoullon

Harry

Understanding is the first step to acceptance, and only with acceptance can there be recovery.

~J. K. Rowling

"Harry has to go," my mother said firmly. "That's all there is to it."

I turned my back on her—slowly, deliberately—and looked out to where our Doberman rushed around the yard. He looked like a clown with the yellow collar the vet insisted he wear. I could imagine how humiliating it must be and how it must itch. I'd try to pull it off, too, if it were me.

I bit my lip as I thought of life without my best friend. *How could Mom do this?* "You just don't care about Harry anymore," I muttered. "You think he's too big and too much trouble."

"That's not true, young lady," she said sharply. "Maybe I shouldn't have gotten Harry in the first place. But I did, and now he's hurting himself almost every week trying to jump the fence. This yard is just too small."

I didn't think the yard was too small. It had always seemed an endless space with its fruit trees, the prickly forest of raspberry bushes, the large shed, and the huge walnut tree that towered over everything. Every corner of the yard reminded me of an adventure—and beside me, in every adventure, had been Harry.

Sometime later in the week, my mother announced she had found

Harry a good home: a farm with acres for him to run in and where he had work to do. *Work? Why would Harry want to work when he could have fun with me?*

It wasn't long until I was out in the yard with Harry for the final time. The pain in my chest was so bad; I thought it would never go away. Harry, too, seemed to know it was our last day together. He walked slowly with his head down and his feet dragging through the grass. I was blinking to keep back the tears, angry at Mom and angry at Harry. "It's your fault," I told him. "If you hadn't kept jumping the fence, you wouldn't have to go."

At my harsh words, Harry looked up at me. His eyes were like little black pools, sad and helpless. I couldn't stand looking at him anymore, so I went back into the house.

Later, my older brother, Paul, came looking for me. "Aren't you coming? Don't you want to see Harry's new home?"

"You go. You think it's just great that Harry's leaving us," I said, my eyes never leaving the drawing I was coloring.

"Don't be so selfish," Paul said in that superior voice of his, like he was a hundred years older than me, not just two. "Harry will be much happier on a farm."

I didn't say anything, hoping he'd eventually give up and go away, which he did. I covered my ears when I heard the car start and pull away. I could block out any noise in the world, but I couldn't stop thinking of my last hurtful words to Harry. They followed me for days after.

"What's wrong with you?" Paul asked me one morning.

"Nothin'," I said sullenly.

"It's probably something stupid," Paul sniggered. "Did you lose one of your dolls again?"

I glared at him. "It's none of your business."

"It's none of your business… it's none of your business…." Paul sang, mimicking my voice and dancing around my room.

"Oh, just be quiet!" I snapped at him. "I didn't lose a doll…. I lost Harry… and when he went, I told him it was all his fault…." I could feel my eyes brimming over with tears, but this time I didn't try to stop them.

"Don't be such a baby," Paul said. "Harry's a dog—he wouldn't have understood what you said."

But I knew that wasn't true.

I woke up on Saturday to a funny feeling in the air. It seemed to crackle all around me like it did when there was going to be a storm, but the sun was out. I heard whispering as I walked down the hallway, but it stopped abruptly when I reached the dining room. My whole family was eating breakfast around the table, and they were all smiling at me. I could see Paul's feet dancing under the table as he struggled to keep still. His eyes gleamed at me with excitement. "We've got a surpri—"

"Shh!" Mom slapped his hand lightly.

I didn't ask what was going on. I didn't care about anything, unless it was Harry coming home. And so I didn't say anything when Mom ordered us into the car or when Dad drove us across the bridge and out into the country. We went past rolling hills topped with trees, miles of fields dotted with cattle and sheep, and winding creeks. Finally, we stopped.

"Come on!" Paul gave me a push as he jumped out of the car. I opened my door slowly and stood on the rough path. I stretched and breathed in deeply. The air was fresh and cool, and it seemed as though there was never-ending space, miles and miles of it.

My mother marched up to the gate that surrounded the house, and we all followed. A man near the house put down his bucket and walked slowly toward us. He gave a long, low whistle, and two dogs came running down from one of the far sheds. One of the dogs was a shaggy sheepdog, and the other was a Doberman who looked strangely familiar.

"Harry?" I called. I started running toward him, but then stopped as I watched how his long legs seemed to fly across the endless space between us. He could never have run like this in our backyard.

Harry danced around me and barked.

"He wants to show you around," the man said with a grin. "Why don't you go with him?"

So I did. I let Harry show me the sheds where the pigs burrowed in straw and the chickens laid their eggs, the paddocks where he rounded up sheep, and the veggie garden he helped to protect from wild animals.

I was still smiling when we all got back into the car. There was no need to feel upset and sad about Harry anymore. I realized that sometimes changes can be hard, but still be for the best. It helped when I finally saw that Harry was where he belonged.

~Kristie Jones

The Courage to Roar

The difference between school and life?
In school, you're taught a lesson and then given a test.
In life, you're given a test that teaches you a lesson.
~Tom Bodett

The details of our dreams usually vanish quickly upon awakening. But, when I was twelve years old, I had a vivid dream that branded itself in my memory forever.

In it, a tiger sunk his razor-sharp teeth into my ear. I lay there paralyzed with fear, frozen in pain. All I could do was listen to my heart boom loudly in my chest. My eyes flew open, shattering the dream, but I was certain there was a tiger under my bed. I needed proof that the big cat was really gone, so I slowly lifted the bed skirt and peered under the bed. No sign of a tiger, only an old pair of Keds tennis shoes, big, fuzzy slippers with puppy dog heads, three *Teen* magazines, and a few dust bunnies.

Mom called from the kitchen, "Helen, are you awake? Your breakfast is almost ready."

"Yes, Mom. I'll be right there."

I got dressed in front of the full-length mirror. It proved to me every day that my butt was too big, my skin was too oily and my curly red hair defied taming. My eyes were the only good feature I had going for me. They were almond-shaped, caramel-colored with tiny, golden specks that reflected the color of my curvy lashes. When

I looked closer into the mirror, I found a huge, cherry-red zit sitting on the very tip of my nose. I wanted to jump back into bed and pull the covers over my head, but I knew that Mom would still make me go to school.

I slumped down the stairs dragging my backpack, and when I walked into the kitchen, my nine-year-old brother took one look at me and said, "Hey, look! It's Rudolph the Red-Nosed Reindeer."

I shot him an angry glance. "Shut up, you little dork. Mom, can we trade Todd in for a dog or a cat, or even a gerbil?"

"No, we can't," she said. "He's your brother, so you're stuck with him. Todd, apologize to Helen."

Todd gave a heavy sigh. "Okay, I'm sorry that you look like Rudolph the Red-Nosed Reindeer."

I raised my fist in Todd's direction and said, "You're gonna look like vomit soup."

Mom extended her arm like a cop stopping traffic. "That's enough from both of you. That blemish doesn't look so bad, Helen. I'll put some make-up on it right after breakfast."

I gulped my breakfast, brushed my teeth and waited for Mom to work her magic on the red balloon that sprouted from the tip of my nose. "This should do the trick," Mom said, as she opened a bottle of cover-up and dabbed some on my nose. Todd studied my face for a moment and said, "Anyone up for mountain climbing?" I opened my mouth to protest just as Mom spotted the school bus coming down the street. She quickly coaxed us out the door saying, "Don't worry, it'll be fine."

We boarded the bus and I plopped myself down on a seat near the back. I turned my face to the window, closed my eyes and thought how great it would be to rule my own world. There would be no school, no parents to tell kids what to do, no brothers, and no more pimples.

My thoughts drifted, the air became warm and heavy and my eyelids closed. My earlier dream flowed back into my thoughts, and I found myself in a jungle of tall trees.

As I picked my way through the tall grass, I had a feeling that I was not alone. I heard a growling, rumbling noise and turned to find an enormous tiger, posed in a valiant stance, gazing at me. The sunlight filtered through the trees and flickered over his majestic body. Prominent black stripes were perfectly painted over his ivory-white to reddish-orange fur. His nostrils flared in anger at my impudence in invading his habitat. He let out a mighty roar, and I started to run.

I knew that I couldn't outrun the tiger, so I grabbed onto a golden-colored vine hanging from a tree and climbed. When I looked down in my dream, the tiger was clawing his way up the tree trunk. I could think of nothing else to do, so I opened my mouth and roared with a thunderous clap that echoed through the air. At the sound of my roar, the tiger began to shrink. I gave one last powerful blast, and the tiger shrunk down to the size of a kitten. I now felt confident enough to come down from the tree, so I swung down to where the kitten sat. I felt powerful and free.

I woke up, hearing laughter in the distance that became so loud it disturbed my thoughts. I squirmed in my seat and remembered that I was on the bus, not in a jungle.

Kids were laughing as two boys tossed Todd's lunch bag back and forth across the aisle. Todd was getting more upset with each toss. After a couple more throws, I got up and stood in front of the boy who just caught the pass.

"Hand it over," I said, giving him my best steely-eyed glare.

"Oh yeah?" he said. "Whaddaya gonna do if I don't?"

"I'll go straight to the principal and rat you out as a bully. I have lots of eyewitnesses here to support my story. You'll probably get detention or worse."

He paused for a moment, gave me a silly grin, and pitched me the lunch bag. "Take it. We were done anyway."

The bus pulled up to the school, the doors opened, and kids started piling out. Todd remained in his seat with a soulful look on his face. I walked over to him, handed him his lunch and said, "Don't worry about it, Todd. Those guys are jerks. Come on; walk with me up to the school."

We walked together quietly for a while and then Todd said, "Hey, Helen? Did you know that you look really pretty today?"

"Sure, punk. I'm positively glowing—especially around my nose."
I gave Todd a playful push, and we both laughed.

~Helen Stein

Conversation Starters

1. In the short story "The Treasure" on page 121, what exactly is Charlotte's treasure?

2. "Fifty-Six Grandparents" starts on page 125. How did Machille know all of the residents in the convalescent home before the class field trip?

3. In the story "The Courage to Roar" on page 133, Helen dreams about a tiger. How does her courage to roar surface in her real life?

Be the Best You Can Be

Handling Bullies

Kindness
Is More Powerful

As the sun makes ice melt, kindness causes misunderstanding,
mistrust, and hostility to evaporate.
~Albert Schweitzer

"Is she coming?" my shaky voice cracked. I didn't dare look behind me. My sister, Kayleen, turned to see the front of the middle school where eager seventh- and eighth-graders were pushing their way to carpools or making their way down the sidewalk toward an evening of television and homework.

"No," she whispered, "but if we walk faster, maybe we'll miss her completely. I'll bet she's still waiting for you outside the gym door."

I walked faster with my head bent down because tears were stinging my eyes and my nose had started to run. My heart was beating furiously and I had a sick feeling in my stomach.

Who was "she?" You might be wondering. Her name was Sabrina, and she was a bully. We were in gym class together, and I was less than athletic—more like pathetic! I didn't run very fast, and I was afraid of being hit by a ball, so I was a ducker not a catcher.

That day during gym class, we had played soccer. I not only embarrassed myself, I also made Sabrina mad—basically because she was on my team, and we didn't win. So, in the shower, she threatened me! "I'll meet you after class," she sneered, "and you will wish you and I had never met!"

I didn't need to wait until after class, I already wished we had never met!

As soon as class was over, I snuck out the teacher's entrance and ran to my locker where Kayleen was already waiting for me, so we could walk home together.

"What's up with you?" she asked, noticing the look of panic in my eyes. "Sabrina!" I choked. "We lost the soccer game in gym and it was my fault. She was on my team."

"Oh," Kayleen simply stated, but she patted my back in understanding. "Well," she said, "we'll walk down Seventeenth South instead of Harrison. It's out of the way enough that Sabrina won't have a clue."

Kayleen and I lived straight down the hill about a mile from Clayton Middle School. Sabrina lived somewhere in the middle. She had followed us most of the way chanting harassments since the first day of school. I couldn't figure out what I had ever done to her. She couldn't have had an idea of how bad I was at sports on the first day of school!

My mother said it was because I was quiet and kind and non-confrontational that made me an easy target for bullies. I just felt like a loser! I was grateful for Kayleen, though. I always knew I could count on her. I think because she was my older sister, she felt like she needed to be my protector, and she was, always thinking of ways to avoid Sabrina or any of her sidekicks who enjoyed harassing me on a daily basis.

"Slow down!" Kayleen gasped. "You're practically running. We're far enough away now to be safe."

I looked up and Kayleen noticed my tears. "What about tomorrow?" I sobbed. "She'll just make it worse tomorrow!"

Kayleen stopped dead in her tracks, causing me to stop, as well. I turned to look at her. She stood there with her hands on her hips. "Well, then," she said in her favorite grown-up voice, "I guess you just might have to tell someone, then!"

"It will just make it worse," I mumbled.

The next day arrived in record time. As Kayleen and I made our way up the steep Harrison Avenue hill, I felt sick. "I still think you should tell somebody," Kayleen chirped every few minutes.

I never replied until she had said that at least ten times, and then I burst out, "Tell somebody *what*? That Sabrina is mean and scary and just creeps me out? She's never actually done anything! Am I supposed to just tell them I am a big, fat baby who can't handle seventh grade because she is in it, too? What am I supposed to say?" Kayleen didn't respond. We walked the rest of the way in silence.

In homeroom, Sabrina's best friend passed me a note that stated, "At lunch, you will pay for running away!" I didn't even look up, but I accidentally swallowed my gum and choked until Mr. McKonkie excused me to go and get a drink.

Walking down the hall, I felt a slight sense of relief and freedom. Still, the note had me scared, and I ducked into the girls' bathroom and just cried. When I calmed down enough, I washed my face so I could go back to class without it being totally obvious. As I made my way down the hallway, I had a sick feeling that I was being followed.

Suddenly, someone kicked me in the back of the leg, hard. I almost fell over. "You little chicken!" Sabrina's voice sneered. I didn't turn around, I just walked faster. *Why wasn't she in class?* I wondered in my panic. I turned to go into Mr. McKonkie's class, but Sabrina blocked me. I turned again and started running down the hall. I had no idea what she was going to do, but three months of constant harassment was weighing heavily on my mind, and I was really freaked out.

Sabrina was now chasing me. At last, she caught up with me enough to kick the back of my legs, trying to knock me down. In a panic, I swung around to the staircase that led to the science and math department. Sabrina was so close to me by then that my sudden shift in direction knocked her off balance and she toppled down the stairs. I stood there watching her fall.

At first, I felt a sudden independence and victory. I turned to walk away from her when I noticed she hadn't stood up yet. Instinct took over, and I suddenly wasn't afraid of her anymore. I practically jumped down the stairs and touched her shoulder. "Can I help?" I asked. When she looked up, I could tell she was in pain. "I can't walk," she moaned. I helped her into a standing position, put her arm around my shoulder and together we hobbled to the nurse's office.

Sabrina never harassed me after that. We never became friends, but from that moment at the foot of the stairs, I knew I had earned her respect. She still hated being on my team in gym class, but things were different. Her best friend would still start in on me sometimes, but Sabrina would shake her head and quietly say, "Leave her alone."

And she always would.

~Janalea Jeppson

EDITORS' NOTE: For more information about how to deal with bullies, log on to www.kidshealth.org (keyword search: "bullying").

The Little Girl Who Dared to Wish

Never be bullied into silence. Never allow yourself to be made a victim.
~Tim Field

As Amy Hagadorn rounded the corner across the hall from her classroom, she collided with a tall boy from the fifth grade running in the opposite direction.

"Watch it, squirt," the boy yelled as he dodged around the little third-grader. Then, with a smirk on his face, the boy took hold of his right leg and mimicked the way Amy limped when she walked.

Amy closed her eyes. *Ignore him*, she told herself as she headed for her classroom.

But at the end of the day, Amy was still thinking about the tall boy's mean teasing. It wasn't as if he were the only one. It seemed that ever since Amy started the third grade, someone teased her every single day. Kids teased her about her speech or her limping. Amy was tired of it. Sometimes, even in a classroom full of other students, the teasing made her feel all alone.

Back home at the dinner table that evening, Amy was quiet. Her mother knew that things were not going well at school. That's why Patti Hagadorn was happy to have some exciting news to share with her daughter.

"There's a Christmas wish contest on the radio station," Amy's mom announced. "Write a letter to Santa, and you might win a prize. I think someone at this table with blonde curly hair should enter."

Amy giggled. The contest sounded like fun. She started thinking about what she wanted most for Christmas.

A smile took hold of Amy when the idea first came to her. Out came pencil and paper, and Amy went to work on her letter. "Dear Santa Claus," she began.

While Amy worked away at her best printing, the rest of the family tried to guess what she might ask from Santa. Amy's sister, Jamie, and Amy's mom both thought a three-foot Barbie doll would top Amy's wish list. Amy's dad guessed a picture book. But Amy wasn't ready to reveal her secret Christmas wish just then. Here is Amy's letter to Santa, just as she wrote it that night:

Dear Santa Claus,

My name is Amy. I am nine years old. I have a problem at school. Can you help me, Santa? Kids laugh at me because of the way I walk and run and talk. I have cerebral palsy. I just want one day where no one laughs at me or makes fun of me.

Love,

Amy

At radio station WJLT in Fort Wayne, Indiana, letters poured in for the Christmas wish contest. The workers had fun reading about all the different presents that boys and girls from across the city wanted for Christmas.

When Amy's letter arrived at the radio station, manager Lee Tobin read it carefully. He knew cerebral palsy was a muscle disorder that might confuse the schoolmates of Amy's who didn't understand her disability. He thought it would be good for the people in Fort Wayne to hear about this special third-grader and her unusual wish. Mr. Tobin called up the local newspaper.

The next day, a picture of Amy and her letter to Santa made the front page of the *News Sentinel*. The story spread quickly. All across the country, newspapers and radio and television stations reported the story of the little girl in Fort Wayne, Indiana, who asked for such a simple yet remarkable Christmas gift—just one day without teasing.

Suddenly the postman was a regular at the Hagadorn house. Envelopes of all sizes addressed to Amy arrived daily from children and adults all across the nation. They came filled with holiday greetings and words of encouragement.

During that unforgettable Christmas season, over two thousand people from all over the world sent Amy letters of friendship and support. Amy and her family read every single one. Some of the writers had disabilities; some had been teased as children. Each writer had a special message for Amy. Through the cards and letters from strangers, Amy glimpsed a world full of people who truly cared about each other. She realized that no amount or form of teasing could ever make her feel lonely again.

Many people thanked Amy for being brave enough to speak up. Others encouraged her to ignore teasing and to carry her head high. Lynn, a sixth-grader from Texas, sent this message:

"I would like to be your friend," she wrote, "and if you want to visit me, we could have fun. No one would make fun of us, 'cause if they do, we will not even hear them."

Amy did get her wish of a special day without teasing at South Wayne Elementary School. Additionally, everyone at school got another bonus. Teachers and students talked together about how bad teasing can make others feel.

That year, the Fort Wayne mayor officially proclaimed December 21 as Amy Jo Hagadorn Day throughout the city. The mayor explained that by daring to make such a simple wish, Amy taught a universal lesson.

"Everyone," said the mayor, "wants and deserves to be treated with respect, dignity and warmth."

~Alan D. Shultz

Bullied
to a Better Life

*It's wonderful when you can bring sparkle into people's lives
without fading away from your own true color. Keep the hue in you.*
~Dodinsky

was in third grade and my parents said I was a cute kid with a great personality who loved to laugh. The problem was that I was overweight, and that year the bullying began. A couple of kids at school started picking on me. Before school, after school, at recess, on the bus. "Fatty, Tubbo, Jelly Roll" were names I was called every day. They would throw stuff at me too. I was so scared I wouldn't ride the bus and my mom had to take me to school. Even when I got to school I would scream and cry, begging my mom not to leave me there.

I didn't tell my mom and dad why I didn't want to go to school anymore, so instead I would fake being sick all the time. I just wanted to stay at home where I was safe. My parents talked to my teacher, my principal, and a school counselor. They finally found out I was being bullied and I got to switch to a new class with an awesome teacher, Mrs. Willhoite. There were not any bullies in her class and she would let me bring my lunch to her room and eat with her so I didn't have to go to recess and be around those mean kids from my old class.

The bullies were still picking on me in fourth, fifth, and sixth grades. I would see them in the halls. They'd be there at recesses. But I had finally been truthful and asked for help. My mom and dad worked with the school to make sure I was in good classes and protected as much as possible. Would the bullying have been so bad if I had asked for help in the very beginning? I don't know, but I do know that once my parents found out they got me help. And once I got help, I didn't have to deal with the bullies by myself.

By sixth grade, even though I was hardly being bullied, I started to get sick for real. I weighed 206 pounds by the time I was eleven. I had solved the bullying problem, but now I had to take care of my health. I started drinking water instead of soda, eating fruits and veggies instead of chips and candy. I even put down my Xbox controller and went outside. I got active and started getting healthier. I lost some weight and felt great. I lost some more it was awesome! The harder I worked, the more I lost. The better I felt, the harder I worked. By the time I got to seventh grade I lost 85 pounds! My friends hardly recognized me. The bullies didn't even think I was the same kid and left me alone. I was back to being what my parents had described when I was in third grade — a cute kid with a great personality who loved to laugh.

I started a project called Strive for 85, since 85 is the magic number of pounds that I lost. I shared my story with 85 important people, including Michelle Obama. I inspired 85 other kids. I hosted or attended 85 events that raised awareness. I've been on TV, in magazines, even got to fly to Washington, D.C.... twice. I've spent the last year traveling around to schools and telling them bullying is never okay. I was overweight but I didn't deserve to get picked on.

Here's what the bullies say to me now: "Can I have your autograph?"

If you are being bullied, get help. You don't have to deal with this alone. You have to believe in yourself and not let mean kids decide who you will be and what you can do. If you are being the bully, stop! Come run with me instead or go ride a bike, climb a building, hit a punching bag. Do anything other than try to make a kid, like me, feel bad about himself. You never know… the person you're picking on could turn out to be the president one day.

~Mason Carter Harvey

The Kindness Cure

If you can, help others; if you cannot do that, at least do not harm them.
~Randy Rind

"Hey!" the voice called from behind me. "Are you a girl or a duck?" I ignored the comment even though I knew it was directed at me.

I ran to my class, causing my slight limp to become even more apparent. I didn't care. I just wanted to get away from the group of mean girls behind me. It was my first day at a new school and I was still trying to learn how to find my class. I wasn't prepared to handle this type of treatment also.

Already, I could see that things would be different here. At my old school, I had a group of friends to protect me. If those friends had been there, I just knew they'd be yelling back, "Hey! Leave her alone!" I could actually see Maryann and Elisa waving their fists at the name-callers and howling their warning, "Or else!"

Yet starting today, in this new school, I was on my own. I took my place in the first row of desks, grateful for alphabetic seating. My last name came at the beginning of the alphabet and the mean girl Betsy's last name came at the end of the alphabet. That put a full five rows between us.

By the time lunch hour arrived, I was feeling better about my situation. Betsy and her group had been quiet during class and polite when speaking to the teacher. Surely, they had calmed down and wouldn't be repeating their behavior. Or so I thought. The minute I walked into the hallway, I felt a hand at my back. It was Betsy.

"I don't like being ignored," she said. "I asked you a question before and I expect you to answer it."

"Yeah," chimed her chorus of friends, "answer it."

I looked at her, "What question?"

"Are you a girl or a duck?"

"I'm a girl."

"Then why do you walk like a duck?"

I felt my face redden. "I don't walk like a duck," I insisted.

"Yes you do," Betsy smirked. "Quack, quack."

"Quack, quack, quack," sang her chorus. Then they all broke into fits of laughter and went off to take their seats for lunch. I, however, went to the far end of the cafeteria and ate my lunch alone and in silence. Was this how I would spend the rest of my school days?

As the weeks went on, though, I made friends with two girls named Fran and Lisa who sat near me in class. They didn't seem too thrilled with Betsy either and whenever she made one of her snarky remarks they would wave it off and tell me to ignore her. Eventually, I also gained skill in avoiding Betsy and her group of crazy quackers. I didn't linger in the hallway before and after class and I went directly home at dismissal time.

Still, I hated that I didn't walk like everyone else. I didn't like not being able to run as fast or as straight as the other kids and I didn't like getting picked last for teams in gym class. Mostly, though, I really hated it when people like Betsy made dumb remarks about how I walked. Yet I learned to live with it until one day the game changed.

"Class," our teacher addressed us one morning, "you've been in the same seats for a full semester and you've become friendly with the students around you. Now it's time to change seats and make some new friends."

The class let out a collective moan, yet our teacher would not be dissuaded. As she assigned the new seating, Fran, Lisa, and I looked at each other while we waited for our names to be called. We didn't want to be separated. And we especially didn't want to sit anywhere near Betsy.

Fran and Lisa's names were called first. Though they weren't sitting right next to each other, they were sitting close. Then my name was called. I took my seat. Then Betsy's name was called. She took her seat — directly behind me.

I knew this wasn't going to be good and I soon discovered I was right. For Betsy, her new seat assignment was like hitting the bully jackpot. I could practically hear her rubbing her hands together in delight. She was as close to her target as she could get and she didn't waste any time getting to work. The torment started within minutes. Betsy leaned into my back: "Quack, quack." When I ignored her, she kicked my seat. When that didn't work, she poked me. This went on daily until one morning I simply refused to go to school.

My mother sat me down after I told her the details of my harsh treatment. "Look," she said, "there will always be mean people in this world. That will never change. But you can change the way you handle them. Did you ever hear of the saying 'Kill 'em with kindness'?"

I shook my head, no.

"It's simple. Just give Betsy a compliment from time to time. If she drops her pen, pick it up and hand it to her. Things like that. Just be so nice to her that it takes the fun out of teasing you."

I was doubtful, but I was also desperate. Even though Mom's "kill 'em with kindness" idea didn't seem logical to me, I was still willing to give it a try. After I took my seat that morning, I turned toward Betsy. Her hair was a mess. She was wearing a pair of old jeans and the same worn pink and purple shirt she wore every Monday morning. How could I possibly compliment her?

"Betsy," I squeaked, "did I ever tell you how much I like that shirt? Those colors are my favorites."

She looked back at me blank-eyed, "Uh, thanks."

Maybe my mother was on to something because Betsy only quacked once and poked me twice that morning. My new tack seemed to be working and I kept at it. Instead of rushing out of class on Friday afternoons, I began to wish her a good weekend. On Monday mornings,

I'd ask her if she'd done anything special on Saturday and Sunday. She usually would only answer with a mumble, but I did notice she was being less mean to me and some Fridays she would even wish me a good weekend first. It almost seemed as though Betsy was starting to like me.

Then one day I really had the chance to shine. Our teacher was in a pretty serious mood that day. Spring break had passed and most of the students were starting to forget about schoolwork and think about summer vacation. Grades were down and homework assignments were late. In an effort to get us back on track, the teacher began to quiz us with questions from our studies throughout the year. She sat at her desk, asking questions at lightning speed and expecting fast replies. Whenever a student would give an incorrect answer, she would remark, "Wrong!" and move on to the next student.

When my turn came, I answered quickly and correctly. Then it was Betsy's turn. "What year did Columbus discover America?" the teacher asked.

I stood still, sensing Betsy's terror. I knew she couldn't possibly remember the answer. The day we learned that lesson, Betsy had been too busy jabbing me to have heard anything the teacher said. But I knew the answer. And I wrote it down on a piece of paper and slipped it over the side of my desk where the teacher couldn't see.

Startled, Betsy looked down. "1492!" she answered in triumph.

I had saved the day.

In the days that followed, something interesting happened. Betsy started to open up to me. Her parents were recently divorced and her dad was somewhere where she said she couldn't visit him. Also, her mom had become ill and was awaiting surgery. I could see the pain in her pale blue eyes and, for a minute, I felt sorry for her. Betsy's teasing soon stopped altogether.

On the last day of school, Betsy turned to me. "You're really nice," she said. "I don't know why I was so mean to you."

But, by that time, I had figured out why she had been so cruel. She was so unhappy at home that she took out her frustrations at school—on me. However, when I was kind to her the teasing lost its appeal.

We parted that June day and I never did see Betsy again. Apparently, her mother's illness was serious and she and her sister were sent to live with grandparents in another part of the state. While I hoped Betsy found happiness there, I couldn't say that I missed her. Honestly, part of me was glad that she was gone. But a bigger part of me was even gladder that I had listened to my mom and turned on the kindness. It was just what I needed. And probably just what Betsy needed, too.

~Monica A. Andermann

The Smile
that Beat the Bully

Be excellent to each other.
~Bill and Ted's Excellent Adventure

Have you ever had a bully who scared the skin off you? The one bully who you have nightmares about? It's the face you see when you get up in the morning with your stomach all tied in knots. Rosalie Bangeter was that for me—she was a bully in every sense of the word, and I was terrified of her. She was one of the meanest girls I'd ever met, and I have a sneaking suspicion that I was not the only person in the seventh grade who lived in mortal fear of her. I'll never forget the day I saw her pulverize another student in the cafeteria. As if pounding the girl wasn't bad enough, she topped it off by dunking her head in a half-eaten tray of meatloaf and mashed potatoes.

To this day, I don't know why Rosalie hated me so much. The fact that I merely existed and had the nerve to breathe in and out seemed to tick Rosalie off, and she never missed an opportunity to threaten or ridicule me. I would hear her jeering remarks when I walked out to catch the bus home. I could feel the heat of her glare when I cowered in my seat in the cafeteria and avoided looking anywhere near her direction. I would've walked the length of two football fields to avoid coming in contact with Rosalie Bangeter if I could have, but unfortunately there just wasn't enough time to do that and still get to my fifth period class before the bell rang.

So I had to face the reality that, for two or three excruciating seconds every day, I had to walk past Rosalie Bangeter in the hall. I tried hanging out in my fourth period class a few extra seconds and walking a little slower to my locker in the hope that Rosalie would have already gone to class, but that never worked. I would still pass her. Of course, I didn't dare make eye contact with her, but I caught sight of her sneer in my peripheral vision while I scampered past. I knew it would only be a matter of time before she lashed out at me.

I was one of those quiet, timid seventh graders who talked up a blue streak at home but wouldn't say two words at school. I had a couple of close friends who were just as shy as I was, and we usually huddled together and tried to stay out of everyone's way. Deep down, I was envious of those outgoing, cheerleader girls who would be the first ones to raise their hands to do a math problem on the chalkboard. I felt like life was passing me by and that if I disappeared one day, no one at school would even notice or care.

My family lived in a small town of about three thousand people, and it seemed as if my dad knew every single one of them. What was even more astonishing was that everyone seemed to know him. One day, I asked my mom how this was possible. She thought about this a minute and then said, "Well, Jenn, your dad never lets anyone stay a stranger. He talks to everyone he sees, and then he gives them that big smile of his. I guess it's contagious because people just love him."

I wanted to be more like my dad. I wanted to get to know people and to somehow leave my mark on the world. But more than anything, I was tired of being that girl who cowered in a corner and got picked on.

I thought about what my mom had said. I knew I had to take action, but how? There was no way I could just go to school one day and start talking to everybody. Forget for a moment that they would have thought I was a raving lunatic—I knew that, as good as my intentions were, I would never be able to force the words out of my mouth. So, I caught hold of the phrase where she talked about his smile. I could smile. I mean, everyone could do that, right? I decided to try it out, but I knew that there was only one way to go to the heart of my fears. I would take my experiment straight to the biggest bully of all—Rosalie Bangeter.

I don't think I heard a single word my math teacher said that day in fourth period because I was too busy thinking about what I was about to do. Finally, the bell rang. I gathered my books and headed to my locker. My heart was pounding in my chest, and my hands were so sweaty I was afraid I'd drop my books. Somehow, I managed to shove my math book in the locker and pull out my English book. I ran my tongue over my teeth that felt dryer than the Mojave Desert. Then I did a practice smile that I was sure looked more like a grimace. I took a deep breath and willed my feet to keep moving forward.

I saw her in the distance coming toward me, looking as mean as ever. For the first time in my life, I made eye contact with her, and then I did it! I actually managed to squeak out a smile through my chattering teeth. Rosalie looked downright shocked, and then she scowled. I hurried past, sure that she was going to turn around and pounce on me. I don't think I took another breath until I made it to my next class and collapsed in the chair.

The next day, I tried again. This time, my teeth weren't chattering quite so badly. Rosalie was no longer surprised, but her snarl remained. This went on for several days, until one day, she didn't glower. I hurried past her. Maybe she was in too big of a hurry today, I thought.

The next day, she didn't glower at me either. In fact, she gave me a little half-smile for my effort. Over the next few weeks, Rosalie actually started smiling back. And then came that memorable day when I got the nerve to nod and say hi. I couldn't believe it! She said hi back! At the end of the year, Rosalie looked me up and asked me to sign her yearbook.

In the years that followed, I broke out of my shell one small chip at a time. I made many new friends and became an active participant in my classes. Looking back now, I can trace it all to that fateful day when I had the courage to smile in the face of the bully. The next time you're in a jam, give it a try—it's amazing how far a smile can go.

~Jennifer Youngblood

The Bully and the Braid

Kindness is in our power, even when fondness is not.
~Samuel Johnson

"Somebody's gonna get beat up," announced May Jordan while casually leaning against the monkey bars. Frozen by fear, the group of students surrounding May silently hoped that her latest victim wasn't among them, but they knew full well that there was always a chance. "We'll see after school," she said before flexing her large muscles for effect. Meanwhile, I hugged my Cabbage Patch Kid on a nearby bench, trying desperately to ignore the lump in my throat; it now felt the size of a small tangerine. I couldn't wait for recess to end.

I loved school, I really did. But since May had transferred in, Elliott Elementary had become an uncomfortable place. At approximately five feet eight inches, May was the tallest kid in our fifth grade class, and, in fact had already sprung well above every student in the school. Although her height was intimidating, it wasn't a problem—her attitude was. No part of the student population was beyond the reach of May's menacing taunts: She routinely hurled insults at innocent third graders who were too afraid to defend themselves; she blatantly bullied boys during gym class; she even threatened to snatch the patches off the sashes of Girl Scouts.

After carefully looking over their shoulders so as to ensure that May wasn't within earshot, many students contended that she was all bark and no bite. But I wasn't so sure. I had managed to fly under May's radar—and I wanted to keep it that way. But all that changed when I showed up for school one morning with a new (albeit unoriginal) hairstyle. Apparently, by wearing my hair in a French braid, I had managed to change my fate.

It all started when my best friend, Jaime, said my hair looked nice. I noticed May's piercing glare—and it made me uncomfortable—but I remained focused on my math worksheet. Then came May's daunting proclamation as she passed me in the cafeteria: "Nice braid. Somebody might cut it off."

I was scared. But what really sent me into a tailspin was when May, who was now clear across the room, moved her fingers to imitate a pair of scissors in motion. My stomach dropped to my knees, and I immediately came up with a plan, which involved hiding out in the bathroom at the end of the school day so as to avoid running into May on the walk home.

I awoke the next morning with a start and scurried to the bathroom to watch my mother get ready for work. Although my watching her had become routine, she knew something was up.

"What's wrong, Courtney?" my mother said, while sweeping the apples of her cheeks with blush.

"Nothing," I replied.

"You're lying. Tell me the truth," she persisted.

"May Jordan wants to cut off my braid," I sputtered with a mouth thick with saliva; tears began to fall.

"She's a bully," my mother said earnestly while taking my chin in her hand. "She thrives on making others scared, that's all. Don't be afraid of her, Courtney. If she can see that you're not afraid, she will stop. I'll bet she's like everybody else—she just wants to fit in and make friends. Perhaps she just doesn't know how."

I rolled my mother's words around in my head. She did have

a valid point. May wasn't so great at making friends. Maybe — just maybe — underneath all that toughness was a regular fifth grader who simply wanted to be liked. Did I have what it would take to befriend May? I wasn't sure, but I wanted to find out.

Later that morning, I told Jaime that I had made the tentative decision to talk to May.

"You're crazy," she said. "Do you know what she could do?"

"Maybe not," I replied. I didn't quite believe my own words, but I realized that, for the first time, my curiosity outweighed my fear.

After lunch, I approached May at the pencil sharpener and went for broke: I invited her to come to my house after school. "We could walk home together, if you'd like. Maybe watch the Nickelodeon Channel?" I offered. (I'd be lying if I didn't admit that I was somewhat pacified by the idea that I'd be on home turf, under the watchful eye of my parents, where little could go wrong.) Still, I was proud that I had extended the invitation.

Then, something unprecedented happened. Something that I would not have believed had I not seen it with my own eyes. May smiled. And then she said yes.

I don't remember what we watched on television, or what my mother prepared for our after-school snack. But I do know that I went from ruing the day I wore a French braid to school to realizing that it had become the catalyst for a new friendship.

May Jordan never bullied me again, and, in fact, we became pretty good friends. After spending countless afternoons at my house, I quickly realized that, yes, underneath the tall girl's armor was an insecure fifth grader who wanted nothing more than to be accepted.

I've since learned that the old adage, you can't judge a book by its cover, certainly rings true, and that someone who looks different on the outside can really be just like you.

~Courtney Conover

Losing an Enemy

If your enemy is hungry, feed him;
if he is thirsty, give him something to drink.
~Romans 12:20

Last year, my brothers were enrolled in Pioneer Clubs, a weekly kids program at our church. Daniel was nine, and Timothy was seven. My sister, my dad and I were all teachers at the same church program. At one point during the year, my brothers began to complain that a boy named John was picking on them.

John, an eleven-year-old foster boy, was in my dad's class. He was the type of kid who always seemed to be in trouble. Worse, he didn't consider that it was his behavior that was the problem, but instead decided my dad was picking on him. He often took it out on my brothers by knocking off their hats, calling them names, kicking them and running away. Even I received the occasional rude remark from John. We all thought he was a real pain.

When my mom heard about the problem, she came home from town a few days later with a bag of wrapped butterscotch candies.

"These are for John," she told Daniel and Timothy.

"For *who?*"

"For John." Mom went on to explain how an enemy could be conquered by kindness.

It was hard for any of us to imagine being kind to John; he was so annoying. But the next week the boys went to Pioneer Clubs with butterscotch candies in their pockets—one for themselves and one for John.

As I was heading to my class, I overheard Timothy saying, "Here John, this is for you." When we got home, I asked Timothy what John's response had been.

Timothy shrugged. "He just looked surprised, then he said thank you and ate it."

The next week when John came running over, Tim held on to his hat and braced himself for an attack. But John didn't touch him. He only asked, "Hey, Tim, do you have any more candy?"

"Yep." A relieved Timothy reached into his pocket and handed John a candy. After that, John found him every week and asked for a candy, and most times Timothy remembered to bring them—one for himself, and one for John.

Meanwhile, I "conquered my enemy" in another way. One time as I passed John in the hall, I saw a sneer come over his face. He started to open his mouth, but I said, "Hi, John!" and gave him a big smile before he had a chance to speak.

Surprised, he shut his mouth, and I walked on. From then on, whenever I saw him I would greet him with a smile and say, "Hi, John!" before he had a chance to say anything rude. Instead, he started to simply return the greeting.

It's been a while since John picked on my brothers, and he's not rude to me anymore, either. Even my dad is impressed with the change in him. He's a nicer John now than he was a year ago—I guess because someone finally gave him a chance.

He wasn't the only one to change. My whole family learned what it meant to love an enemy. What's strange is that in the process, we lost that enemy—he was "conquered" by love.

Love: It never fails.

~Patty Anne Sluys

Solving a Fifth Grade Problem

Never be bullied into silence. Never allow yourself to be made a victim.
Accept no one's definition of your life, but define yourself.
~Harvey S. Firestone

"Hey Alena, nice leggings!" Britney yelled from atop the slide. Her voice carried mockingly to where I was swinging. Then, with a burst of laughter, she glided to the sand to join her posse of girls.

Britney Palmer was the elected point person of The Pink Ladies, a group of elite fifth graders to which I desperately wanted to belong.

Shoot. They were all wearing jeans. The Spandex I wore hadn't been in style in five years. Aside from the fact that my mother proudly dressed me in my cousin's hand-me-downs, I was chubby. Thus, I was The Pink Ladies' favorite target.

"I told my mom they are stupid but she made me wear them anyway." My attempt to explain my embarrassing choice of wardrobe just encouraged more laughter. I stared down at my swinging feet.

They joined hands and skipped to the corner of the playground where they plopped down in a circle. I couldn't decide which felt worse, when I was the object of their scorn or when they forgot I existed.

"Okay, so tomorrow we all have to wear pigtails," Britney addressed the six girls who circled her. "And if you don't, you can't play with us all day. This way, everybody will know who is a Pink Lady and who is not."

The next morning, it was clear what I had to do.

"Mom, can you put my hair in pigtails?" I stood in the dark at the edge of her bed, looking intently at her sleeping face.

"Alena, I'm sleeping. Maybe tomorrow," she muttered.

"But I need them today."

"Then you'll have to do it yourself," she replied, turning over. I left her room in defeat and headed for the bathroom.

I studied my reflection, comb in one hand, two hair ties in the other, trying to see what it was that caused The Pink Ladies to explode in laughter every time I smiled in their direction. I could understand my round face and straggly hair, but why didn't they like my blue eyes or the beauty mark next to my mouth like Cindy Crawford's? I placed one hand on my stomach and the other on the small of my back, making a hasty measurement of my waistline. Would they like me if my hands were closer together?

I had never made pigtails before, and I knew it would be no easy feat. I pulled, pushed, maneuvered, tightened and loosened, but my efforts were fruitless. My pigtails were hopelessly lopsided. After a ten-minute struggle, I had to surrender to my fate and run to the bus stop.

As soon as I entered the classroom that day, I felt the burn of The Pink Ladies' stares on me. If I had been fortunate enough to possess telekinetic powers, I would have willed the hair ties to the floor.

For the first half of the day, despite the many superficial compliments I gave them, they ignored me. Not exactly the reaction I had imagined. I was discouraged, but too proud to relent and untie my hair.

At snack time, I sat in a corner, chewing on peanut butter crackers and bemoaning my situation to my friend Amy, when I noticed Emily Kaplan and Elizabeth Hawkins approaching. Sure that I was about to be reprimanded for my false indication of popularity, I swallowed hard and prepared myself for verbal war.

"We know you are wearing pigtails just because we are, and you aren't allowed to. Pigtails are the way we are wearing our hair today and you aren't one of us," Emily said, propping her hands on her hips and pursing her lips.

I wanted to tackle her to the carpet. It could have made me a legend, exalted at Mill Hill Elementary for my courageous act. I could have formed my own army—The Red Ladies or The Blue Ladies—the strongest social force in the academic district. It would be I who had the power to proclaim the fashion for each week. Every fifth grade girl would beg her mother to take her shopping to purchase Spandex leggings in a variety of colors and fabrics. They would all have to rush to Goodwill since stores stopped carrying leggings three seasons before, but still! That stupid Emily Kaplan would have begged for mercy. That moment had potential for greatness.

At the very least I could have said something to the effect of, "Emily, who made you queen of the world?" But those types of lines only seem obvious later that day. At that particular moment, my mind went horrifyingly blank. My eyes darted around the room, looking for any inspiration. Nothing. The only pathetic words I could manage to choke out were, "Oh. Sorry. I didn't know," as I sheepishly tugged the hair ties at either side of my head and stole an embarrassed look at Amy.

"Oh, you knew. You are just a poseur." Emily issued a satisfied sneer, spun around with a pompous toss of those stupid pigtails, and sauntered away with Elizabeth at her heels.

Emily was right, I was an imposter—a desperate, pathetic mimic. All of my rage and shame gathered in my stomach. I felt nauseous. The moment reeled over and over again in my mind, a mental documentary of my fifth grade tragedy.

"She can wear her hair any way she wants!" Amy shouted.

Emily and Elizabeth slowly turned. "What?"

"She can wear her hair however she wants," Amy repeated with just as much confidence.

The two girls were stunned. Never before had anybody dared to question their authority. They looked at each other, hoping the other knew what to do. But no protocol was established for such a circumstance. Finally Emily stammered, "I-I guess so. Sorry."

I was baffled. For months I cowered beneath the power of The Pink Ladies, hungry for their approval, accepting their pressure, never realizing there was an obvious solution. Stop—stop caring about what they think or say. My thirst for acknowledgment was what fed them. They didn't torture me because I was chubby. They tortured me because I let them. I gazed at Amy in awe. This ten-year-old girl with freckles and spunk held the answer all along. I just never looked in the right place.

"Thanks," I managed.

Amy shrugged. "Can I have a peanut butter cracker?"

~Alena Dillon

Compassion
for a Bully

There is always time to make right what is wrong.
~Susan Griffin

My sixth-grade year was one of confusion, intimidation, strength and friendship. There was a girl in my class named Krista. She was taller than me and very skinny, with bony arms and legs. I remember her beady brown eyes and the hard look on her face. Krista didn't like me. In fact, I think she hated me. I was always the smallest in the class and maybe that made me easy to pick on. She would say, "C'mon, little girl, show me what you got! Or are you scared? No one likes you, little girl."

I tried to act like it didn't bother me and walk away. Sometimes it would just get to me, and I would say, "Stop it!" I definitely didn't want her to see me crying in the bathroom. As the year went on, Krista began to get more aggressive. She started coming up to me and punching me in the arm with her bony knuckles. My friends told me to ignore her as we walked away. But those punches hurt. *Why me? What did she have against me?* I had never done anything to invite this kind of behavior.

One day at recess, I decided to face the bully. I had been imagining this moment for weeks. Oh, how good it would feel to punch her back. I wanted to show her that I wasn't scared. So right as the bell was about to ring, I went up to Krista and kicked her in the leg, and then ran as fast as I could into the classroom. I was safe with the teacher in the room. But Krista beamed an evil look my way and said, "Be scared. I'll get you later."

I worked hard at avoiding her the rest of the year. I remember telling my mom about it, and her consoling me with open arms and kind words. She said, "Nobody can tell you how little you are—you decide how big you will be." I really liked that saying. I would say it in my head often and find strength in these words. Krista continued to punch my arm periodically, but eventually it slowed down. But the thought of Krista and her torment didn't die so quickly in my mind.

A year later, in seventh grade, I received a letter from my temple letting me know the date of my Bat Mitzvah, the biggest day of my youth. Then I read who my partner would be for this special occasion. KRISTA. How could this be? I would stand in front of family and friends and read from the Torah, become a woman and share this moment on the pulpit with *Krista*? She was the source of all my anxiety and insecurity and yet this day was supposed to show my strength, pride and wisdom. I was supposed to become an adult. And she would be there, waiting to belittle me. It wasn't fair.

I practiced my portion for months and planned a wonderful reception. I tried to put the thought of Krista out of my head. When the day came that Krista and I saw each other for the first time in a year, we both acted civil. I could tell she wasn't pleased either. Of course, she couldn't punch me in the temple.

I was all dressed up, standing before a huge audience, wanting so much for things to go smoothly, especially in front of Krista. I would have died if I messed up in front of all these people and then had to deal with the laughing and teasing of this bully. I imagined all the names she would call me.

When I read my Torah portion and my speech, I read loudly and confidently. I knew it well. I had practiced long and hard. I saw my friends and family smiling to me, and I focused just on them.

Then Krista came up. She was shaking. I was shocked at how

nervous and scared the bully seemed. I had never seen that side of Krista. She was always so strong. But as I watched her fumble through words and chants, I saw this tough girl become weak, flawed and human. I hadn't thought of Krista as human and emotional. As she sat back down in her seat, she quietly cried in her hands. I suddenly felt something that I never imagined feeling toward Krista—compassion. I had always dreamed of the day I could laugh in her face and make her feel as little as she made me feel. But now that the day was really here, I didn't want to anymore. I sat down next to the sad girl, as her hands remained over her eyes.

"I know I messed up; you don't need to gloat. Go away!" she said.

"You were nervous. Everyone understands. No one remembers the mistakes. They love you and will focus on all the good. That's what family and friends do," I told her.

"Not my family. They love to tell me my mistakes," she answered. And then it made sense to me. This is why she was a bully. This is all she knew.

I put my hand on her shoulder and told her again that she did great. She could barely look me in the eyes, and then she whispered, "Thank you. I don't know why you are being so nice; I was never nice to you."

"I know. But it is in the past; it's over."

"I'm sorry," she finally said. I smiled and gave her my forgiveness. I told her what my mom had told me the year before, "Nobody can tell you how little you are—you decide how big you will be." Hopefully, those words gave her the strength that they gave me.

I truly believe I became an adult that day.

~Melanie Pastor

Conversation Starters

1. Page 145 is the first page of the story "The Little Girl Who Dared to Wish." What was Amy's wish?

2. "The Kindness Cure" begins on page 151. Betsy acted like a bully to Monica while Monica was nothing but kind to Betsy. Why did Monica choose to be kind to someone being mean to her? How did Betsy change from the beginning to the end of the story?

3. In the story "Solving a Fifth Grade Problem" on page 165, The Pink Ladies are a group of girls who bully Alena. It's Alena's friend Amy who comes to her defense at the end. If you were Alena, how would you have solved the problem yourself?

Chapter 6

Be the Best You Can Be

Having Confidence in Yourself

Find Yourself a Dream

One's dreams are an index to one's greatness.
~Zadok Rabinowitz

"Never let it be said that you can run faster than you can read, or that you can jump higher than your grade point average."

I was the last person in my family to be born on a plantation. We were very poor, and I used to work in the fields picking cotton for $2 to $3 a day. As a young man, I dreamt about becoming a great public speaker, even though I suffered from a severe stuttering disability. Though I could barely put two words together, let alone speak a full sentence, I was able to overcome those handicaps because I had a dream.

I was raised by my grandmother, Ella Mae Hunter. She instilled in me the belief that anything was possible. She gave me so much love and so much confidence, and she always had words of wisdom for me. She taught me that nothing in life was free; that if you wanted anything in life, you had to earn it, and you should want to earn it. She made me do my lessons. She told me I had to go to college. And she let me play sports.

She taught me to never give up, to find myself a dream, to hold on to it, and to never let go. Naturally, I wanted to make my grandmother proud of me and I wanted to get an education so that I could get a good job. Fortunately, basketball enabled me to realize that dream.

Every time the other kids would make fun of me because I couldn't speak, I would practice even harder. In a way, my speaking disability was a blessing in disguise.

I received a scholarship to Southern University, where I averaged thirty-one points and eighteen rebounds a game, I was a two time All-American and even played against the Russian National Team, and I was the first black player to make the All South team. I was drafted by the Cincinnati Royals in 1965 where Oscar Robertson was my mentor. My first year's salary was $8,000 and my signing bonus was $200 cash! (My, how times have changed!)

In those days the NBA was made up of only nine teams, and there was a limit to how many blacks could be on a roster. After a short time with the Royals and the Milwaukee Bucks, I was traded to the Chicago Bulls, where I went on to lead the team in scoring for seven straight seasons with a total of 12,623 points. I was an NBA All-Star in 1971, 1972, and 1973... All-NBA Second Team 1970-71, and 1971-72... NBA All-Defensive Second Team 1971-72, 1973-74, and 1974-75. Many of these team records were only finally surpassed by Michael Jordan. Of course, if they had the three-point line when I played, Michael might still be chasing me! My jersey, #10, was officially retired on January 14, 1994.

Even though I had a stellar career with the Chicago Bulls, I kept my stuttering disability a secret from my fans. Instead, I decided to do my talking on the basketball court. But when my career ended early due to a back injury, I found that none of my records meant anything when it came to getting a job. Because I could not put two words together without stuttering, no one would hire me. In spite of a degree in food and nutrition, in spite of all my athletic achievements and records, I had to start at the bottom, earning $4.45 per hour as a dishwasher and busboy at Nordstrom's in Seattle.

I could have given up then, but I remembered what my grandmother told me. She said, "Robert Earl, everybody has a handicap; everybody has a disability. What you've got to do is have a dream, and hold on to it. It's not how many times you get knocked down. It's whether you can get up or not that matters." So I decided to become the best dishwasher, the best busboy in the world. I wasn't going to let anything keep me from reaching my goals.

After a while, the owners of the company came to me and told me that they had noticed my hard work, and that if I would be willing to go to a speech therapist, they would pay for it. After several years of intensive therapy I was able to move up in the company and I eventually became their corporate spokesman.

Today, as Director of Community Affairs for the Chicago Bulls, I make over three hundred appearances each year, and I speak to over 250,000 young people about the importance of staying in school, getting an education, perseverance over adversity, and achieving one's dreams. I am considered one of the top motivational speakers in the sports field in the country. After forty-five years of being unable to speak, my dream has finally come true.

Today, when people ask me what I do for a living, I tell them, "**I talk**."

~Bob Love, former Chicago Bulls star

Embracing My Uniqueness

The one thing I've learned is that stuttering in public
is never as bad as I fear it will be.
~John Stossel

My grandfather stuttered, as did my uncle. My brother stuttered, too. And, at forty-one years old, I still stutter.

I'm fine with it now but that wasn't always the case.

It wasn't too terribly difficult the first couple of years of school. In fact, I don't recall being made fun of at all, although there was a great deal of curiosity about my abnormal speech.

In the second grade, one of my classmates asked me why I talked funny. With a straight face, I told her that I had a piece of meat lodged in my throat, which caused my words to get stuck. She believed me.

Several years later, she asked me if I still had that meat stuck in my throat.

To this day, stuttering can be difficult, in more ways than one, to explain.

Less than one percent of the world's population stutters; however, there was only one stuttering kid in first grade at Jeter Primary in Opelika, Alabama, and that stuttering kid was me.

Kids love recess, naps, and show and tell, and I was no different. Recess and naps came easy, and in spite of my speech disorder, I still took part in show and tell just like all the other kids. I just did a whole lot more showing than I did telling.

At the time, I didn't like being different. I felt that I stood out for all the wrong reasons.

It's never easy being a kid, but it's especially tough when you're different. Just imagine the pain, shame, and embarrassment of not even being able to say your own name. I would often give fake names when meeting new people, because it was easier. It was not uncommon for me to be Jason or Mike, Chris or Kevin or just whatever sounds I was confident I could say at that particular moment.

Most little boys are shy when talking to girls, but I was downright terrified. I can probably count the number of times on one hand that I talked to a girl in elementary school. Years later, many of those same girls told me they thought my stuttering was cute. I wish I'd known that then.

As I got older, some kids started getting meaner and the teasing started. Unfortunately, I let it bother me. I shouldn't have, but I did. I put more stock in what they had to say rather than being thankful for the overwhelming majority of kids who treated me with kindness, respect and compassion. In hindsight, I know that it was a reflection of them and not me. Again, I wish I'd known that then.

I had sessions with Ms. Watson, my speech therapist, biweekly. Although challenging, my time with her was special. While in therapy, there was no pain, shame, or embarrassment. I could simply be myself and work on my speech at the same time.

Class was a different story altogether. It was a constant struggle.

It was not uncommon for me to know the answers to questions, but it was quite common for me to remain silent out of fear of being ridiculed.

Reading aloud in class was pure torture. The buildup and anticipation of being called upon created more stress and anxiety than I am able to put into words, which often resulted in tension headaches.

When it was my time to read, I would lower my head, focus, and stop breathing. I would instinctively hit my thigh with my fist over and over to literally beat the words out of me, whereas other times, I would hit the underside of my desktop. This technique helped me get my words out but there was also a shadow side to it. When talking to my friends, I would often beat their arms until I finished saying what I had to say.

Could anything be worse than that? Yes, it could.

Giving an oral presentation in front of the class was the ultimate challenge, which usually resulted in ultimate shame. There was nowhere to hide. All eyes were fixed upon me as the secondary effects of stuttering stole the show. My eyes closed and my face contorted as I struggled to get out each word. There was no desk to pound and beating my leg in front the whole class was incredibly awkward.

Kids were mean and I let that bother me. There were very few days this future soldier didn't find himself crying by the end of the day. I didn't like who I was and didn't want to be me. The pain, shame, and embarrassment were too much for me to bear, or so I thought.

The funny thing, though, was that it wasn't the stuttering that caused any of the negative feelings I had, and it wasn't the bullies, either. It was my reaction to both the stuttering and the bullying.

I let it bother me, but it didn't have to be like that.

Sometime in the eighth grade, my attitude changed. I don't recall exactly when, where, how, or why, but I turned what I'd always perceived as a negative into a positive.

I wasn't a star athlete and I wasn't a genius. I wasn't in the band and I certainly couldn't sing, but everyone still knew me, because I stood out, and that was a good thing. I was different and I finally embraced that difference and ran with it.

Instead of waiting in fear for the teacher to call my name, I raised my hand when I knew the answer to a question. I always volunteered to read and even used oral presentations as an opportunity to showcase my comedic talents.

I was in control and would not allow the anxiety or insecurity to control my feelings, attitude, or behavior.

In subsequent years, I'd go on to speak in front of the entire student body on multiple occasions.

Being in control eased most of the tension; inevitably, there were fewer headaches, secondary effects, and, to a degree, stuttering.

I surrounded myself with good kids and didn't overly concern myself with the occasional wisecrack. At this point, I knew it was a reflection of them and had no bearing on my character whatsoever. Besides, my own wisecracks were much better than anything they could dish out.

Self-acceptance is crucial to happiness and success in and out of the classroom. It doesn't mean we can't strive to improve upon our so-called flaws, but it doesn't mean we shouldn't love ourselves and embrace our uniqueness either.

Individuality should be celebrated, not suppressed, and certainly not mocked.

I went from a stuttering kid who seldom spoke a word to a stuttering man who now speaks for a living. Self-acceptance continues to be essential in the success I've experienced as a speaker, comedian, writer, and soldier.

My lone regret is that it didn't happen sooner.

It's never easy being a kid. It's especially tough when you're different, but it doesn't have to be.

The time to embrace your uniqueness is now.

~Jody Fuller

Fireplug and Dad

Sometimes the biggest act of courage is a small one.
~Lauren Raffo

I used to play football when I was a little kid. Okay, let's face it. I was never really a *little* kid. I was always chunky, hefty, short for my age, pudgy, stout, tubby, round, robust, portly. You get the picture.

In fact, I was so big that I got to play football a whole year ahead of my friends. Our Mighty Mites football league didn't have an age limit, it had a weight requirement. If you were heavy enough, you got to play. I was heavy enough at eight years old.

The only problem was, by the time I turned eleven I was too heavy. You had to weigh a certain amount to start playing, and if you weighed too much they made you stop.

Not playing would have been just fine with me. I would have been happier sitting at home reading a book.

But Dad was one of the team's big sponsors and friends with the coach, so I figured quitting wasn't an option. I went, day after day, week after week, and year after year… until I was eleven and weighed more than two hundred pounds. I thought that would be the end of it, once and for all. And, in a way, it was.

To make sure each kid was under the official weight limit every Saturday, the referees lugged doctor's scales around with them to every game. All of the "chunky" kids had the honor of joining the referees before each game to weigh in.

If the scales tipped past two hundred, off went the unlucky player's cleats. Then the helmet and the shoulder pads. Sometimes the jersey and the pants, and even the undershirt and the socks! Coach knew I was heading for trouble the day I had to step out of my underwear just to make weight. So he came up with a bright idea. The very next practice he presented me with a T-shirt made out of a black garbage bag.

"Put it on," he grunted, pointing out the ragged holes for my head and arms. "Start running around the practice field and don't stop until I say so."

I'd wave at him questioningly after every single lap, while my teammates sat on their helmets and talked—in between laughing and pointing at me, that is.

"Keep going, Fireplug," Coach would grunt around the mushy cigar in his mouth. "Fireplug" was the nickname he had given me. Although no one ever explained it to me, I figured it had something to do with me being shaped like a fire hydrant.

Every day at practice, I had to run laps in that stupid garbage bag. I'd hear it crinkling beneath my underarms as I stumbled through the stickers and weeds lap after lap. My short, stocky legs weren't exactly graceful, and often I'd trip or fall. The other players would laugh, but not as loudly as Coach.

I used to sit in class toward the end of each school day and dream up excuses why I couldn't go to practice. Nothing worked, and so there I'd be, stumbling around the practice field with the sound of my plastic shirt drowning out my ragged breathing.

When the garbage bag T-shirt didn't exactly work wonders, Coach arranged for me to use the sauna at one of the local high-rise condominiums.

I rode my bike there the next Saturday. Coach handed me my garbage bag T-shirt and wedged me into a cedar-lined closet with two benches and a red metal shelf full of glowing hot rocks. He poured water on the rocks to build up the steam, and then shut the door on me with a wicked smile.

Outside the little porthole window, I could see him chomping on glazed donuts and sipping a cup of coffee. My stomach roared. Since it was a game day, I hadn't eaten since dinner the night before. Nor would I be eating again until after the weigh-in, when, as usual, I would be too weak to do anything much but sit there and pant until Coach shoved me full of candy bars from the concession stand so I could play ball again.

I sat there swimming in sweat and wondering how long this could go on. I'd been trying my best to lose weight ever since I was ten years old. I brought a bag lunch to school and skipped breakfast, but nothing seemed to work. I tried to be strong, tried to be brave, but there I still was… teetering on the brink of two hundred pounds and hoping to make it through yet another weigh-in.

Periodically, Coach would pop his bullet-shaped head into the steamy room to see if I was still alive.

I sat there dripping in sweat and realized something was very wrong with this picture. It was Saturday morning, and there I was, sitting in a sweatbox while the rest of the team chomped on Frosted Flakes and watched cartoons. They were still in their pajamas, while there I was in a garbage bag sweat suit! Why?

Was I being punished for something? Wasn't the running, sweating, hunger and pain enough? What more did they want? I suddenly realized that I'd been knocking myself out for something I didn't even want to do in the first place! It was then that I decided that I didn't have to do it anymore.

My heart fluttered and my stomach flip-flopped, but I finally stood up on wobbly legs and walked out of the sauna. At the time, it didn't exactly seem brave. It just seemed right. It made sense. I had finally realized that there was no law in the world that said I had to keep knocking myself out just so Coach would have another strong player and my Dad could have extra bragging rights!

"Did I say you could get out of there?" Coach bellowed when he returned from the pool deck a few minutes later and saw me sipping on a cup of water and enjoying one of his glazed donuts.

I shook my head, but Coach was waiting for an answer. So I told him.

"I quit," I said in a shaky voice that had nothing to do with heat stroke.

"You quit?" he fairly laughed, looming over me. "You can't quit. What would your dad think? Don't you want him to be proud of you anymore?"

But that was just it. If my Dad couldn't be proud of me for just being me, then what was the point? I was a good kid. I stayed out of trouble, made good grades and even made him a Father's Day card every year. Did I have to torture myself, too?

I shook my head and told Coach it was over. All of it. I wasn't going to starve myself anymore. I wasn't going to make myself try to throw up anymore, or run around the practice field in a garbage bag dress while the rest of the team pointed and laughed.

That was when he called my dad. But it didn't matter to me anymore. I had finally made up my mind. It was time to be proud of myself for a change, no matter what anyone else thought.

After Coach had explained the situation to my dad, he grunted and handed me the phone. Although my hands were shaking, I was glad I wasn't doing this face-to-face!

"Son," my dad said quietly. "Is what Coach said true?"

"Yes," I whispered into the phone.

"You don't want to play football anymore?" he asked simply.

"I never did," I gasped. Well, if I was going to do this, I was going to do it right.

Dad's laughter surprised me. "Then why did you go through with all of those shenanigans?" he asked. "I thought you wanted to be the next big football star!"

I hung up the phone and headed for my bike. Coach just stood there fuming as I pedaled away.

I started carrying myself differently after that. Respecting myself more. I grew a little, shaped up, learned a lot, and eventually, the name Fireplug just seemed to fade with time.

Except for one night, that is. My family and I were waiting for a table in a local restaurant when Coach sauntered in. He greeted my Dad rather coolly and then eyed me with open disdain. "What's the word, Fireplug?" he asked.

Dad looked at me for an instant, and then he finally corrected Coach. "You meant 'Rusty,' right, Coach?"

Coach grumbled something through the mushy cigar in his mouth, but it didn't matter. Our table was ready and Dad kept his hand on my shoulder the whole way there.

And no one ever called me Fireplug again.

~Rusty Fischer

Be Proud, Be Strong, Be You

When you have decided what you believe, what you feel must be done, have the courage to stand alone and be counted.
~Eleanor Roosevelt

At my school, I was the foreign girl. I was also short, I didn't dress fashionably, I had a problem saying my R's and I was Russian. I was usually teased about my hair or my clothes or my height. I did feel bad but I had lots of friends who cared about me. I was called midget, shortie, and the worse name of all—Russian spy. But people thought of me well too, well at least the girls. Over the years, I was also the smart one, the one who could give good advice, the one who could share and the one who would never give up on you.

One day, when school ended, I was walking to the buses with my best friend Macy and her friends. One of them was having serious girl trouble. I was about to give some advice when suddenly a kid stepped in front of me and said, "No one cares what you say, Ruthy." The other guys laughed.

"Back off!"

"Russians are so violent and dumb," he said. All the guys laughed and started talking about movies, games, books and all these other things that made Russians look cruel. I turned away. Macy ran up to me.

"Ruthy, don't listen to them; they are just stupid and jealous," she said. Wow, who would be jealous of me? I got teased every day. Macy went on to say, "Ruthy, do you know why I became friends with you?"

"What does that have to do with this problem?" I asked while trying to fight back my tears. I actually never knew why she wanted to hang out with me. We had started talking and then we started hanging out and we became friends.

Macy said, "Because you aren't like anyone else I know. It's cool that you are Russian. You teach me words in Russian and you are also caring, helpful and the greatest friend I have ever had."

"Really?"

"Absolutely," she nodded with a smile.

We walked a little more and talked about schoolwork. But, I still didn't feel totally okay. I was still sad inside even though I was relieved to hear why she was my friend.

Later that day, I was digging through my backpack when I found a rectangular piece of pink paper. It had my name on it. Then I remembered. My science teacher, Miss Ostapuk, had taught us about self-esteem. She had told us to keep these pieces of paper because we might need them one day.

The paper was a questionnaire that we had filled out. We had to answer questions about what we liked about ourselves. I remembered having a hard time doing the assignment because we had to brag about ourselves and I never really did that. But then I had decided to answer the questions by writing down what other people had said about me.

"What is your best feature?" I had put my eyes because I remembered my older sister commenting on my eyes. "What is your proudest achievement?" I put playing the piano for old people. At the very bottom of the paper there was a comment. It said, "Never let people bring you down because of who you are. You are special." I realized that maybe I was teased not only because I was different but also because I could do things that other kids couldn't do, like speak two languages and play the piano for an audience.

The saying on that paper is my guide now. I live by it. I learn by it. I achieve because of it. I think of my qualities and strengths, not weaknesses. My unique traits and thoughts make me who I am. I still feel sad sometimes and I still get teased but it doesn't affect me the way it did before. So if you are different, like I am, be proud, be strong and most importantly, be yourself.

~Ruth Anna Mavashev

More Than Good Enough

He who trims himself to suit everyone will soon whittle himself away.
~Raymond Hull

It seems like the second you step into middle school, you get judged. Not by other people, but instead by yourself. It's like a constant buzzing going on in your head—an endless circle of thoughts composed of questions for yourself like, "How does my hair look?" or maybe, "Would answering this history question make me look like a snob?" and the always persistent, "Am I good enough?"

I made the bulk of my friends during the first month of school. I always talked to a wide group of personalities, so I knew people who listened to music that screamed at you, people who wore heels bigger than their feet, people who listened to hip hop (which I am much more inclined to listen to, although I never told anyone), and ones who looked like they walked straight out of one of those teen novels, fully equipped with tubes of lip gloss and pink purses.

Then I knew a boy—his name was Brian. He almost always had his earphones placed firmly in his ears (but heard and responded to everything I said), wore what he called "vintage shoes," and was an active member of the Boy Scouts. He was the guy who was different from everyone else. I thought people's stares would faze him, but they didn't. In fact, Brian welcomed negative comments and simply questioned others about the way they lead their own lives. Something about him always made me feel nervous but oddly at ease: Brian never judged me or said anything about the way I looked or what I said. Looking back, it made me nervous because I wasn't used to it.

When I wasn't with Brian, I was constantly trying to be like the people I would speak to. My grades started to slip, the loud music I listened to started to give me headaches, and I was spending the little money I had on clothes and shoes. In short, my life was a complete mess. It was clear I had caved into the pressure of middle school. It was like I was in a hole and I just kept digging.

One day, somewhere in the middle of the third month of school, I was sitting behind Brian in Algebra class. I had just gotten back a polynomial test with a big red sixty-eight percent scrawled across the top. That test was the worst grade I had gotten in at least five years. I was usually such a good student—I did not understand what was happening to my grades.

Before I had the chance to shove the paper in my bag so no one would see it, Brian turned around with a neutral expression, a one hundred percent test in his hand.

"That's because you focus too much attention on what other people think about you," he said to me, gesturing towards my not-so-stellar test. "For someone so smart, you act like such an idiot when it comes to other people." I wasn't even sure how to respond.

"What's that supposed to mean?" I asked.

"It means that you never act like yourself. I always see you change the song you're listening to when certain people walk by. And you never answer questions in class that I'm sure you know."

"That's not true," I lied.

"Yes, it is. Just stop caring about what people think. Don't try to change yourself; you're just fine the way you are when you talk to me," he said before turning around to face the blackboard.

I could feel my mouth hanging wide open, but I couldn't concentrate long enough to close it. Had Brian just told me that I shouldn't try to fit in? I thought this was middle school, where people had to make friends if they wanted to make it through high school. Yet there Brian was, sitting comfortably in his own little world, with perfect grades and a collected life. And then there was me—breaking down on the inside, horrible grades, and a generally miserable life. I must have been missing something.

I realized that Brian was right. It was time for me to listen to the music I wanted to listen to, dress the way I wanted to dress, and to take control of my middle school life regardless of what my other classmates thought of me. I realized that if you're not happy with yourself, you can't have a happy middle school experience. So I took Brian's advice and started to act like myself, and I noticed that I was more than good enough. Finally.

~Jackson Beard

Danny's Courage

Patterning your life around others' opinions is nothing more than slavery.
~Lawana Blackwell

I was in seventh grade when Danny transferred to my school and became my first real crush. He had the darkest of brown eyes and light blond hair with a dark complexion. I fell for Danny the first day he arrived, and many of the girls in my class felt the same way. That, however, soon changed.

Danny had been going to our school for about a week when his parents picked him up in an old beat-up car that spewed exhaust and made loud banging sounds. The girls who had previously adored him looked disgusted. It was obvious that Danny was poor and that was that. He was no longer boyfriend material.

I had a poor family as well; I just hid it from everyone. I was so ashamed of how we lived that I never had kids come over to my house. Even though I couldn't do a thing about it, I felt like the kids in my class would judge me if they knew the truth. It was a lot of work keeping my secret, but I figured it was easier than it would be to not have any friends.

One day, our teacher, Mr. Sims, announced that the seventh-grade field trip would be to an amusement park. The classroom buzzed with excitement as the girls discussed what they would wear and what they should bring with them. I sat back and listened, knowing that my parents did not have the money to send me. It made me angry to feel so left out. But not Danny. He simply told everyone that he wouldn't be going. When Mr. Sims asked him why, Danny stood up and stated, "It's too much money right now. My dad hurt his back and has been out of work for a while. I'm not asking my parents for money."

Sitting back down in his seat, Danny held his head up proudly, even though whispering had begun. I could only shrink in my seat, knowing those whispers could be about me when they found out I would not be going either.

"Dan, I'm very proud of you for understanding the situation that your parents are in. Not every student your age has that capability," he replied.

Glaring at the students whispering in the back, Mr. Sims spoke again, only louder.

"This year, we're going to do things differently. The trip is not until the end of the month, so we have plenty of time for fund-raising. Each student will be responsible for bringing in at least one idea for a fund-raising drive. Bring them in tomorrow. If a student does not want to contribute to the drive, then he or she will be spending the field trip day here at the school. Any questions?"

Of course, Shelly, the most popular girl in the class, spoke up.

"Well, Mr. Sims, my parents can afford it. Do I still have to help?"

"Shelly, this is not a matter of being able to afford it. Money is not just something that is handed to you when you get older. This will be a great learning experience for everyone, whether you have the money or not."

While walking home from school that day, I noticed three of the boys from our class talking with Danny. I worried that they were giving him a hard time, but as I got closer, I realized they weren't harassing him. They were all just debating about the best ideas for a fund-raiser.

Although not everyone accepted Danny after that day, he won over the respect of many of us. I was especially awed by how he didn't cave under peer pressure. For so long, I could never admit to my friends that I could not afford to go somewhere. Instead, in order to continue to fit in, I lied about why I couldn't do things and came up with excuse after excuse.

By standing up and admitting he was poor, Danny changed my life. His self-confidence made it easier for all of us to understand that what his parents had or didn't have did not determine who he was. After that, I no longer felt I had to lie about my family's situation. And the funny thing was, those who were truly my friends stuck by me when I finally let them get closer.

And Danny, more because of his courage and honesty than his great looks, is someone I will never forget.

~Penny S. Harmon

Scarred But Not Different

Being happy doesn't mean that everything is perfect. It means that you've decided to look beyond the imperfections.

~Author Unknown

When I was fifteen months old, I was burned by hot grease falling on me from an electric skillet on the stove of my parents' home. This was an accident caused by a precocious, strong-willed, or as my sisters would say, bratty child who wanted her way and wasn't getting it. In plain terms, I pulled a pan of hot grease on myself that caused first, second and third degree burns on my face, arms and chest, leaving me with permanent scars, the worst of which is having one breast. Growing up with scars was and has been all I have ever known. My body as it is now is my "normal."

Going through grade school I never saw myself as different, other than the fact that I was overweight. The boys teased me of course, and some girls did too, but my parents taught me that these kids didn't feel good about themselves so they didn't want anyone else to either. These words always helped me get through the teasing and find friends that liked me for me.

My scars followed me from elementary school to junior high school and at eleven years old I learned that not all kids are cruel.

On the first day of school we found out that we would be required to take showers in the open locker room during physical education. This meant that I would have to undress in front of the other girls and shower with them. They would see my scars.

"Would you feel better if I talked to your teachers to see if you can take your shower after the other girls are gone?" my mother asked.

"Yeah," I said quietly. "I'm afraid they'll laugh at me."

My mother looked at me. Even though she may have been hurting for me inside she didn't let me see it. "Remember Stacie, anyone who would make fun of you because you have scars isn't worth the worry. They just do that because they think that will make them feel better about themselves." The next day my mother went to the school and met with my P.E. teacher and together they worked out a solution: I would wait until the other girls showered and went to the next class and then I would shower and be allowed to be late for my class. I was relieved. I would avoid all of the stares and ridicule that I knew would come from my scars.

But that night as I lay in bed I felt like a coward. I didn't want to be different and I didn't want to be picked on because I was allowed to do things the other girls didn't get to do. It was then that I knew what I had to do.

The next morning as I got ready for school I had a talk with my mother. "Mom, I think I might go ahead and shower in P.E. like everyone else."

She looked at me surprised. "You don't have to, honey. The teacher has already worked the schedule out for you."

I nodded, "I know Mom, but I don't want to be different because of my scars."

She hugged me and said, "I'm proud of you, but Stacie, if you change your mind, you don't have to." I hugged her back. I knew that no matter what happened, my mom would always understand.

That day I dreaded P.E., not just because it meant running, but because I knew that no matter what, I was going to shower when the other girls did. "Okay girls, it's time to go in and shower!" the teacher said, blowing her whistle. The one hundred yard walk to the locker room felt like one hundred miles. I went inside the locker room to my locker and stood there, taking deep breaths. It was now or never. As I undressed and picked up my towel, I saw some of the girls looking at me. To my surprise, not one of them laughed or made fun of me.

After we showered and dressed, all of the girls in my class walked over to me and asked how I got my scars. I told them my story and one girl asked, "Do they still hurt?"

I shook my head. "No, I can't feel anything," I said, which was true — I didn't have any feeling in my scars — not then, not now. They walked with me to our next class, talking about school and boys, but none of them talking about my scars. From that day on, P.E. was not the class I dreaded… math was. I didn't worry that I was different from the others. We were all the same; we were friends.

That day is when I realized I didn't have to be different. I just had to be me, and in doing so, friendships that began then followed me into my adult life. We all finished high school together as friends, and none of them ever made fun of me for my scars or my weight. As for the boys, when any of them tried to make fun of me, I had a whole class of friends to set them straight.

That P.E. class taught me that even though my body is different, I'm not. My scars don't make me who I am — my heart does.

~Stacie Joslin

Chicken Soup for the Soul

Who Said There's No Crying in Softball?

Character building begins in our infancy and continues until death.
~Eleanor Roosevelt

Our team was playing softball against a team that we were tied with for third place. I was toughing out the position of catcher, and we were winning. However, my knees started to not feel so tough. In the bottom of the second inning they had started to hurt.

I've had bad tendonitis in my knees, and I just couldn't take any more abuse to them that day. So I limped over to the manager, who is also my dad, and told him that my knees were hurting. I asked if he could have the back-up catcher, Jill, catch for the rest of the game. He called Jill into the dugout and told her to put on the catcher's gear.

One of the other coaches overheard this conversation and came running over. I could tell that he was mad at my dad's decision because he was steaming like a whistling teapot.

He yelled at my dad, "Are you crazy? Jill can't catch — she has a huge cut on her finger!"

My dad explained to the coach about my knees.

"So what!" The coach rudely yelled at my dad.

Then he furiously walked over to me. His face was red, and I could feel my heart pounding in my chest.

"You'd better get that gear back on and get back out there right now. If you don't, I swear this will be the worst softball season of your life! Every game! Every game you complain about your stupid knees! If your knees keep hurting so much, I don't understand why you even play! You certainly aren't even good enough!" he screamed at me.

I couldn't believe what he said to me. Amazingly, I was able to choke through my tears, "I'm sorry! My knees hurt so bad! If I catch any more I'll collapse!"

"So what! Do you think I care?" he yelled.

By that time I was sobbing hard. The coach stormed off grumbling something over and over, leaving me in tears.

Later that night, I was lying in my bed thinking. Then a very important question came to my mind.

Why should I continue my softball season if I don't even have any respect? I asked myself.

Then, from somewhere deep inside my heart, I found the answer.

It doesn't matter what the coach thinks about me, it only matters what I think about myself. I love softball and I have a right to play, even though I may not be the best catcher in the world. That doesn't make me a loser. But I would be a loser if I believed what he said instead of believing in myself. I would lose my self-respect. No one, even the coach, can make me quit. All I have to do to be a winner is to keep showing up, sore knees and all. And I will.

~Amy Severns, 12

Conversation Starters

1. "More Than Good Enough" starts on page 192. In this story, Jackson and Brian are both middle school boys trying to find their way. What lesson does Jackson learn from Brian in this story?

2. On page 195, the story "Danny's Courage" begins. How does Danny show his courage in this particular passage?

3. The story "Who Said There's No Crying in Softball?" begins on page 201. Why is Amy crying?

Chapter 7

Be the Best You Can Be

Being Generous

Nice Catch!

When I do things without any explanation, but just with spontaneity...
I can be sure that I am right.
~Federico Fellini

From the moment Kyle heard the loud crack of the Red Sox bat, he was sure the ball was headed over the fence. And he was ready for it. Without ever taking his eyes off the ball, he reached up and pulled it out of the air.

"I caught it!" he yelled to his dad and his grandpa. "And I caught it with my bare hands!"

It was opening day of spring training and they had come out to the ball field to watch the Red Sox play. Kyle's grandma and grandpa lived near Ft. Myers, Florida, where the Boston Red Sox come in late February to prepare for the season.

Later, on the way home to Grandma's house, Kyle kept his head down. He tried to think of a way to convince his parents to stay a few more days.

"Wish we could go back to the ballpark tomorrow," he said. "Maybe I'd catch another ball to put with my Little League trophies and stuff. And maybe I'd even get some autographs."

"You know that's not possible, Kyle," his dad said. "We're flying out early tomorrow morning."

"I know, I know," Kyle said, rolling the baseball around in his hand. "I just thought you and Mom might decide to stay a few more days. We don't go back to school until Monday, and tomorrow's only Thursday."

"We were lucky to get that flight!" his dad said firmly. "The airlines are booked solid this week."

That night, a huge snowstorm moved into the Northeast. When they arrived at the airport early the next morning, they were told that all flights into Logan Airport in Boston had been cancelled for the day.

On the drive back to his grandparents' house from the airport, it was obvious to Kyle that his dad was upset. It was definitely not a good time to bring up going back to the Red Sox ball field.

But by the time they were back at Grandma and Grandpa's house, Kyle's dad began to joke about the cancelled flight.

"Another day in sunny Florida isn't so bad," he said. "I'm in no hurry to get back to Boston, where my car's probably buried in snow."

"We could go out to the ball field again," Grandpa said. "Unless there's something else you'd rather do."

"The ballpark's fine," Kyle's dad said with a grin. "I'd never go against the wishes of anyone with so much power over the weather."

It was mid-afternoon when another loud crack of the Red Sox bat sent a ball flying over the fence. Again, Kyle reached up and caught the baseball in his bare hands.

As he rubbed his fingers around the ball, a small voice from behind him called out, "Nice catch!"

Kyle turned around to see a small boy in a wheelchair. Without a moment of hesitation, Kyle handed him the baseball.

"Here," he said. "You can have it. I already got one."

The grin on the boy's face was a mile wide.

"Thanks," he said. "I never held a *real* baseball before."

Kyle's dad and his grandpa looked surprised—very surprised.

But they were no more surprised than Kyle was himself. He couldn't believe what he'd just done. But he wasn't sorry. He could never forget the happy look on the small boy's face. It was worth a million baseballs.

"I'm gonna get some autographs," Kyle said, rushing off to meet the players as they came off the field.

With three Red Sox autographs in hand, Kyle walked back to the parking lot.

"Think the Red Sox will have a good season?" Grandpa asked.

"They looked pretty good today," Kyle said. Kyle's dad tapped him on the shoulder.

"You looked pretty good today yourself, son."

And three avid Red Sox fans left the training grounds, each carrying with him a special feeling of pride. The proudest of all was Kyle.

~Doris Canner

Secret Santa

Generosity is giving more than you can
and pride is taking less than you need.
~Kahlil Gibran

Manuel and I work in the same building. I'm a music talent agent with a firm on the eighteenth floor. Manuel has his own space near the escalator from the garage to the lobby. He sells newspapers, magazines, gum and candy. I pass Manuel each day as I make my way from the underground parking to the lobby.

Hundreds of people working in the building pass by Manuel each day, and he seems to know everyone's name.

Each morning I stop to buy a newspaper, and Manuel greets me. "Good morning, Miss Tanja. How are you today?"

Last year I convinced him to stop calling me "Miss Crouch," but he refuses to drop the "Miss" in front of my first name. Some mornings I stop to chat a moment and marvel at the fact he supports a wife, three boys and a daughter on his salary.

Prior to Christmas, my assistant learned that Manuel not only supported his own family but had recently taken in his widowed sister and her two children. Manuel's wife, Rosa, stays home to care for the six children while Manuel and his sister work to support the family. When my assistant heard about this, she decided we needed to become secret Santas to Manuel's family.

Throughout the month of December, several of us made it our mission to learn all we could about Manuel and his family. We rejoiced as something new was discovered, such as Manuel's oldest son, Jose, was ten years old. He loved baseball and hoped to one day play professionally. He would get a baseball, bat, glove and cap. Manuel's only daughter Maria was just learning to read and she loved bears. A special teddy bear and books were selected.

We charted facts, listed gift ideas, then cross-referenced them with what had been purchased. One of the partners in the firm got into the spirit and bought a VCR, then charged a new television set to another partner! Everyone was caught up telling stories of how Manuel had touched our lives with his warm spirit and the details we were learning about his life.

We arranged for UPS to deliver our gifts the day before Christmas. The return address was simply North Pole. We speculated at how surprised Manuel would be and could hardly wait to return from the holidays to hear if he would mention it. We never in our wildest dreams anticipated what we would learn.

Manuel had packed up all the gifts and sent them away! The television and VCR went to a nursing home where Manuel's sister worked as a maid. Clothes were shipped to relatives in Mexico. Food was shared with the neighbors.

On and on it went. Manuel considered his family so blessed that they had shared all the wonderful gifts they received with others less fortunate.

"We had the best Christmas ever, Miss Tanja!" Manuel beamed.

"Me, too," I smiled.

~Tanja Crouch

Flowers of Forgiveness

*Forgiveness is the fragrance that the violet sheds on the heel
that has crushed it.*
~Mark Twain

The Children's Theater was actually an old mill building with cement walls, twisting passages and big staircases. Everything smelled of mothballs, metal, and old grease. Static crackled in the air and every footstep echoed eerily.

One afternoon, my eight-year-old sister Brittany and I were with the drama group rehearsing *A Little Princess*, a children's play based on a book by Frances Hodgson Burnett.

"Break a leg!" I whispered as Brittany adjusted her boarding school costume.

"Take your places for act one, please. Everyone, places for act one!" called the director, a woman with spiky blond hair and rings on every finger.

The lights went out and the rehearsal began. Halfway through the first act, Brittany finished her part and went backstage. She grabbed her script from the make-up table and read along with the rehearsal that was still at full swing in front of the curtain. A small group of fellow actors joined her, and started practicing lines. Suddenly, something wet exploded on the back of Brittany's head! Spinning around, she saw a tall girl with a bottle of Febreze in her hand. She aimed it at Brittany's ear, grinning widely. Splat! Gooey blue liquid slid down Brittany's face. The older girl guffawed and looked to the other girls for a reaction. Brittany glanced at them, expecting them to speak up and defend her. Instead, they shrieked with laughter and pointed mocking fingers at Brittany, who ran out of the make-up room in dismay.

Ten minutes later, Brittany met me backstage. "A big girl just sprayed me with this stuff and laughed at me," she said, trying to wipe the chemical out of her curly hair. "All the other girls laughed, too."

I didn't even know the girl's name, and she was bullying my sister!

When we got home, we looked at the cast list and found that the girl's name was Jessica. Our mom e-mailed the director, who said she would talk to Jessica and arrange time for an apology right before the next rehearsal. Nobody really expected a heartfelt apology from Jessica, but Brittany was prepared to forgive her.

Next rehearsal, the director met Brittany at the door and announced that we had a problem on our hands. "Jessica swears that she was never even near you yesterday."

But Brittany knew the truth. As she glanced across the room full of young actors, she glimpsed Jessica slouching defiantly in a metal folding chair. For a split second, their eyes met. Jessica quickly whirled away to stare in the opposite direction. For weeks afterwards, no matter how hard Brittany tried to talk to her, Jessica refused to look her way.

It was very difficult for Brittany to work with Jessica every rehearsal, for three hours each week. But finally, we were ready to perform. There would be three performances over the course of the next weekend. Brittany and I were glad that the ordeal was almost over.

After the first show, Brittany and I each got a beautiful bouquet from our church's pastor and his wife. Jessica didn't get a single flower.

The second night, we received flowers from our grandparents. Again, Jessica received nothing.

On the way home, Brittany spoke up.

"Mommy," she said quietly from the back seat of the car, "I've been thinking, and I decided I want to buy some flowers for Jessica."

Mom smiled in surprise. "That would be very nice."

Before the last performance, Brittany met Jessica on the way into the theater. She handed the older girl a big bunch of yellow roses, bought with her own savings. "Great job with the show last night, Jessica. These are for you."

Jessica's eyes popped in astonishment. "For me?" she faltered, squinting incredulously at Brittany's warm smile. "These flowers are for me? Are you sure?"

"Yes, I want you to have them!" Brittany skipped towards the dressing room, leaving Jessica staring after her with a bewildered look on her face and a bouquet of beautiful flowers in her arms.

That night, Jessica finally received some flowers from her dad. She pulled out a sprig of carnations and smiled shyly as she gave them to Brittany.

Maybe Jessica will never apologize to Brittany. Maybe she won't ever even admit her wrongdoing. But she is just beginning to realize what wonderful things God's love does in people like Brittany.

~Caitlin Brown

Help by the Bagful

Sometimes when we are generous in small, barely detectable ways
it can change someone else's life forever.
~Margaret Cho

lmost immediately, when I walked into my third grade classroom, I spotted the bag in the corner by my desk. It was thick cream-colored plastic, making it impossible for anyone to tell what was inside. I picked it up and asked, "Who does this belong to?"

No answer. Opening it up, I rooted around and saw a blue and red shirt, some shorts, and what looked like some tennis shoes. Unaware of whose bag it was, I asked again, but nobody volunteered. I scanned the faces of my students. They all looked clueless until I got to Timothy. Looking up, he glanced at me and shook his head a little—side to side—just enough to make me stop digging into the bag. I sensed he was responsible for the bag of stuff. I also sensed that if I made him stand out from the rest of the class or if I exposed what was in the bag, I would embarrass him.

Later in the day I took him aside. "Timothy, are those your clothes? Are you going to a sleepover after school? What's going on?" Timothy scuffed his tennis shoes and told me the clothes were for his friend—one of the other boys in our class—a kid he saw every day. He was concerned that his buddy wore the same two outfits and the same pair of shoes every week. He told me he'd noticed that the clothes didn't always fit, and since they had been worn by two older brothers before being passed down to his friend, they were kind of ragged. Also, the shoes were sometimes smelly.

I was curious, because most kids in third grade are just worried about themselves. They don't often reach out to others like this. Later, when I asked Timothy why he had done it, he looked me in the eyes and said, "He's my friend. I just wanted to be nice."

I asked him if his mom knew about it. There was no way I wanted one of my students giving away his clothes without his parents' permission, but Timothy reassured me.

"First," he said, "I asked my mom if it was okay and she said, 'If somebody needs something and you've got it, you can give it to them.' So I went into my closet and drawers. I picked out things that were getting too small for me, things I thought he would like. I picked out that blue and red shirt, with a polo guy on the front, especially for him."

Pulling it out of the bag and examining it, I said, "It's a colorful and sharp-looking shirt, Timothy. I'm sure he'll love it."

"It still kind of fits me but soon, I'll be too tall to wear it anymore, and my friend is shorter than me."

I looked at the expression of pride on Timothy's face, touched his shoulder and said, "Instead of shoving the shirts and pants to the back of your closet, you decided to give them away to someone who could wear them?"

"Yeah, and my mom taught me how to do laundry last year, so I washed the clothes and put the stuff in a bag."

I asked Timothy when he was going to give them to his classmate. He said, "I already did. I handed him the plastic bag this morning and said, "I have some clothes for you."

Timothy looked around to make sure no one was close enough to overhear us. "He said he'd take 'em. So together, we decided that the safest place for them would be in a corner by your desk until the end of the day."

That afternoon, I walked out with the car riders and talked to his mom. Leaning into her car window, I told her, "You have such a kindhearted son. You should be really proud of what he did."

Timothy just shook his head and smiled. From the expression on his face, it looked like he didn't think he had done anything special. All he had done was help his friend. But when I saw his friend wearing his "new" clothes in the weeks that followed, I knew both boys had learned a life lesson: little gestures from the heart mean so much.

~Sioux Roslawski

Friends of the Heart

Kind words and good deeds are eternal.
You never know where their influence will end.
~H. Jackson Brown, Jr.

A riana caught another whiff and tried to hold her breath. She moved away slightly, but Ashley only moved closer and continued talking.

Ariana thought to herself, *Why does she always have to sit next to me?* She inched away some more until she touched elbows with the girl next to her. Ashley didn't seem to notice that Ariana was trying to move away, and she leaned in closer. Ariana felt trapped. She wanted badly to tell Ashley that she didn't smell very good. But how could she without hurting her feelings? Instead, she gathered the remains of her lunch to throw in the trash, thankful for the excuse to get some fresh air.

She looked back to see Ashley eating quietly. Ashley's hair was stringy and tangled, like it needed a good washing, and her clothes were wrinkled and stained. All the other kids talked and laughed with each other. No one talked and laughed with Ashley.

Ariana forced herself to go back to the table and take her seat. She was stuck with Ashley today, but vowed that she would not get stuck with her tomorrow.

When Ariana got home from school, she complained to her mother. "There's this girl named Ashley who likes to sit next to me in school, but she smells bad."

"She's probably having a tough day," said her mother.

"No, it's not just one day. She smells bad a lot," Ariana explained. "Nobody else likes to sit next to her, either."

"Well, try to be nice to her," said her mother. "Maybe she's having a hard time at home. You never know what a person's home life is like."

For the rest of the week, Ariana tried to be a good friend to Ashley. There were times when they had fun talking and playing together, especially on the days that Ashley bathed. But the days when she smelled bad, which was most of the time, Ariana still found it very hard to be her friend.

One morning, while getting her hair combed for school, Ariana brought the subject up again with her mother.

"I don't want to be friends with Ashley anymore," she told her.

"Why? Is she mean to you?" asked her mother, twisting Ariana's hair into a ponytail.

"No. She stinks!" Ariana scrunched up her nose. "And her clothes are dirty. She wore the same shirt two days in a row. That's disgusting."

Her mother's hands froze in midair. Ariana turned to see what the matter was. Her mother looked upset. Ariana wondered what she had said to make her mother react this way.

"I don't think you understand Ashley's situation, so let me ask you this...." Her mother's tone was serious. "Who makes sure that your hair is combed every morning so you'll look nice when you go to school?"

"You do," answered Ariana.

"Who makes sure you're bathed and cleaned every day? And your clothes are washed and neatly ironed?"

"You and Daddy," Ariana said again.

"Do you live in a nice home? Do you have enough to eat?"

Ariana nodded, beginning to feel guilty. She was starting to understand now. Ashley couldn't help her situation because she was only seven years old—the same age as Ariana. Grown-ups are supposed to take care of kids.

"Why doesn't her family take better care of her?" Ariana asked.

"Not all children live in the best situation," her mother said. "The best thing you can do for Ashley is to treat her with kindness and compassion."

Ariana bit her bottom lip. Sadness for Ashley filled her heart. She vowed that from now on she would be the best friend that she could be to Ashley.

At school, Ariana kept her vow. She let Ashley sit next to her. Other times, she voluntarily sat next to Ashley. She partnered with Ashley to help with her schoolwork. On the days that Ashley smelled bad, she moved away a little or politely asked Ashley for a little room. She was always careful not to hurt Ashley's feelings.

As the months passed, Ariana discovered that she enjoyed talking and hanging out with Ashley. She no longer saw her as the girl who smelled bad, but as a friend with a kind and warm heart.

At the end of the school year, the second grade prepared to go on a field trip to the zoo. The day before the field trip, the teacher announced that the class needed to bring in a lunch from home. Ashley was absent, and Ariana worried that her friend would not have a lunch because Ashley always ate the school lunches.

Ariana couldn't call Ashley because she didn't know her telephone number. So, the next day, Ariana asked her mom to make an extra lunch and some snacks for Ashley—just in case.

"You have a good spirit, Ariana," said her mother. "I'm very proud of you!"

When Ariana got to school, she discovered that she had been right. Ashley had not brought a lunch for the field trip.

When Ariana gave the lunch to Ashley, she saw tears well up in Ashley's eyes. Ariana was surprised at Ashley's reaction because after all, she was only doing what true friends do for each other. Ashley was her friend—and they were friends of the heart.

~Ariana Morgan Bridges as told to Robin Smith Bridges

A Little Hand Up

Never worry about numbers. Help one person at a time,
and always start with the person nearest you.
~Mother Teresa

I bundled up my six-year-old daughter, Renee, against the Minnesota cold and a forecasted snowstorm for her short walk to school. Snow pants, coat, scarf, gloves, and her new wait-until-payday boots, all princess pink and a half size too big to allow for growing. Renee was so excited about her new boots that she had worn them in the house all weekend, only giving them up for bath and bed.

It pleased me to slip her feet into them, knowing each precious toe would be warmly nestled into the deep soft lining. It pleased me almost as much as throwing out her old ones with the sticky zippers. They definitely hadn't made it into the box of freshly laundered and packed clothes that Renee and I had spent Saturday morning sorting out of her closet for her younger cousin.

Kissing Renee on her eyelids, the only uncovered part of her body, I opened the front door. Her two big brothers tossed me a kiss and a "Love you, Mom," as they each grabbed one of their sister's hands and run-skipped the block to the crossing guard.

I poured myself another cup of coffee, turned on the radio and began mentally checking my things to do. I wasn't too far into dance-cleaning the kitchen before "Get up and Boogie" was interrupted by the happy news that school was closing early due to the snowstorm.

Within a few minutes, my boys exploded into the house and out of their winter wear. They gave me a "Yippee!" high-five and headed for their game system.

Renee wasn't able to wiggle-dance out of her winter bundling.

"Mommy, I'm stuck all over," Renee said, doing an off balance, toe to heel, boot push move until she plopped to the floor, thankfully cushioned by the seat of her snow pants.

I bent over to help her. "Renee?" I asked, surprised at the grimy boot in my hand. "Where are your new boots?"

"These are my new, new boots," she smiled at me.

"No, honey, these aren't your new boots. Look, they're dirty. The clasps are broken and the snow got in through the hole in the side."

"Yup," she agreed, not realizing the implied question in my statement. "My friend's clothes are all like that and these boots were too small for her."

"But what happened to your pretty-princess boots?"

"Mommy," she smiled at me, "My friend needed boots. She outgrew hers and her feet were cold. My boots were warm and they fit her, and she looked pretty in them. She was happy and that made me happy too. She gave me her boots as a hand-me-down and I gave her mine as a hand-me-up."

Suddenly, the ugly boot in my hand became as beautiful as the fabled glass slipper. The simple clarity of truth filled my heart. I had felt generous setting an example for Renee by giving away outgrown and no longer needed clothes because it was the right thing to do.

But, not only had Renee done the right thing by giving her new boots to someone who needed them, she had done it the right way. She was a cheerful giver. She reminded me that God hands us down His blessing so that we may cheerfully hand-me-up His abundance to others.

~Cynthia Hamond, S.F.O.

A Coincidence?

Give and it will be given to you; good measure, pressed down, shaken
together, running over, they will pour into your lap. For whatever measure
you deal out to others, it will be dealt to you in return.

~Luke 6:38 NIV

I was very proud of my daughter Emily. At only nine years old, she had been carefully saving her allowance money all year and trying to earn extra money by doing small jobs around the neighborhood. Emily was determined to save enough to buy a girl's mountain bike, an item for which she'd been longing, and she'd been faithfully putting her money away since the beginning of the year.

"How're you doing, honey?" I asked soon after Thanksgiving. I knew she had hoped to have all the money she needed by the end of the year.

"I have forty-nine dollars, Daddy," she said. "I'm not sure if I'm going to make it."

"You've worked so hard," I said encouragingly. "Keep it up. But you know that you can have your pick from my bicycle collection."

"Thanks, Daddy. But your bikes are so *old.*"

I smiled to myself because I knew she was right. As a collector of vintage bicycles, all my girls' bikes were 1950s models—not the kind a kid would choose today.

When the Christmas season arrived, Emily and I went comparison shopping, and she saw several less expensive bikes for which she thought she'd have to settle. As we left one store, she noticed a Salvation Army volunteer ringing his bell by a big kettle. "Can we give them something, Daddy?" she asked.

"Sorry, Em, I'm out of change," I replied.

Emily continued to work hard all through December, and it seemed she might make her goal after all. Then suddenly one day, she came downstairs to the kitchen and made an announcement to her mother.

"Mom," she said hesitantly, "you know all the money I've been saving?"

"Yes, dear," smiled my wife, Diane.

"God told me to give it to the poor people."

Diane knelt down to Emily's level. "That's a very kind thought, sweetheart. But you've been saving all year. Maybe you could give *some* of it."

Emily shook her head vigorously. "God said *all*."

When we saw she was serious, we gave her various suggestions about where she could contribute. But Emily had received specific instructions, and so one cold Sunday morning before Christmas, with little fanfare, she handed her total savings of $58 to a surprised and grateful Salvation Army volunteer.

Moved by Emily's selflessness, I suddenly noticed that a local car dealer was collecting used bicycles to refurbish and give to poor children for Christmas. And I realized that if my nine-year-old daughter could give away all her money, I could certainly give up one bike from my collection.

As I picked up a shiny but old-fashioned kid's bike from the line in the garage, it seemed as if a second bicycle in the line took on a glow. Should I give a *second* bike? No, certainly the one would be enough.

But as I got to my car, I couldn't shake the feeling that I should donate that second bike as well. And if Emily could follow heavenly instructions, I decided I could, too. I turned back and loaded the second bike into the trunk, then took off for the dealership.

When I delivered the bikes, the car dealer thanked me and said,

"You're making two kids very happy, Mr. Koper. And here are your tickets."

"Tickets?" I asked.

"Yes. For each bike donated, we're giving away one chance to win a brand new men's 21-speed mountain bike from a local bike shop. So here are your tickets for two chances."

Why wasn't I surprised when that second ticket won the bike? "I can't believe you won!" laughed Diane, delighted.

"I didn't," I said. "It's pretty clear that Emily did."

And why wasn't I surprised when the bike dealer happily substituted a gorgeous new girl's mountain bike for the man's bike advertised?

Coincidence? Maybe. I like to think it was God's way of rewarding a little girl for a sacrifice beyond her years—while giving her dad a lesson in charity and the power of the Lord.

~Ed Koper

A Healing Haircut

There are two primary choices in life: to accept conditions as they exist,
or accept the responsibility for changing them.
~Denis Waitley

I t was about ten o'clock in the evening when I crept across the kitchen floor. My feet seemed to make a whole lot of noise. Luckily for me, Mom was on the phone, so she wouldn't immediately send me back to bed. I had an *American Girl* magazine clutched to my chest, my finger marking a certain page. I waited behind a wall until Mom was off the phone before walking into the room.

"Mom," I called softly as I walked in.

She looked at me, so I knew she was listening.

"Mom, you know how you want me to cut my hair? Well, now I want to do it, and I want to send my hair here…." I said, and I showed her the article I had read about Locks of Love.

Locks of Love is a company that takes donations of hair, makes the hair into wigs, and provides the wigs to kids who are suffering from alopecia areata or other diseases that make them lose their own hair. Locks of Love provides the wigs for free or on a sliding scale based on financial need.

Until I read the article, I had always insisted on keeping my hair long. Now I wanted to cut it short. Mom looked shocked.

"Are you sure you want to do this?" Mom asked.

"Yes, I am," I answered seriously.

"Why?" Mom asked.

"When I read that article," I began, "I thought of all those kids who need my hair more than I do. I knew I had to help them."

Mom gave me a hug and told me how proud she was that I was doing this.

The next day, Mom called the number in the article for more information.

"You need ten inches of hair or more," she informed me when she got off the phone. Mom measured my hair with a ruler. "You have twelve inches!" she told me.

Two weeks later, I went to get my hair cut. I told Jenny, the stylist, what I wanted to do.

First, she washed my hair, and then she cut it. She told one of the other stylists to put it into a bag. She gave it to me before we left.

When we got home, Mom told me to set my hair on the dining-room table to dry in the sunlight that came in from the window. It took about a week. When my hair was finally dry, Mom and I wrapped gold ribbons around it and sent it off to the address Locks of Love had given us. I had typed up a letter asking that my hair go to a burn victim. My mom had told me horror stories about when she worked in the burn unit, and I felt especially sorry for them.

I was very proud of what I did. I knew some child, probably a girl, was delighted, at least for the moment. She would be wearing a wig with curly brown hair.

A few months later, I got a thank-you card. I didn't need it. The good feeling I got doing it was thanks enough. I learned that acts of love aren't just hugs and kisses, but that thoughtful gestures to complete strangers are acts of love, too.

~Angela Rooker

EDITORS' NOTE: If you're interested in donating hair to Locks of Love, go to www.locksoflove.org for information on how to make your donation. Following are the charity's guidelines for donation hair:

1. Ten inches minimum hair length (tip to tip). They cannot accept wigs, falls, or synthetic hair.
2. Please bundle hair in a ponytail or braid.
3. Hair needs to be clean, dry, placed in a plastic bag, then in a padded envelope.
4. They need hair from men and women, young and old, all colors and races.
5. Hair may be colored or permed, but not bleached or chemically damaged (if unsure, ask your stylist).
6. Hair swept off the floor is not usable.
7. Hair cut years ago is usable if it has been stored in a ponytail or braid.
8. Hair that is short, gray, or unsuitable for children will be separated from the ponytails and sold at fair market value to offset the cost of manufacturing.
9. You may pull curly hair straight to measure the minimum 10 inches.
10. The majority of all hair donated comes from children who wish to help other children.
11. Layered hair may be divided into multiple ponytails for donation.

Truly Cool

Maturity begins to grow when you can sense your concern for others outweighing your concern for yourself.
~John MacNaughton

My heart was in my throat. As Mom and I entered the store, I had only one thought, *I hope my pretty pink bike is still there.* It would be my first bike ever. But since it was about a week before Christmas and the stores were in total chaos, Mom gently reminded me that it was possible that the bike I wanted would be sold out.

I could feel the excitement in my stomach, and my hands were jittery. I was so anxious to get the bike. I crossed my fingers as we came around the corner to the bike section. My stomach did somersaults when I finally spotted it near the end of a long row. There it was, my big, shiny pink bike! I thought it was too clean and pretty to touch, so I stuck my hands in my pockets to keep from smudging it.

The week went by really slowly. The only thing that we were looking forward to, besides school letting out, was a charity drive that our school was doing for a homeless children's shelter. We had made little toys for the kids who were living there. I was surprised to see how many were on the list—so many who didn't have a real home where they could spend Christmas.

Still, I didn't think as much about helping them as I was thinking about my bike. I couldn't wait for winter break to end so that I could ride my bike to school for everyone to see. I would be the cool kid for once.

While we waited in the classroom for the bus to come and take us to the children's shelter to deliver our presents, I sat at my desk writing my mom a thank-you letter. I explained how I had never wanted anything as badly as I did that bike. Just as I finished, the bus driver came into our room to let us start getting on the bus. I ended up sitting next to a guy who was getting a skateboard for Christmas. We talked about how excited we were about our big gifts.

We chatted all the way there and were still talking as we came through the shelter doors. Suddenly, my mouth dropped, and I stopped in mid-sentence. I was in shock seeing kids wearing torn-up and worn-out ragged clothes. I felt sad as I looked around the place.

Our teacher encouraged us to find a kid who was staying in the shelter and visit with him or her. I noticed a little girl sitting in a corner by herself. When I walked up, it seemed like she didn't want to say "hi" or anything, but I felt like I should say something to her. So I started out by asking her if she was excited about Christmas coming. I told her about how I was getting a bike. Suddenly, her eyes lit up, and a huge smile came across her face. She told me that she would be the happiest kid in the world if she could ever get one.

Then she explained to me what her life had been like. To say the least, she didn't have a normal childhood. She had never known what it was like to live in a real home of her own with pets and everything. Her parents had been alcoholics and constantly had money problems. They moved around often because they either couldn't pay the rent or would be thrown out for some reason. Things got so bad with them that they finally abandoned her, and she ended up in this shelter.

She no longer had anyone to call family.

I realized that her getting a bike anytime soon was out of the question. I mean, who would buy it? Her parents were gone, and she was alone in the world, other than for the people who ran the shelter. My heart just ached for her.

We got so involved in our conversation that my teacher had to come and tap me on the shoulder to tell me that it was time to leave. I grabbed my bag and told her that I hoped she'd have a merry Christmas and get everything she wanted. Before leaving the room, I looked back and gave her a little smile.

Later that night, I lay in bed remembering what the girl had told me about what it was like to live at the shelter. I thought about her life and about mine as well. All I had ever done was want and want and think that I never get enough. Now I'd met a girl my age who had barely enough to get by and took nothing for granted. I never understood when people would tell me how lucky I was. Now I finally understood.

Over the next three days, I kept thinking about ways that I could help make this girl's life better. Then on Christmas Eve, while sitting in church listening to the preacher speak, it dawned on me. I wanted to give her my new bike (which I had not yet received)!

When I explained everything to my mom, she gave me a smile that I could never fully describe — one like I have never seen before. My mom found the paper that told what children's shelter I had gone to and, on Christmas morning, we headed for the shelter with my new bike in the trunk of my mom's car.

I walked in feeling somewhat sorry that I would not be the one getting the bike, but I also felt really good inside. When I finally found her, she was sitting in the corner where I had first met her. Her head was down, and she seemed to be sad. I walked over and said, "Merry Christmas." Then I told her that I had something for her.

Her face brightened, and she smiled as she looked up at me. She looked happier than I have ever seen a kid look before. I grabbed her hand and walked her over to the door. Parked outside was my bright pink bike with a big red bow on it. I was expecting a bigger smile than what I had seen moments before, but instead I saw a tear running down her cheek. She was so happy that she was crying. She thanked me over and over again. I knew then that what I had done was truly cool. I knew I had made her the happiest kid in the world.

What I didn't know was that giving away the only bike I'd ever had would change the way I thought about things. But over time, I found that I wasn't as greedy as I was before.

I now realized that receiving a great gift gives you a good feeling, but giving from the heart gives you a feeling that's even better.

I also realized that I had been counting on that bike to make me cool. Although I never got to show up at school riding it, my mom was proud of me and so was everybody else. In the long run, that meant more to me than the bike, or looking cool, ever could have.

~Brittany Anne Reese, 15

Conversation Starters

1. In the story "Flowers of Forgiveness" on page 212, Brittany shows forgiveness by giving flowers to Jessica. Jessica bullied Brittany, so why did Brittany decide to give her flowers?

2. "Help by the Bagful" is the story that starts on page 215 and teaches a life lesson. What is a gesture? What is the gesture shown by Timothy in this story?

3. After reading "A Little Hand Up" on page 221, we see that Renee also shows a gesture to a friend. How are Renee and Timothy in "Help by the Bagful" similar?

Chapter
8

Be the Best You Can Be

Making True Friends

Three Dimensions: My Unexpected Best Friend

A friend who is far away is sometimes much nearer than one who is at hand.
~Kahlil Gibran

I sat on the plane and wondered if I would end up hating her. That same part of me also wondered if I should have gone at all. What if I was stuck for three days wearing a false smile and pretending I found her halfway tolerable? Or what if, instead, I was the one who ended up on the receiving end of the false smiles, being regarded with minimum tolerability? What if we found each other so unbearable we would never speak again? There were so many things that could go wrong.

First of all, she was Jewish. And she lived in an entirely different part of the country: Alabama. I had never been to a Bat Mitzvah before, nor had I ever visited any of the southern states, except for Disney World, which hardly counts. I had no clue what "opening the ark" entailed. And I had never been very graceful—what if I tripped and knocked something over in the middle of the service?

Then there was also the fact that I had never met her.

In person, at least. In theory, I knew her better than anyone. We had been writing back and forth as pen pals for two or three years, and we shared so many similar interests, primarily horseback riding and writing. Most importantly, we could tell each other everything and vent all of our problems without fear that we would be judged. I assumed I would never meet her, so there was never any reason to hold back any thoughts that seemed insane or dreams that seemed improbable. After exchanging messages daily for those three years, she invited me to her Bat Mitzvah, which was three months away.

Somehow, although I'm not exactly sure how, I convinced my parents to take me to a different city and spend three days with a family they had never met.

After arriving in Alabama, we checked in at the hotel where most of Emily's family was staying. When we got in the elevator, I wondered if I was standing next to Emily's sister or cousin. But I had no way of knowing.

We had agreed to meet at a nearby restaurant. Unfamiliar with the city, my parents and I arrived at the wrong restaurant — one with the right name but an incorrect location. I remember walking in with reluctant excitement. I was so thrilled that I was going to meet her, but I was also kind of scared, too. When I realized we were at the wrong place, however, I was really disappointed, because I had never really doubted that Emily would be exactly the kind of person I thought she was.

When we finally arrived at the correct restaurant, I was able to spot Emily immediately in her trademark rain boots. I recall my dad making some comment about a rooster to break the ice, because at first it was kind of like: *Whoa. You are a real three-dimensional person.* To me, she was always the person who replied to my letters and spoke to me through the magic device called a telephone. Somehow, I don't think it sunk in that she was going to be here in all her three-dimensional glory. And then my thoughts slowly changed. It became, instead, *Oh my God! You're here! Yay! I've wanted to meet you forever!*

That weekend, I went horseback riding with Emily, stayed at her house, and attended her Bat Mitzvah ceremony, where I was honored to open the ark (without tripping), as well as attend her amazing party.

In other words, one of the most important events in my life was a Bat Mitzvah. It wasn't my own, but the Bat Mitzvah of a girl I had met over the Internet who lived halfway across the country. When people ask me how I know Emily, I just smile. Some people don't understand how I could possibly have gone to visit a girl I had never met in person. But in many ways, I know her better than the friends I see every day. We still keep in touch, and I hope that we continue to do so forever. She's one of the few friends I can imagine calling when I am a little old lady living in a nursing home (or in my own house, with a walker, if I'm too stubborn).

I almost said no to her pen pal request when I was ten years old. At the time, I was very busy, and I wasn't sure if I had time to write to another pen pal. If I had said no, I never would have met my creative, intuitive, smart, and funny best friend, Emily. But I said yes. And I can only say I'm glad that I did.

~Julia McDaniel

Meeting Julia

The language of friendship is not words but meanings.
~Henry David Thoreau

I was around ten years old when my pen pal craze started. I had always loved meeting new friends—I would try new activities to meet people and talk to people my age I saw in stores or other places. However, when I was ten, I wanted to make friends from other states. I thought it would be fun to communicate with people all over the country and learn new things about other places. I also thought writing letters might help with my writing, which was one of my favorite hobbies.

I told everyone I knew that I wanted a pen pal, but no one knew of any way that I could meet one. Then, one day, I found an online pen pal site where people could create a profile and find other pen pals who had similar interests. One girl was named Julia. She was ten years old and liked horseback riding, writing, and animals. She lived in Ohio. She sounded a lot like me, and I wanted to be pen pals with her.

That night I asked my parents if I could join the pen pal club. They told me I could as long as I didn't give out any personal information and didn't get my hopes up about meeting a pen pal in real life. I agreed, but I secretly thought I could get them to change their minds about the meeting.

The next day, as soon as I got online, I wrote Julia a letter describing myself and asking her if she wanted to be my pen pal. She wrote back saying that she would love to.

Julia and I talked about everything. I told her about novels I was writing, and she told me about her various publications. We told each other about horses we rode and good books we read. One time, Julia told me about a project she was working on about passing a law against horse slaughter in the U.S. She told me about the fashions and events in Ohio and I told her what was happening in Alabama.

Later, when we were twelve, we were both going through difficult times. I was bullied at school, causing me to have low self-esteem. Also, Julia took three sixth grade classes and three seventh grade classes. She had trouble fitting in with friends since she was caught between two grades. We stuck by each other through these times and gave each other support.

My writing skills also improved because of Julia. Not only did we write letters back and forth, but we wrote stories together. In June we signed up for Script Frenzy, a program in which writers all over the world write a twenty-thousand-word script in a month. We chose to write the script together. We didn't finish our script, but we laughed a lot and became even better friends because of it.

My Bat Mitzvah was coming up on September 29th. A lot of camp friends and out-of-town family would be coming to it, and I wanted Julia to come too. My parents told me that I would never be able to meet a pen pal in real life, but Julia and I had been writing for almost three years and knew each other pretty well, so I decided to ask my parents if I could invite her to my Bat Mitzvah.

My parents said they would consider inviting Julia, but they wanted to talk to her parents first. They exchanged e-mails with her parents and eventually talked to them on the phone. After they had gotten to know each other well, my parents agreed to send Julia an invitation. Two weeks later, she RSVPed, and her answer was yes. Julia would be coming to visit me from September 28th to September 30th.

The Friday before my Bat Mitzvah, September 28th, I talked nonstop about Julia at school. I had only seen a few pictures of her, and they were from a year or so ago, so I wondered what she would look like.

I wondered how she would act in person and if things would be the same between us in person as they were online and on the phone. I also became nervous about making a good first impression for her.

After school, Julia and I met at a restaurant. She looked a lot different than I had expected, but she was the same talkative, creative, fun person I had always known her to be. We talked a lot, laughed a lot, and after meeting, we went horseback riding together. It was one of the best days of my life.

At dinner that night, all of my family and out of town relatives ate with us. Julia enjoyed meeting my grandparents, aunts, uncles, and cousins. Most of my family thought that we talked and laughed together as if we were life-long friends, and they were surprised when they found out that we had met just hours ago!

Saturday morning was the service. Julia got to participate in the ceremony by opening the ark, and it was fun to see her on the bema with me. We also had a blast at the Kiddush luncheon and the party. She had to leave Sunday, and I told her I would miss her a lot. We hugged each other goodbye and promised to keep in touch.

Now it is mid-March, and we have kept our promise. In November, we both wrote fifty-thousand-word novels for a program called NaNoWriMo (National Novel Writing Month) and edited each other's novels. We write e-mails to each other almost every day and call each other every weekend. This summer, I plan to go to Ohio to visit Julia.

Julia is nice, smart, creative, funny, and such a great person. I am so happy that I got to meet her and know her. We'll always be best friends.

~Emily Cutler

A True Friend

My friend is one... who takes me for what I am.
~Henry David Thoreau

Makayla and I have always clicked. In kindergarten, we were both very athletic and loved racing against each other. Then during the first grade, Makayla and her family went on a trip. On their way home, a bus hit her family's car. At that moment, my friend Makayla's life changed forever.

She was in the hospital for a long time. Every day I hoped and prayed that Makayla would come back to school. After what seemed like forever, Makayla finally returned. When I saw her, I knew my life would change, too. She was in a wheelchair, paralyzed from the waist down.

From that time on, when it is too wet or too cold for Makayla to go outside during recess, I stay in with Makayla and we play together, just the two of us. We have been in the same classes for the last five years. She is an A+ student who never gets into trouble.

Some people think Makayla should be in the "special" class, but that's just not the case. When people try to treat Makayla like she is helpless, she doesn't get down—she just goes that extra mile to prove them wrong. Makayla can do eleven or more pull-ups, hang on the bar longer than most boys, reach up as far as the tallest girl in school (when she is sitting down) and tons of other things.

Sometimes the classroom is crowded with a lot of kids. If you think that stops Makayla, you had better think again! She will get up out of her wheelchair and use the desks and her strength to get to wherever she wants to go. When she needs to go upstairs, and the elevator is occupied or isn't running, then Makayla will crawl up the steps and have somebody bring the wheelchair upstairs for her.

Every springtime at school, we have a day where our whole school does outdoor activities all day, and we keep track of what we have done on a card. Half of the activities include running, which Makayla can't do. I pair up with Makayla, and she will do whatever activities she can. Then I do my running events. After that, I run Makayla's events for her. At the end of the day, I am extremely tired—but happy—knowing that I helped Makayla fill out her whole card. Makayla stands beside me 150 percent, and I do the same in return.

Sometimes people think Makayla doesn't go through the same things that they go through because she is in a wheelchair. But that's not true. She goes through dealing with crushes, issues with her brothers and sisters, school and everyday stuff that every other girl goes through.

So when you see somebody who is handicapped or different, take the time to get to know them. Who knows... they may become your very best friend.

~Kelsey Temple, 11

The Gift of Friendship

*When you are sick, friends can sometimes be a better medicine
than the kind the doctor gives you.*
~Julie Anne, 12

About two weeks before my tenth birthday, I fell while I was Rollerblading and broke my wrist. I had been planning on having my birthday party at a roller rink, and now I wouldn't even be able to skate at my own party! But because we had sent out the invitations and everything was already planned, we still had to have the party at the roller rink anyway.

On the day of my party, I was standing by the front door of the roller rink greeting my friends while they came in. When one of my friends, Sarah, came in the door, I noticed that she was limping. Sarah told me that she had hurt her leg, and that her parents had told her that she could come to my party anyway if she just took it easy and only skated around the rink one time.

Sarah didn't even skate once during the whole party. All of my other friends were busy, having a great time skating—but Sarah stayed with me the whole time. We talked about all kinds of stuff: school, our teachers, what boys we like and who we think is cute—and we laughed our heads off. Because of Sarah, my party was a lot more fun than I thought it was going to be.

A few weeks later, I saw Sarah's mom at the store, and I asked her if Sarah's leg was better. Her mom looked very surprised, and then she told me that she didn't know what I was talking about. She said that Sarah had never hurt her leg.

It was then that I realized that Sarah had stayed with me at my birthday party just to make me feel better. My true friend, Sarah, gave me the best present of all.

~Ashley Russell, 10

Thanks, Y'All!

We all take different paths in life, but no matter where we go,
we take a little of each other everywhere.
~Tim McGraw

I have distant friends, neighborhood friends, basketball friends and friends online. However, I have one group of friends that has really been special to me.

In the fifth grade, my twin sister, Monica, and I transferred to a new school. Without any hesitation, I went. I didn't argue. Since my mom taught there, I would no longer have to ride the bus with a bunch of rowdy boys and worry about stuff like getting kicked in the head. No kidding—they actually accidentally kicked me in the head one day!

At my old school, I hadn't made any real friends. I was treated like a complete dork because of the way I looked. I had glasses, baggy clothes, pimples and blemishes. I rarely smiled and hardly ever laughed, wore a belt and was overweight. I was also dealing with the reality of my parents getting a divorce.

So, on the first day at my new school, I just hoped that I would make friends. For a few weeks, I was always alone. Monica ended up having a different lunch period than I did, so I would just read during recess and lunch.

Then one day, a girl in my class named Cori came up to me at lunch and asked if she could sit by me. We began to talk, and since we both are twins, it gave us a lot to talk about. Soon, Cori introduced me to friends of hers—Adriane, Hannah and Toni—and I introduced them to Monica. Then Cori's twin, Cole, and his friends Matt and Ross started hanging around with us. We became one big inseparable group. At recess we played basketball and other games. We did everything together.

Ever since we've been together, my friends have always been there for me—even the boys. They liked me, for me. Having them in my life changed the way I felt about myself. Their friendship gave me a sky-high feeling. We barely ever argued! We were really tight. They seemed to understand how hard it was to change schools and have stuck with me through the tough times, like dealing with my parents' divorce.

One time, when Monica and I couldn't go outside with our friends after school, Toni supplied us with a pair of walkie-talkies to keep us all in touch!

I began being more outgoing, like getting involved in student council and entering writing contests—some that I even won! Then came the sixth grade, our last year of elementary school and the last year for all of us to be going to the same school together. Adriane, Hannah, Toni, Matt and Ross were going to Tison. Monica and I would at least still be seeing Cori and Cole since the four of us were all going to Hall Junior High.

I'd also be seeing my "old" classmates from the other elementary school, including some I had run into recently. Boys who had teased me in my old school, stood staring at me not even knowing who I was. The girls who previously had treated me like vapor now paid attention to me and called me by name. I couldn't figure it out. I didn't know why. I thought that I was the same old me. But then when I looked in the mirror, I realized that I was a lot different than I had been before.

I wasn't short and stubby anymore. I had grown tall and slender and my complexion had cleared up. The glasses were gone and my belts were pushed to the back of my closet. I realized then that my friends had done more than just make me feel good—they had made me feel confident because they had supported me, and slowly my appearance had changed.

With their help, I had pushed my weight off. Toni helped me with that by encouraging me not to eat some of the more fattening foods and telling me that I could do whatever I set my mind to. I had been trying to lose weight since I was nine, when the doctor had said to my mom, "Michelle has a weight problem."

I learned to properly wash my face with the help of my friend Hannah and her magical beauty tips. "Just wash your face every night, it doesn't take too long!" she instructed.

With the help of Cori, my belt was gone. "Believe me, it's a lot less painful on your stomach. I used to tuck *all* my clothes in, even sweaters!" she exclaimed.

Adriane suggested that I wear my glasses only when I really needed them. "If you can see how many fingers I'm holding up, you are okay," she said. "Just wear them when you need to see the homework assignment on the board."

My sister, Monica, loves clothes and helped me pay attention to how I dressed. She would give me feedback about what looked good and what didn't. It really helped to hear her say, "Wow, Michelle, that looks FANTASTIC on you! Man, why couldn't I have gotten that?"

With the help of Cole, I learned a little bit more about athletics. "No! No! The receiver receives the ball! No! No! The quarterback doesn't flip the quarter! That's the referee!" he explained.

With the help of Matt, I learned to smile. "It won't hurt you," he encouraged.

With help from Ross, I learned a laugh a day keeps the frown away.

"B in math? Awesome! That's not failing—it's just not perfect," expressed my friends.

As I gaze into the mirror, I turn to the left and then to the right. I smile at my reflection, because I now realize that these people, my true friends, never saw me as a dork. They saw the beauty in me. They brought my personality out.

The best friends that anyone in the world could ever have will be missed when we go to junior high. But I will cherish the memories that we have created, and whatever happens, I'll always remember that my friends helped me become who I am. In conclusion, I have to say… thanks, Cori, Cole, Hannah, Matt, Adriane, Ross, Toni and Monica.

Y'ALL ARE THE BEST!!!

~Michelle Strauss, 12

Seeing, Really Seeing

Friendship is a sheltering tree.
~Samuel Taylor Coleridge

His nose was all smooshed looking, like maybe his mom had dropped him when he was a baby. His ears were two—maybe even two and a half—sizes too big for his head. And his eyes! His eyes bulged like they were ready to pop right out of their sockets. His clothes were nice, Tim had to admit. But he was still the homeliest kid he'd ever seen.

So why was the new kid leaning on Jennifer Lawrence's locker like they were best friends or something? She was a cheerleader and one of the coolest girls in school. And why was she smiling at him instead of twisting her nose all funny like she did when she looked at Tim? *Strange,* he thought. *Really strange.*

By lunchtime, Tim had forgotten about the new kid. He sat down at his usual table—in the corner, all alone. Tim was a loner. He wasn't as ugly as the new kid—just a little on the heavy side and kind of nerdy. Nobody talked to Tim much, but he was used to it. He had adjusted.

About halfway through his peanut butter and ketchup sandwich (he put ketchup on everything), Tim looked up and saw that kid again. He was holding his lunch tray and standing over Jennifer, grinning like he'd just aced a math test. And she was grinning, too. Then she moved over and made room on the bench next to her. *Strange. Really strange.*

But even stranger was what the new kid did. Tim would have plunked into that seat so fast, his lunch bag would have been left behind, just hanging in the air. But not this new kid. He shook his head, looked around and walked straight to Tim's table.

"Mind if I join you?" he asked.

Just like that. *Mind if I join you? Like the entire eighth grade was fighting to sit at my table or something,* Tim thought.

"Sure," said Tim. "I mean no. I don't mind."

So the kid sat down. And he came back, day after day, until they were friends. Real friends.

Tim had never had a real friend before, but Jeff — that was his name — invited Tim to his house, on trips with his family and even hiking. Right — Tim hiking!

Funny thing was... one day Tim realized he wasn't so heavy anymore. *All that hiking, I guess,* thought Tim. And kids were talking to him, nodding to him in the hallways, and even asking him questions about assignments and things. And Tim was talking back to them. He wasn't a loner anymore.

One day, when Jeff sat down at the table, Tim had to ask him. "Why did you sit with me that first day? Didn't Jen ask you to sit with her?"

"Sure, she asked. But she didn't need me."

"Need you?"

"You did."

"I did?"

Tim hoped nobody was listening. *This was a really dumb conversation,* he thought.

"You were sitting all alone," Jeff explained. "You looked lonely and scared."

"Scared?"

"Uh huh, scared. I knew that look. I used to have one, too, just like it."

Tim couldn't believe it.

"Maybe you didn't notice, but I'm not exactly the best-looking guy in school," Jeff went on. "At my old school I sat alone. I was afraid to look up and see if anyone was laughing at me."

"You?" Tim knew he sounded stupid, but he couldn't picture Jeff by himself. He was so outgoing.

"Me. It took a friend to help me see that I wasn't alone because of my nose or my ears. I was alone because I never smiled or took an interest in other people. I was so concerned about myself that I never paid attention to anyone else. That's why I sat with you. To let you know someone cared. Jennifer already knew."

"Oh, she knows, all right," Tim said as he watched two guys fighting to sit near her. Tim and Jeff both laughed. *It felt good to laugh and I've been doing a lot of it lately,* realized Tim.

Then Tim looked at Jeff. Really looked. *He isn't so bad looking,* thought Tim. *Oh, not handsome or anything like that. But he isn't homely. Jeff is my friend.* That's when Tim realized that he was seeing Jeff for the first time. Months earlier all he had seen was a funny-looking nose and "Dumbo" ears. Now he was seeing Jeff, *really* seeing him.

~Marie P. McDougal

Friends Forever

Best friends: it's a promise, not a label.
~Author Unknown

"Hey, Jenna, do you think we'll still be friends when we're eighty-two?" I stopped bouncing on the trampoline when I saw a puzzled look on my friend's face. Boy, did her look say it all! It was clear she was wondering where in the world I had come up with such a random question. Being such good friends, it had become easy to read each other's minds. So, while I waited for Jenna to answer, I started wondering what life would be like without her.

Definitely not the same, that's for sure! Losing Jenna would be like losing a very close sister. We hang out together as often as we can. We laugh together. We cry together. We give each other advice. We even look a little bit alike. When I spend the night at her house, I feel like part of Jenna's family. If it weren't for Jenna, I don't know where in my life's journey I would be, but I'm sure it wouldn't be here.

Suddenly, my thoughts were interrupted. "Of course, we'll still be friends when we're eighty-two," Jenna announced loudly. I gave Jenna a friendly stare, and she returned it. We stared at each other until we were laughing so hard that tears were streaming down my face. That moment was one of the most important in our friendship together and, as you might have guessed, eighty-two was our new magic number. But that's not where the story ends.

The next year, in fourth grade, we met Jamie. Jamie had just moved from California, and since she lived in the same neighborhood as Jenna and me, the three of us soon clicked into a really tight group of friends. We played together almost every day. We shared our biggest secrets and crushes, and even came up with crazy ideas to make a little extra cash for the summer. I was happy to have reached out to Jamie as well as getting even closer to my other good friends. Things couldn't have been better, and I thought even time couldn't pull us apart, but that is where I was sadly mistaken.

The three of us started fighting a lot — and not just small fights where your friend won't return a CD you let her borrow. No, these fights involved hurt feelings, crying, taking sides, nasty e-mails, and mean glares. Before Christmas, we had a really big fight, and it was just my luck that Jamie and Jenna were ganging up on me, both saying I was bossy and couldn't keep my mouth closed. I felt helpless and alone. They wouldn't even talk to me at school unless they had some mean insult for me. I had very little hope for the future, and I was almost positive that Christmas, my birthday, and New Year's Day would be horrible! *Why is this happening to me?* I thought. *How can I not even know what I did and have things end up this bad?*

That's why I was surprised when Jenna came to my house and gave me an awesome Christmas card she had made for me. I was so sure that she was still disappointed with me, and now I was getting a really nice card that she even made herself. *Is time going to prove me wrong once again?*

"Wow," I said, breaking the silence as we stood on either side of my front door. "Thanks."

"Okay... well... I have to go," she said softly.

"Okay. See you later then...." and I closed the door and headed back to my mom's bedroom to finish watching a movie.

"Who was that at the door?" my mom asked.

"It was Jenna," I explained, showing her the card. I pressed play on the VCR, but I wasn't watching the TV screen. Instead, I was admiring the front of the card, which was decorated with snowmen, snowflakes, and a perfect image of Santa Claus. After a few minutes of admiring the front, I decided to peek inside.

The card started off with "Merry Christmas" (what else would you put in a Christmas card?), but then, farther down the page, it said, "I am so glad we're friends. I am sorry about what I said when we were fighting. A fight won't stop us from being friends. Besides, we said we were going to be friends even when we're eighty-two."

I stopped reading and started laughing. I couldn't believe I had forgotten what she said that day in her back yard. I couldn't believe I had been so selfish in trying to get even and making my friends feel sorry for me that I had forgotten about real friendship.

Instead of drifting farther and farther apart, and eventually going our separate ways, like my friendship with Jamie, Jenna and I held strong, even through the bad times. Jenna ended up being my true friend. Isn't that what a true friend is? Someone who chooses to stick with you every day of your life, even when you're eighty-two.

~Darian Smith

Trouble in Neverland

An apology is the superglue of life.
It can repair just about anything.
~Lynn Johnston

The clock struck twelve, and my third-grade classmates and I ran from our desks and out the door. It was time for recess, the only part of the day anyone really cared about. Jamie, my best friend, was also in my class, and as soon as we hit the playground, we ran to the farthest basketball court. No one played there. If they wanted to play basketball, they would usually play on the court closest to the water fountain. Kickball was also a popular sport, and if you weren't playing kickball, you were probably on the swings and slides. Since no one played at the farthest basketball court, Jamie and I could play whatever we wanted and not have to worry about anyone complaining or interrupting our game.

We liked to pretend we were in different places, like the jungle, the desert, or off in some fairytale world. One day, we decided to play Peter Pan.

"All right, here is where Wendy lives," I said, pointing to a four-square section of the court. "And Peter Pan will live near that basketball hoop." Jamie liked my idea and started to make up our situation.

"Peter will be in trouble, so Wendy has to come in the middle of the night and save him," Jamie told me.

"That sounds good…. I think I'm going to be Tinker Bell," I said. Suddenly Jamie looked at me.

"But I want to be Tinker Bell…." she complained.

I told her that I'd thought of the idea first, but she still whined.

"Come on, Jamie… you can be Tinker Bell tomorrow," I said, hoping she would drop it.

"No! I'm going to be Tinker Bell today. It's only fair," she yelled.

"How is it fair?" I asked.

"It just is!"

I sighed. This fight was going nowhere. "Okay," I said, "either I get to be Tinker Bell, or we won't play this game at all."

"Wow!" Jamie yelled. "Not only is that a stupid idea, but its mean, too! I guess that's how Jewish people are." She walked away.

I stared at her back and watched her walk toward the swings. *What happened? What does me being Jewish have to do with the both of us wanting to be Tinker Bell?* I knew that it really didn't mean anything, but it still wasn't a right or nice thing to say. Just then, the teachers blew their whistles, and recess was over.

I told my teacher that Jamie and I had gotten into a fight, and she let us talk outside the classroom. The talk was useless. Jamie didn't seem to care that she had hurt my feelings. I didn't know how much it had hurt until I realized I was yelling at her. I stopped and told her I was sorry.

"It's okay. What I said was really rude. I shouldn't have said it. I guess I'm the one that's sorry," she said.

"Thank you," I whispered.

"No problem. And I promise never to say anything mean about your religion again. Do you forgive me?" she asked.

"Of course, I forgive you!" I laughed, taking her hand and walking back into the classroom.

Jamie and I stayed best friends until middle school, when we went to different schools and eventually drifted apart. But I'll never forget her or the fact that she never did insult my religion again, just as she promised.

~Carly Hurwitz

Now You See It, Now You Don't

*One is taught by experience to put a premium on those few people
who can appreciate you for what you are.*
~Gail Godwin

could hardly wait to get to school and see my friends. What would their reactions be when they saw me? I didn't know, but I was sure it wouldn't be like it was the day when I had started school there three years before.

On that terrible day my stepfather, Buddy, had to take me to school early so that he wouldn't be late for work. When he stopped in front of the school, I didn't want to get out of the car. I looked out at the small group of students standing outside the building and suddenly felt sick, but it was too late to back out now. Swallowing hard and trying not to cry, I slowly opened the car door and pushed myself around to get out. I felt awkward and ugly. The body brace I wore held me so stiffly that I couldn't move very easily, but at last I was out of the car. Buddy said good-bye, then drove off leaving me standing there alone.

I felt abandoned. I didn't know anyone there. I wished I were still in my old school with all my friends. My old friends knew all about my brace. They had also known me before I got the brace, so they knew I wasn't really this... this... monster that I felt like now.

Some of the kids had gathered near the front doors, which were still locked. I didn't have to look at them to know they were staring at me. I could feel it. And who could blame them? I was sure I had to be the ugliest, strangest thing they had ever seen. *So let them stare,* I thought defiantly. *I'll just ignore them.* I turned my back to them and sat down stiffly on the steps that led from the sidewalk up to the school. Hot, angry tears fell on my new dress, but I quickly wiped them away.

I looked down at my dress. It would be a pretty dress — on someone else. The brace ruined everything. I felt like a freak. I wanted to cry, to run and hide so no one could ever stare at me again. But I was trapped. Trapped inside this hideous contraption made of leather and steel. The leather wrapped around my middle and rested on my hips. Two narrow metal bars ran up my back. A wider bar came up the front to support the neckpiece, which held my head in place. The only way I could turn my head was by turning my whole body.

That morning though, I didn't try to turn my head. I didn't want to see the curious stares of strangers. I should have been used to it. People were always staring at me, or worse, asking me what was wrong with me. I hated being different. And the brace made it even worse. There was no way to hide the ugly thing. It just stuck out there, inviting everyone to gawk.

As I sat there on the steps, I didn't think I could be more miserable. I was wrong. Even though it was September, the weather was still warm and as the sun rose higher, the shade disappeared. I could feel the sweat begin to trickle down my back and under my arms. *Great! Now I would smell sweaty on top of looking weird.* I wanted the earth to swallow me up right then and there.

But, of course, the earth didn't oblige by swallowing me up. I managed to get through that day, and the next, and all the days for the following three years. In spite of the horrid brace, I managed to make friends, once everyone got used to seeing it. I still felt awkward and ugly most of the time though, and I could hardly wait to get the brace removed for good.

That day finally arrived, one rainy Thursday in spring. I remember being so thrilled when the doctor said I could leave the brace off that I threw my arms around him and gave him a big hug. I told him I would always love rain from that day on. I was free at last!

At first I was going to call my best friend and tell her what happened, but then I decided just to surprise her at school the next day. I could hardly wait for the oohs and ahs that I expected to hear from everyone when they saw me without that dreadful brace. I danced up the stairs to the school building that morning. *Just wait until they see me*, I thought. *Just wait!*

And so I waited. In my first class, no one said a word. What was the matter with them? Couldn't they see how much I had changed? Maybe they were just too surprised to say anything. Probably in the next class, they would notice. Again, I waited. Still nothing. I was beginning to feel awful. Maybe I was just as ugly without the brace! Or maybe my friends just didn't care as much about me as I thought. Then on to the next class, where I waited again.

By the end of the day, I was feeling hurt and confused. Even Danielle, my very best friend, hadn't said anything, and she knew how much I had hated wearing the brace. I didn't know what to think. I at least had to know what Danielle thought. I was spending the night at her house, so I decided to bring it up if she didn't say anything about it by then.

After a few hours at her house, she still hadn't said a word. At that point, I chickened out and asked Danielle's younger sister, Ann. "Ann, don't you notice anything different about me?" I asked her cautiously.

"Did you do something to your hair?" she asked.

"No. Not my hair," I said impatiently. "It's the brace. The brace is gone!" I turned in a circle and nodded my head up and down to show her. "See? It's gone!"

Ann just looked at me and shrugged her shoulders. "Well, I kinda thought something was different, but I just didn't know what it was!"

It wasn't until later that I realized my friends had long since accepted me for who I was, and they simply didn't notice the brace anymore. With or without the brace, what they saw when they looked at me was their friend.

~Anne McCourtie

Conversation Starters

1. In the story "A True Friend" on page 243, we meet Kelsey's friend Makayla. Makayla is handicapped. What does handicapped mean? How did Makayla become handicapped?

2. "Thanks, Y'All!" on page 247 is a story in which Michelle says thank you to the new friends she made. Why does she appreciate them so much?

3. "Trouble in Neverland" starts on page 257. Jamie insults Carly's religion during a disagreement on the playground. How do you think Carly felt when Jamie insulted her religion?

Chapter
9

Be the Best You Can Be

Accepting Responsibility

Stolen Conscience

The person that loses their conscience has nothing left worth keeping.
~Izaak Walton

L ast year, my mom tried to tell me that there really is a thing called a "conscience." You know, that little voice in your head that tells you when something you do is wrong? I never really believed her. I thought about hearing a small voice saying, "Brandon don't do this. Brandon, do that." *That's dumb,* I thought.

Then one day, my dad took me shopping, and we went into a toy store. There were lots of things to buy, especially in this one store where they sell collectable Star Wars cards. I really wanted a pack, but my dad said I couldn't have them so I got mad. After my dad left the store, I put the pack that I asked for into my pocket and walked out of the store.

The next day, I had a bad stomachache, and I felt that I needed to say something or let something out.

This is the first time I ever felt this way. I wondered all day if it was my conscience telling me that I did something I shouldn't have done. It was a horrible feeling, as if someone knew what I had done and told me that I was bad. I felt ashamed of myself.

Then that night, I had trouble sleeping. I was thinking scary thoughts about what could go wrong. *What if someone finds out? Will I get kicked out of the store for good? Will I go to jail?* The next day, I asked my mom if someone would feel anything if they did something wrong.

"Yes," my mom answered. "You would feel sort of sick in a way."

I knew I had to confess. So I told my mom what I had done, and she drove me to the store. She gave me money, and I paid for the cards that I stole. I also told the lady who ran the store that I was sorry. She was nice and said that I could come back to the store again.

After I told the truth, I felt better. But I was still embarrassed that I committed a crime, which I never thought I would do in my life. Even today, anytime I think about stealing, I get the shivers and feel just like I did when I stole that pack of cards. I also learned an important lesson during that week: Listen to your head and heart, not your greed.

~Brandon Deitrick, 12

I Can't Believe
I Did That

Only surround yourself with people who will lift you higher.
~Oprah Winfrey

was dangling my legs in the pool when Linda swam up and
blocked me. Something about Linda always made me a little
uncomfortable. I wanted her to like me, mostly because none
of my classmates lived close enough to hang out after school.
Linda lived only two houses down from mine. But this warm spring
afternoon, her words made me shiver.

"You've got to do what I say," she commanded, her voice low.
"Otherwise, I'll tell your mom you did it anyway."

"She won't believe you," I protested.

Linda glanced a few feet away at our moms in their pool chairs.
We could hear them laughing and chatting. They weren't listening
to us. Linda tossed her wet ponytail over her shoulder. "Oh, I don't
know… maybe she will. And even if she doesn't, my mom wouldn't
talk to yours anymore either."

Uh-oh. Linda's ideas weren't always fun. And sometimes they were
downright mean. "What do you want me to do?" I squeaked.

"You know those new people in the house on the corner?"

"Yeah," I answered.

"We-ell… they're such pains," Linda declared. "All I have to do is put a toe on their precious lawn and they come running out to make sure I didn't run over their flowers with my skates. I have an idea that will show them."

Linda pulled me down into the shallow water beside her and whispered her hideous plan.

"Soooo.... you just bring me a bag of your grossest garbage tonight," she said. "Then, when it's dark enough, we can pull our stuff down there in my wagon...." Her voice sounded mysterious, like a kid detective. Only she wasn't solving crimes. She was planning one.

"But..." I tried again. "I don't like this. What if they see us?"

"Don't be a baby," she said flatly. "They won't."

Maybe I could do it after dinner when I was supposed to be taking the trash out anyway. But I was feeling sicker by the minute. Why was I doing this? So what, if Linda dumped me. I knew it was wrong. I didn't even know those people. But it was like Linda had some sort of hold on me that I couldn't explain.

As Mom and I left, Linda wrapped her dripping arm around my shoulders and laughed loudly like we were best buds. "See you later!" she said.

"Feeling okay, hon?" Mom asked when I could barely eat my dinner.

"I'm just... not... too hungry, I guess," I said. Now I was lying too! How did I get in this mess?

I pulled the kitchen trash bag to the door. "Be back in a bit," I called.

Outside, I nearly abandoned the whole idea. But there was Linda, waiting at the end of our driveway. She must've known I'd chicken out and she wasn't going to let me.

"C'mon!" she urged, tugging our cargo down past her house to the corner. The home was dark. "Perfect!" she said in her director's voice. "Now!"

And suddenly, there we were, tossing all that yucky grossness onto the clean driveway. Lettuce leaves and greasy foil wrappers and wads of smelly tissue landed at my feet. I could hear cans dinging and rolling behind the bushes.

My heart was pounding, and my feet felt glued to the pavement in horror at what we'd just done. Somewhere a light went on in the back of the house. "Run!" Linda cried, yanking the rattling wagon and pulling me down the street. I never ran so fast in my life.

The next morning I truly did feel sick. But somehow I made it through the door, into the car with Dad, and on to school. "Have a great day!" Dad called. I hugged my books to my chest and clunked the door behind me. I didn't think I'd have a great day ever again.

I flubbed the easiest math problem when Mrs. F. called on me. I couldn't concentrate on my favorite reading book. I could barely swallow my peanut butter and jelly sandwich at lunch. And by the time I got home, my insides felt as wobbly as Jell-O Jigglers.

"Is something bothering you?" Mom wondered when I turned down Toll House cookies. Her voice was quiet, but I could hear a firmness in it. I knew she wouldn't let this one slide.

Suddenly, I couldn't hold it in any longer. "I think I did something... terrible!" I blurted on a sob. "And I'm... not sure... how... to fix it."

Mom just listened, pushing my bangs away from my eyes as I choked out the whole disgusting story. I was sure she was going to be so disappointed in me. More than I was in myself... and that was huge.

But she only looked into space for a moment. "I saw the husband out trying to scrape his driveway this morning," Mom told me then. "His wife is recovering from a fall she had last month and he told me how glad he was she didn't trip over any of that slop today."

I looked into her eyes, miserable. She reached over and tucked her finger under my chin. "I think you know what it feels like to be the new kid in school. And how they feel being new on our block...."

"Yes," I admitted softly. Then, after a moment, it was like I suddenly woke up from a nightmare. Yes! I did know. And I also knew how much I wanted people to like me and to fit in. So much that I let someone talk me into doing something so unlike me that it left me heartbroken. I had hurt someone for no reason. And like Mom always said, "hurting someone else hurts God, too."

Suddenly I was angrier than I was afraid. Mostly at myself — for letting Linda talk me into such a plot. I wanted to march two houses down and tell her my own plan. And if she didn't care to join me, that was her problem.

Linda did go with me, hanging behind as I rang the bell. I stuttered our apology to the woman in her wheelchair. At first, her black eyes flashed, reminding me of dark skies on a stormy day. I could tell she wasn't sure if we were really sorry, or if someone was making us confess. But after we finished hosing down her driveway she asked us in for lemonade. She told us about her grandchildren, who were our age and lived in another state. I confided how I loved to read and that Linda was a great swimmer. By the time we left, I had a new friend, and dinner sounded good again.

Even Linda seemed relieved. It was almost like she had needed me to stand up to her. Maybe all her crazy ideas were because she tried too hard to feel… important. Because she wanted me to like her, too. I hadn't thought of that before.

"Hey! Race you to your house!" I dared.

I was through doing whatever old thing Linda said. But after today, maybe, we could be real friends….

~Pam Depoyan

Oops,
I Messed Up

The truth brings with it a great measure of absolution, always.
~R.D. Laing

The other day at school we had an assembly. When a speaker is talking, we are supposed to be quiet and listen—that's what I usually do. But this time I kept talking to my friend Jamie. My teacher got up and walked around, trying to figure out who was talking, so I looked innocent and kept quiet until Mrs. Nussbaum gave up and sat down.

Then I started again. What I didn't see was that our P.E. teacher was sitting two rows ahead of me. She got up and came over to tell me to behave and listen, and then she went back to her seat.

After the assembly, my teacher asked me if I had gotten into trouble with the P.E. teacher. "Not me," I answered. "It must have been someone else."

She looked at me and said, "It's a good thing it wasn't you, or you wouldn't be having recess." Then she excused our class and sent us outside. I thought I was off the hook until we came back into the building. My teacher and the P.E. teacher were talking to each other, and they were looking my way.

When we went into the room, Mrs. Nussbaum told our class that we had some thinking to do. She said "someone" had caused a disturbance at the assembly, and until she found out who it was, none of us would be having any more recesses. When some of my classmates pointed to me, Mrs. Nussbaum said she had already asked me, and that I had said it wasn't me. She said that I wouldn't have any reason to lie. She was looking right at me in kind of a funny way when she said that, and then she turned away.

Jamie looked at me and said, "You started it. Why don't you admit it?"

"Because then she'll call home, and I'll be in lots of trouble and probably not be able to go to my soccer game tonight."

"So we all have to suffer because of you? That's not fair."

"Did you want to say something, Jamie?" Mrs. Nussbaum asked.

He looked at me. I wasn't sure if he was going to turn me in or not. "No, nothing," he answered while he glared at me.

After school, I waited until everyone had gone. I walked home slowly, thinking about what I had done. Why did I have to talk when I wasn't supposed to? Worse yet, why couldn't I just admit it when I was wrong? Now I had gotten the whole class into trouble.

I went into the house and stood by the kitchen door, knowing what I had to do. I walked in and saw Dad.

"Hi, son. Your mom is running late, so I've started supper. We'll eat early so we can all go to your soccer game. You'd better change."

I looked at Dad.

"What's wrong?" he asked.

I told him the whole story. He said we had to call Mrs. Nussbaum right away. Dad called the school and had Mrs. Nussbaum paged. When she came to the phone, he handed the receiver to me.

"I have to talk to her?"

"Yes, you do."

I took the phone and told her it was me, that I was the bad kid. She said I wasn't a bad kid; I just had messed up. In the end, I had been honest. She wasn't even going to punish me!

When I got off the phone, Dad said, "I'm proud that you finally admitted what you had done, but I think it's sad that Mrs. Nussbaum almost had to punish the entire class for your misbehavior."

"Does that mean I can't go to soccer?"

"That's up to you. You decide if you think you deserve to go to the game."

I looked at Dad and knew the answer. "I'll call my coach and tell him I won't be there."

When my mom and big brother came home later, they asked why we weren't going to soccer. My dad looked at me, and I explained it all.

"Wow," my brother said.

"What?" I asked.

"Well, I think it's great you told the truth, even when you knew it would make you miss the soccer game."

I like my big brother, and I look up to him. I thought he was only proud of me for the scores I make in my soccer games. Now I realize he could be proud of me for being honest.

That night, my brother helped me write a letter apologizing to Mrs. Nussbaum and the class. Even though I was nervous to go to school, I knew what I had to do. The next day in class, I was shaking as I read from my paper in the front of the classroom. When I finished, I didn't know what to expect. Some of the kids were upset with me, and I don't blame them. But others came up to me and thanked me for being honest.

I try not to talk during assemblies anymore, but let's face it—no one's perfect—least of all me. But now, when I do something wrong, I admit it. Life is just way simpler that way.

~Mike Schneider as told to Nance Schneider

My Bad Reputation

A lie may take care of the present, but it has no future.
~Author Unknown

Every day after school my parents made me sit and write… "I will not tell a lie! I will not tell a lie!" I repeated the sentence over and over until my hand felt as if it might fall off.

It was the middle of third grade and I am not sure what had gotten into me. I lied for no reason at all and about the dumbest things. I lied that I had eaten all my dinner, when in fact I buried it in the bottom of the trashcan. I lied that I had made my bed, when clearly by entering my room it was obvious I had not. I lied that I had brushed my teeth; with a quick check it was obvious the toothbrush wasn't even wet. My lies were not hurting anyone, but for some reason I felt the need to say things that were not so.

My parents tried everything to understand why I felt the need to make up stuff. I was grounded; I was watched closely so that I did what I was supposed to do, I was talked to and lectured while they tried to get to the bottom of where my poor behavior was coming from.

Was I looking for attention? As the middle child, maybe I wanted attention I wasn't getting. I soon realized the new attention I was getting was horrible. I was labeled a liar and my parents did not trust me. I promised to stop telling lies.

A few days later my sisters and I were invited to spend the weekend with my aunt. We all loved the times we were invited to Aunt Kim's house. She did not have children of her own so she spoiled us with her time. Not much of a cook, she gave us the perfect food for a third grader—hot dogs and macaroni and cheese. She took us roller-skating at a park with a long path and she was an amazing artist so arts and crafts were a big part of our afternoons. She had cool pencils, erasers and other supplies that any young girl would love to get her hands on.

The day finally arrived for the fun to begin. As my parents dropped us off and visited a few minutes they made it a point to tell my aunt to keep an eye on me and to not let me fall back into my world of silly lies. I was embarrassed and angry but when they pulled out of the driveway I forgot all about their lecture.

Then it happened… sometime that day someone took one of Aunt Kim's good art erasers and rubbed it across the entire top of the TV. The eraser ruined the shiny finish on the TV's casing. When Aunt Kim discovered the destruction all three of us were called into the TV room and asked to confess. Nobody did! Boy was she mad. I had never seen that side of her. She told us how disappointed she was and that someone would have to take responsibility. Again, nobody said a word. The next thing I knew she was on the phone with my parents and they were on their way to pick me up.

It had to be me! I was the liar. No amount of protesting could convince any of them that I had not committed the crime. I was taken home and sent to my room for the rest of the day. I begged and pleaded my case, but no one listened. Why would they? I had been telling lies for the past few weeks so of course it had to be me.

I stayed in my room the rest of that day thinking of all the things my sisters were getting to do without me. I was labeled a liar and now I sat alone with nothing to do. My parents finally let me out for dinner. And then there was a knock at the front door! Aunt Kim was standing there. I could not believe it. I was sure she and my sisters were already watching a movie from her big collection. Why had she come? It turns out my younger sister finally felt guilty! She confessed that she was the one who rubbed the eraser on the TV. Aunt Kim had come to get me. I was invited back!

Funny, I don't even remember being mad at my sister. I learned a valuable lesson about lying. No matter how big or small your lies, once you are labeled a liar earning trust takes a lot of work and time. I promised myself right then and there to never lie again.

~D'ette Corona

Tennis Anyone?

Character is doing the right thing when nobody's looking.
There are too many people who think that the only thing that's right
is to get by, and the only thing that's wrong is to get caught.
~J.C. Watts

One summer when I was about ten years old, my brother and I received a wonderful gift—tennis rackets and balls. We had never had the opportunity to play tennis, so this was exciting. However, there was one problem—the small town we lived in did not have a tennis court.

One Saturday morning my brother said, "Hey, I've got an idea. Let's take our tennis rackets and balls to the school and hit the balls against the school building."

"Great idea! Let's go," I agreed, not realizing what a lesson we would learn before the experience was over.

When we got to the school ground, no one was around, so we began hitting our balls against the side of the two-story brick building.

"I'll hit it the first time," my brother suggested, "then you hit it the next time. We'll hit it back and forth to each other."

So we began taking turns hitting the ball, getting more confident with each stroke. Actually, we became pretty good at returning the ball and we were hitting the ball higher and faster each time.

Suddenly, the unthinkable happened—the ball got out of control and went crashing through one of the upstairs windows.

We looked around and no one was in sight—except—there was an old man sitting on a porch halfway down the block.

Quietly, I asked, "Now what should we do? Our ball is inside the school."

"Well," my brother responded, "no one will know whose ball it is. And no one saw us, except that old man down there. And he probably can't see this far."

"He probably doesn't know who we are anyway," I added.

"Let's go home," my brother suggested.

"Okay," I agreed. "Should we tell Mom and Dad?"

"I don't know," my brother answered.

As we picked up the rest of our balls and headed for home, the decision as to whether we should tell what had happened was carefully weighed out. But that decision was made for us the moment we walked into the house.

Our mother was always in tune with her children. "What happened?' she asked as soon as she saw us.

"Well," my brother slowly began. "We had a great time hitting the tennis balls against the school."

Then I interrupted, "until we hit it too hard and too high and it went right through the school window."

"Oh, my goodness!" my mother exclaimed. After a short pause, she continued, "You will have to tell your father as soon as he gets home."

And so we did. As soon as he walked in the house, we both hurried to him and poured out our story.

His response was typical. "Well, today is Saturday and tomorrow is Sunday, but first thing Monday, I will call the school janitor and see what we need to do. You will probably have to pay for the window."

We had two agonizing days to wait until our dad got home from work on Monday.

He looked very somber and we were sure that the news was bad. We were sure that every penny we had saved would have to go to fix the window.

Then my dad smiled. "Well, I talked to the school janitor and he was surprised to hear from me. He had been sitting on his porch watching while you two were playing tennis on Saturday. He saw the whole thing and was surprised when I called to tell him what had happened. He said many windows had been broken, but we were the first ones to call and admit that we were responsible. He said the school budget allows for window repair, so we will not have to pay for the window, but he was glad we called."

He could see our relief as he continued. "I am proud of you kids for having the courage to tell us what happened."

I'm not sure at that moment whether we were happier to be able to save our money, or to hear our dad say he was proud of us. But either way, we discovered that there is always someone who sees what we do and we might as well confess our mistakes and be willing to take the consequences.

~Shirley M. Oakes

The Tiny Bear

Have the courage to face the truth.
Do the right thing because it is right.
These are the magic keys to living your life with integrity.
~W. Clement Stone

A unt Evie had a miniature dollhouse. It was the most beautiful thing I had ever seen. Everything about it looked so real, as if tiny people had handcrafted each little doorknob and every piece of furniture.

Every Friday I went to Aunt Evie's because Friday was card night for my grandparents and their brothers and sisters. They would gather around in the dining room, eating pie and laughing, while I looked at the dollhouse for hours.

Sometimes I would pick up the delicate furnishings and place them in different positions. It was fun to decorate with the little items. Once, I asked Aunt Evie where she got the little miniatures so that I could buy some, too, one day. But Aunt Evie said that most of the miniatures were handcrafted and couldn't be replaced.

One such item was a small teddy bear an inch high. I was amazed by how beautifully it was sewn together. It was so tiny and had two little beads for eyes. I wanted the bear badly. *If I take it, Aunt Evie wouldn't even notice it's missing. But I could hold it in my hand and admire it all day long,* I thought to myself.

That Friday night, it took me a couple of hours to get the courage to take the bear and put it in my pocket. I had to wait until nobody was watching me. Once the bear was in my pocket, I couldn't wait to get home and look at it. I would have to hide it somewhere at home, so that no one would know I had it.

That night, I couldn't sleep. I tossed and turned and couldn't get comfortable. *What an awful person I am,* I thought. *I'm a thief, and I stole from my family.* When I woke up the next morning, I had a fever, but didn't seem to have a cold. I stayed in bed to punish myself for what I did. I couldn't tell my grandmother or Aunt Evie. I was too embarrassed about what I did. *There's no turning back,* I thought.

I felt worse and worse. My stomach started aching badly. I started hating the bear. I hated myself, too, and knew that if I didn't do something quickly, I wouldn't be released from the bad feelings I was having.

I decided to tell my grandmother. My hands were shaking, and I couldn't hold back the tears.

"I thought you knew better than to do something like that." My grandmother shook her head in disappointment.

"I feel awful, Granny. I can't live with myself and what I've done," I said.

"There's only one way to make this right. You have to take the bear back and tell Aunt Evie what you did," she said.

I started to panic. Facing Aunt Evie and telling her that her niece was a thief was too much to ask. *Aunt Evie will never forgive me, and for the rest of her life, I will be embarrassed to look her in the face,* I thought.

"You're going to stand up and take the consequences for what you did, whether you like it or not," my grandmother said.

My finger was trembling when I rang Aunt Evie's doorbell. She opened the door as if she already knew what I was going to say. I showed her the little bear and told her I was sorry. Quietly, Aunt Evie picked up a box by the door and handed it to me. Inside was a miniature tea set.

"I admire your courage for coming here and returning the bear. You are my favorite niece even more now," Aunt Evie said.

During the ride home, I looked at the present on my lap. My stomach felt a lot better.

~Lara Anderson

Start with the Truth

When in doubt, tell the truth.
~Mark Twain

t was a beautiful sunny day, and Mary and I were playing in her new basement because it was so hot outside. The two of us were best friends, so we naturally did what best friends do—we did everything together. We went camping together, we trusted each other, and always stuck up for each other.

But that day, something changed.

I'll never forget the look on Mary's face when she knocked over her mother's favorite vase that was on the table. The flowers and vase crashed to the floor, and the vase cracked into tons of tiny little pieces. I looked at Mary and said, "There's no way to fix this!"

Mary burst into tears. "What am I going to do? What am I going to say?" She looked at me while she wiped her tears and asked, "Can you say that you did it?"

I was shocked. I didn't know what to do or say, and I started to pace back and forth.

"Okay, I'll do it," I said.

That very second, her mother came downstairs to ask about the loud noise she had just heard. Mary said, "Mom, we were sitting on the couch, and Michelle put her feet on the table and knocked over the vase."

Her mother looked at me and shook her head. "I don't know

how many times I have to tell you girls, you don't put your feet on the table."

I apologized to Mary's mother and told her I would buy her a new vase. She said not to worry, but just be more careful. I felt so bad—and I didn't even do it! I know that I had kept Mary out of trouble, but I also felt that it wasn't right.

I didn't go over to Mary's for a few days, and she didn't come to my house, either. I was busy cleaning and doing extra chores. Finally, I earned enough money to buy Mary's mother a new vase. I shopped around for a vase that looked like the one that Mary had broken until I found one that I thought her mom would like. Wanting to get it over with, I went straight to Mary's house to give her mom the new vase. When Mary saw the vase that I had worked so hard to buy, she burst into tears again.

"Mom, I have to tell you something. I broke the vase, not Michelle," she confessed. "I asked her to take the blame for me."

Mary and I looked at each other with relief. Now I knew that Mary felt it was wrong to lie about the vase, too. Mary's mother had a talk with us about the importance of telling the truth from the beginning. Then Mary decided that she should do something to make things right with her mother and me. She asked if she would take us to the store where Mary picked out some beautiful flowers for her mom's new vase and a pretty friendship bracelet for me. And she paid for them herself with her allowance.

~Michelle Rossi

Walking with Grandpa

The power of choosing good and evil is within the reach of all.
~Origen

Grandfather was a wise and honorable man. His house was not far from ours, and I would visit him often going home after school.

No matter how rotten I had been, I could tell Grandpa anything. My secrets were safe. He always understood. He loved me.

I remember a time when a bunch of us were playing baseball in the field behind Mrs. Ferguson's house. I hit one pitch just right and... *slam!* It was a home run that soared high and away, and ended up shattering Old Lady Ferguson's kitchen window! We all ran!

Walking home, my best friend, Tom, asked, "How will she ever know who did it? She's blinder than a bat!" He had a point.

I decided to stop by Grandpa's. He must have known something was up by the expression on my face. I felt ashamed. I wanted to hide. I wanted to bang my head against a tree a thousand times and make the world just go away — as if punishing myself could undo things. I told him about it.

He knew we had been warned many times about the dangers of playing where we shouldn't. But he just listened.

"I was wrong," I told him, with my head down. "I hate myself for what I did. I really blew it. Is there a way out? Will she call the police?"

"Well," he said, "she has a problem, just like you. I'll bet if she knew you cared, she would be sad to know that you're afraid of her. I'll bet she wishes you would give her a chance... a chance to be understanding. It's your decision," he said, shrugging his shoulders. "Just so I don't say the wrong thing, is the plan to pretend nothing happened? Just keep quiet and carry your little secret around... hide what you're not proud of?"

"I don't know," I sighed. "Things might get worse...."

"Let's think it through," he said finally. "If you were Mrs. Ferguson, what would you do?"

I had been afraid that Mrs. Ferguson would stay mad at me, so I ran. I didn't know what she might do. On the way home I imagined that she was a mean witch chasing me, and the further away I ran, the more gigantic she grew... until finally she towered over the whole town, seeing my every move with an evil eye.

"Well," I said, taking a deep breath, "One solution is to tell Mrs. Ferguson I'm sorry and offer to fix her window."

"If you call her," asked Grandpa, "what's the worst that can happen?" I had to think for a moment. I realized that even if she did not accept my apology, it could not be any worse than seeing the disappointment on Mom and Dad's faces.

Grandpa smiled when he knew I had figured it out.

"Doing what's right is not always easy," he said, handing me the phone. "I'm proud of you." Grandpa did not make me do it. It was always my choice. I knew I had found the best answer, just by thinking it through. That's how Grandpa did things. As it turned out, things were not anywhere near as bad as I had first imagined.

"Owning up to what you're not proud of is the hardest thing of all," said Grandpa. "Choosing to be honest, on your own—even when you don't have to be—makes others trust you and respect you."

Besides, it made me feel really good about myself. No one can ever take that away. *Thank you, Grandpa.*

Mrs. Ferguson and I eventually became really close friends. She was so kind and grew to take a real interest in me. I started doing all kinds of odd jobs around her house after school, which eventually helped me to save enough to buy my first car. She once told me, "Fear can make the smallest things look so much bigger than they really are."

Just before he passed away Grandpa asked me, "Who will you turn to when I'm gone?"

Holding his hand I told him, "Honor is its own reward, Grandpa. And a good teacher lives on through his student. Thank you."

After Grandpa died, everyone was sad. So many people loved him and would miss him.

I still talk to him, in my thoughts. I imagine how he would approach things, what questions he would ask… what advice he might give… whenever there is a problem. His soothing voice is clear and simple.

Grandpa gave me the tools to fix many problems… and cut them down to size.

And most of all he showed me I was brave.

~Uncle Greg

Mary Lou

If you're secure in yourself, and even if you're not secure in yourself, you don't need to bully.

~Joan Jett

t was my first day as newcomer to Miss Hargrove's seventh-grade class. Past "newcomer" experiences had been difficult, so I was very anxious to fit in. After being introduced to the class, I bravely put on a smile and took my seat, expecting to be shunned.

Lunchtime was a pleasant surprise when the girls all crowded around my table. Their chatter was friendly, so I began to relax. My new classmates filled me in on the school, the teachers and the other kids. It wasn't long before the class nerd was pointed out to me: Mary Lou English. Actually she called herself Mary Louise. A prim, prissy young girl with a stern visage and old-fashioned clothes. She wasn't ugly—not even funny looking. I thought she was quite pretty, but I had sense enough not to say so. Dark-eyed and olive-skinned, she had long, silky black hair, but—she had pipe curls! Practical shoes, long wool skirt and a starched, frilly blouse completed the image of a total dork. The girls' whispers and giggles got louder and louder. Mary Lou made eye contact with no one as she strode past our table, chin held high with iron determination. She ate alone.

After school, the girls invited me to join them in front of the school. I was thrilled to be a member of the club, however tentative.

We waited. For what, I didn't yet know. Oh, how I wish I had gone home, but I had a lesson to learn.

Arms wrapped around her backpack, Mary Lou came down the school steps. The taunting began—rude, biting comments and jeering from the girls. I paused, then joined right in. My momentum began to pick up as I approached her. Nasty, mean remarks fell unabated from my lips. No one could tell I'd never done this before. The other girls stepped back and became my cheerleaders. Emboldened, I yanked the strap of her backpack and then pushed her. The strap broke, Mary Lou fell, and I backed off. Everyone was laughing and patting me. I fit in. I was a leader.

I was not proud. Something inside me hurt. If you've ever picked a wing off a butterfly, you know how I felt.

Mary Lou got up, gathered her books and—without a tear shed or retort given—off she went. She held her head high as a small trickle of blood ran down from her bruised knee. I watched her limp away down the street.

I turned to leave with my laughing friends and noticed a man standing beside his car. His olive skin, dark hair and handsome features told me this was her father. Respectful of Mary Lou's proud spirit, he remained still and watched the lonely girl walk toward him. Only his eyes—shining with both grief and pride—followed. As I passed, he looked at me in silence with burning tears that spoke to my shame and scalded my heart. He didn't speak a word.

No scolding from a teacher or preaching from a parent could linger as much as that hurt in my heart from the day a father's eyes taught me kindness and strength and dignity. I never again joined the cruel herds. I never again hurt someone for my own gain.

~Lynne Zielinski

Conversation Starters

1. On page 275, the story is entitled "Oops, I Messed Up." How does Mike mess up in the story? How does Mike accept responsibility in the story?

2. "Tennis Anyone?" is the story on page 281. How did a new sports activity help Shirley and her brother learn an important lesson?

3. After reading "Walking with Grandpa" on page 289, did you make a connection to the story "Tennis Anyone?" How is Greg's situation in this story similar to Shirley's?

Be the Best You Can Be

Being Kind

being kind

The Carriage House

A hug is a great gift — one size fits all, and it's easy to exchange.
~Author Unknown

My grandfather lives in a nursing home called the Carriage House. That's where my grandmother goes almost every day to visit him.

When I sleep over at her house, we go to see him, too. There are lots of old people there. When I first started going there, they would see me coming and hold their arms open for a hug, but I would pretend that I didn't see them and hurry upstairs to Grandpa's room. Just thinking about the other people with their wrinkly faces and hands made me shiver.

I felt safe up in my grandpa's room with him, even though he can't walk, talk or do anything for himself. I would tell him all about my life and sometimes give him a kiss. Even if I felt like I needed to go to the bathroom or I wanted to go to the soda machine, I didn't leave the room.

The first time my little brother, Ben, came with my grandmother and me, he looked like he was going to cry. I understood how he felt. I didn't blame him because he'd never been around people who were so different from us.

One day, I asked my mom about the old people. She told me that they can't take care of themselves anymore and need special care from the nurses, so they live there at the nursing home. I thought about that for a while, trying to imagine not being able to live in my own home anymore and not able to see my family and friends every day. I began to understand how they feel, and I thought, *They must be so lonely when no one visits them.* So I made a decision.

The next time I went with my grandmother to visit my grandpa, I actually hugged the other old people—and it wasn't as scary as I thought it would be.

Now I am getting used to being in my grandpa's new home, and I'm getting to know some of the other people who live there. And now I know that just because they are old doesn't mean that they don't have feelings or deserve to be loved.

~Victoria Thornsbury, 8

Goals and Dreams—
A Winning Team

Coming together is a beginning. Keeping together is progress.
Working together is success.
~Henry Ford

After relocating to the suburbs of Atlanta, Georgia, I was fortunate to be offered a fifth-grade teaching position. When I accepted the job, I was warned that I was being given a "tough" group with behavioral problems and real attitudes. Being excited just to have a teaching job after relocating, I wasn't even discouraged after warnings from former teachers and parents alike.

The year started out like any other year. Expectations were set, and my single rule of respect was imposed. Within two weeks, I began to notice the attitudes I had been warned about. This was a diverse group of students who were intolerant to differences of others. Getting them to work with partners or in groups was torture for them and for me.

I would not accept their intolerance. I insisted the students team up and respect one another and value their differences. This became my mission for the year. I had the time and situation to work through these skills with them. It was the year of the Olympics in Atlanta so there were teams from many nations all around us preparing for the games. We began to study the different countries that were participating.

We talked about the history and values of each culture. We discussed how every person's role on a team was important. We talked about the respect for each person's talents as the means for success. We learned how winning was not as important as participating with effort. The feeling was contagious, and soon all the students were caught up in the Olympic fever and in doing their best. Away went the disputes when working together, and away went the name-calling, the racial slurs and the insults over mistakes. Instead, they shared feelings of encouragement for each other.

They were doing so well that other teachers and the parents began to notice. I heard things such as, "I used to see these kids and cringe when they came toward me. Now they are one of my favorite groups." I also heard, "A year ago I would never have expected Tricia to get a citizenship award." Parents reported that their children were no longer arguing with siblings or over chores and homework. The rebellious, intolerant attitudes had all but disappeared.

By spring, I felt these students were ready for their final test from me. I had received a small grant from the local community to support my plan. I began a project called Goals and Dreams. The idea was that the class would set a goal, and all the students would participate to make it happen. Having focused so much on sports with the Olympics, the students chose to get involved with a sports activity. Each year the school sponsored a five-kilometer road race to raise money for cancer research. This year my students were going to train for this road race and complete the 3.1-mile course, though none of them had ever run more than a mile and certainly none had ever been in a community road race before.

We began our training program learning about the body and the systems we would need to develop for us to run this race. We studied famous runners from the past and current runners training for the Olympics. We trained each day on the field and charted our endurance, pulse rate, heart rate and speed. Each student chose a running partner so they could encourage each other when one wanted to stop and walk. We kept training logs of activities done at home. We designed team T-shirts to wear on race day and did community service to raise money for the entry fee for the race. We all believed in our goal of participating in and completing the race.

Each day, lessons revolved around our goal, and the students were very excited about working to achieve it — except for one student.

Luke was not excited about running three miles on roads in the local neighborhood. He was not excited about running even one lap around the field. Luke was not a runner. He was the largest boy in the class by at least six inches and thirty pounds. To run for more than two minutes at any speed was a struggle for Luke. Despite this, he never complained and did each of the workouts with the class, always finishing last, always red-faced and gasping as he shuffled to join the class. Luke never seemed upset, and he trudged on like a real trooper each day.

No one in the class said much about Luke's struggle. It became accepted that Luke would come in last. There was never any pity or insults. It was just the way things were, and it didn't bother anyone — or so we thought.

The night before the big road race, Luke's mother called me. Her son was in tears over the idea of coming in last place in the community road race. Luke understood that winning didn't matter, but coming in last place would be humiliating. Luke's mom wanted me to be aware of this and know that she would walk the course so that she would come in last place instead of Luke.

The day of the race we excitedly lined up for team pictures and stretched our muscles. Everyone was confident about finishing the course and achieving our goal. Even Luke was a proud member of the team and showed no worry.

The gun went off and hundreds of runners started making their way around the course at different speeds. In front were runners from the community who had been running in races for years. In the crowd behind them were my twenty-six well-trained students and myself, a runner for several years.

After I crossed the finish line, I stood along with many parents to greet each student with a victory hug. One and two at a time they crossed, each bringing us closer to accomplishing our goal. I lost count of the students who had come across the line and started asking those who had finished to be on the lookout for classmates approaching. Gradually, each student crossed the finish line with gritty pride to be part of the success of our class as well as the personal success of finishing a 3.1-mile race. After some time, the finish line area started getting more and more quiet. Still, there was no sign of Luke. I looked around, and no longer saw my students or their parents. I was so disappointed. This was supposed to be a class goal, which meant that everyone had to cross the finish line, and then we would celebrate success.

Maybe this was too much to ask of ten-year-olds. Maybe parents who had hundreds of things to do on a Saturday morning did not understand the importance of having their child stay to cheer on every last classmate. I just knew I would not let Luke down. I would stay at the finish line until he crossed.

My disappointment soon turned to concern. What if Luke physically could not do it? As these thoughts ran through my head, I heard a huge commotion around the final bend before the finish line. A siren let off a screech that pierced my ears and turned my blood cold. Oh no, it must be Luke. Something was wrong with Luke! I started sprinting from the finish line toward the corner.

Suddenly, I stopped in my tracks to see Luke with the entire class gathered around cheering him on with every bit of energy they had left. Together, the group of twenty-six fifth-graders crossed the finish line screaming and celebrating their victory with Luke in the middle as the hero.

Every member of our team received a medal for our victory, and every time I look at mine in its special case, I am reminded of these special students, who learned and lived what it means to be a team, and of Luke, my running hero.

~Jodi O'Meara

The Hand of Friendship

Labels are for filing. Labels are for clothing.
Labels are not for people.
~Martina Navratilova

The third graders tumbled into the classroom for our after-school Bible study program, screeching metal chairs on the linoleum floor as they found places to sit. Chatter filled the room and the kids couldn't help fiddling with the plastic caddies of supplies in the middle of the table—scissors, glue bottles, markers—for our project that day.

"What are we making, Mrs. Malone?" asked a girl with a green polka dot bow on the top of her head.

"Handprint butterflies," I said, showing them my sample, a paper butterfly made from the outlines of my hands traced on cardstock and glued together at the bottom of each palm. It fluttered at the end of a piece of yarn. Some of the kids grasped at it as I fluttered it over their heads.

I passed out two pieces of cardstock for each of the kids. "As soon as you choose a marker to outline your hands, you can begin," I said. Most were swirling a marker tip around their hands before I finished the sentence.

As the handprints morphed from blank canvases into rainbow-winged creatures, I noticed one boy who hadn't started yet. He tapped the table with the tip of his marker and held his left hand firmly in his lap.

"Why aren't you working, Michael?" I asked.

He shrugged.

"I'd like everyone to at least try to do the project. Do you want me to help you trace your hand?"

"Mine won't look like everyone else's," he said.

"No two people can make their butterflies exactly the same. That's what makes each one special."

He shook his head. "No. That's not what I mean."

Puzzled, I struggled to understand. Michael looked down, clearly upset. Why would a simple coloring project be so troublesome? Never before had he refused to do a craft. Across the table, his best friend Andy's expression was just as grim as Michael's.

I knelt down so Michael and I were eye to eye. "What's bothering you, Michael?"

He sighed and laid his left hand, the one he'd been hiding on his lap, on the table. "My hand is different."

I looked at his hand. For the first time in the four years I'd known him as a classmate of my daughter since kindergarten, I saw his missing fingers. There were only four fingers. Two of his four fingers were partial, pink nubs. He tapped them with the marker in his other hand. "My butterfly wings will look funny."

At first, I didn't know what to say. Here was a boy who was always smiling, surrounded by friends at school and out on the playground, a polite boy who talked easily to adults and who towered over others his age. Not once had I noticed his hand. How could I explain to an eight-year-old that the shape of his hand was not important to the people who mattered to him? At a loss for words, I looked to Andy for his reaction to Michael's words. Then I noticed Andy's picture.

Andy's hand was splayed across the page as he finished tracing his second handprint. Only he had three fingers folded under his palm, creating the same outline Michael would have displayed had he traced his own hand, with its shorter fingers.

The gesture almost brought tears to my eyes. It was a perfect example of what I wanted to tell Michael but didn't know how to put it into words.

"Look at Andy's butterfly," I said to Michael.

Michael looked sharply at Andy. "Why are you doing that?"

"Because we're the same. We're friends," he said without hesitation.

Michael and Andy exchanged looks. Andy made a goofy face at his friend and then picked up an orange marker to color the wings.

I patted Michael's left hand. "Your friends don't care what your hand looks like. I didn't even know about it until you showed me just now. I've known you only as someone who smiles a lot and makes his friends laugh. That is what's important to Andy, too, and your other friends."

Michael nodded. His mouth hinted at a smile. He wiggled his hand from underneath mine and flattened it on the paper. With the black marker, he finished tracing both hands by the time I got up from the floor.

As I walked between the tables, helping those who had finished coloring their handprints to glue them together, one of the adult assistants in the room pulled me aside.

"Whatever was bothering Michael before seems to be forgotten now," she whispered. "What was the problem?"

"He was worried that his project would look different."

"Whatever you said to him worked."

"It wasn't me," I said. "Andy made him feel better."

True friends have that power.

~Dawn Malone

The Eleventh Box

It is more blessed to give than to receive.
~Acts 20:35

What is your most memorable Thanksgiving? For me, it was on the eve of the day. The church had the names of ten families scheduled to receive food baskets. A local merchant donated hams, and groceries were purchased from the food bank. As we packed the boxes in the fellowship hall, these families were excited over the food they were taking home. It would be the best meal many had enjoyed in months. As they were picking up their boxes, another family arrived. Father, mother and three children piled out of an old pickup truck and came inside the hall. This was a new family, not on our list. They had just heard there was food being distributed by a church.

I explained that we did not have enough for an extra family. And as I tried to assure them that I would do what I could, an amazing thing happened. With no prompting, a woman put down the box she was carrying and quickly found an empty box to place beside it. She began removing items from her box to share. Soon others followed her lead, and these poor people created an eleventh box for the new family.

~Pastor Bill Simpson
Submitted by M'Shel Bowen

Adventure from a Stolen Apple

Love is the only force capable of
transforming an enemy into friend.
~Martin Luther King, Jr.

When I was ten years old, I spent the summer at my grandmother's farm. Even though I was older than all of my cousins and most of them were boys, we still hung out together after we did our chores. We would wander the countryside, picking wild blackberries and playing together.

There was one very rundown farm that we stayed away from because my cousins said that a witch lived there. They called her "Old Lady Green." I had never seen her, but one day in late August as we were passing near her farmhouse, we saw that she had a lot of large apples hanging almost over her fence. We stopped to look at them.

Then my cousin Paul climbed over the fence. He reached up, grabbed an apple and handed it to me. Just then, I heard a startled gasp. I turned and saw an old lady watching us.

"Old Lady Green! The witch of Knox County!" my cousin yelled. Then he raced back through the waist-high grass and leaped over the tumbled-down fence.

My eyes couldn't leave the eyes of the old lady. *Why*, I thought, *she's going to cry!* She was leaning heavily and painfully on a stumpy, knotty, worn tree branch. Her head was bald in spots, and her white thin hair hung limply around a face that looked like a shrunken apple. Although she looked about a hundred years old, she was only as tall as I was.

I reached out and handed her the apple. A crooked half smile creased her wrinkled face, and I saw that she only had a few teeth.

"Thank you," she rasped. "Why didn't you run away like the boy did? Aren't you afraid of me?"

"Because at my school we are learning about being kind. I want to help you." This was only half true. I felt like running as fast as I could away from her, but I stood my ground.

Then she sat down on a tree stump, laughed and slapped her thigh. "I'm too old and weak to care for my property. I can only reach the low apples, pears and peaches. I have only a few chickens. I don't want 'em scattered. The only way I've been able to save what I have is to scare the lights out of youngsters by pretending to be a witch. Now I've lost my power over you!"

What should I do? I wondered as I stood there. Even though I was still a little scared of her, I wanted to stay and help her — and I did. I climbed high up to the sweet apples and brought her a bag full of them. I picked green beans from her weedy garden, and washed and snapped them. I dug up some potatoes. Then I searched the grass near the hen house and found some eggs the hens had mislaid.

When I started for home, I found my cousin, my aunt and Grandma almost running down the road to look for me. They seemed very worried. I quickly explained, "She isn't a witch at all! Just a nice old lady who is very weak and can't pick the apples up high, so she chases away people who try to steal the only ones she can reach!"

Now whenever I see an old lady who looks cross because children or dogs are running around her lawn or through her flowers, I remember Old Lady Green who wasn't really mean or a witch, but simply too weak and too poor to replace what others might carelessly destroy.

~Rosemary K. Breckler

Finding Friendship

Don't wait for people to be friendly, show them how.
~Author Unknown

n middle school I was the shy, quiet girl who always did her work, sat in the back of the class, and never raised her hand for fear of giving a wrong answer. My shyness was a problem when it came to meeting new people, but I had a small group of friends who I had grown up with, and I believed they would always have my back. Emily, Vicki, and Michelle were my three best friends in the whole world; they were also my only friends.

Vicki was the leader; she took it upon herself to always invent games and take charge, and she absolutely hated anybody standing up to her. Put simply, she was bossy, and if something didn't go her way, she wouldn't hesitate to fight.

Michelle was Vicki's sidekick, and she was much more passive. She followed Vicki around like a puppy dog, and went along with whatever she said.

Emily was quiet and not as bossy as the others, but she was also more assertive than I was. She never picked fights with anybody for disagreeing with her, and she never had anything bad to say about anybody. I trusted her the most of my three friends.

I was in sixth grade when I finally saw my friends' true colors, and it felt like a slap in the face. I had just finished gym class, and I was walking to the cafeteria with Vicki, Michelle, and Emily. It was time for lunch, which was my favorite part of the day.

We walked in as a group, with Vicki and Michelle in front, while Emily kept pace directly behind them. I brought up the rear, walking slowly and silently. Without warning, the three sat down at a table nearest the entrance, and I suddenly noticed that there were no empty seats for me to sit in.

"Very funny, guys," I said softly, hoping they would move to another table. The one where they had chosen to sit was already full with a group of boys that I barely knew.

"Can you make room for me?" I asked, and I could already feel the flush of embarrassment creeping up my cheeks.

"There's no room," Vicki said simply, looking me straight in the eye.

"Can't we just sit at a different table?" I pleaded. I felt humiliated. I was being abandoned by my best friends, my only friends.

"No. We're sitting at this one. You should just walk faster next time."

"Yeah," Michelle piped in.

I looked desperately at Emily, my last hope, but she stared down at the sandwich in her hands instead of meeting my gaze. She acted like I wasn't even there.

The hurt and embarrassment of this betrayal was enough to shatter what little self-esteem I had, and I could barely make my voice audible, much less keep it from breaking.

"Wow, thanks guys," I choked. I had tried to make it a sarcastic, biting comment, but I couldn't maintain my composure. I wanted them to feel a fraction of the pain I was feeling, I wanted them to regret this. But Vicki had already moved on and was starting a new conversation with Michelle.

I shuffled away from the table, holding onto my lunchbox for dear life. I refused to let myself cry, but I couldn't stop my face from turning what must have been an unsightly shade of red. I glanced at every table I passed, skimming each one for a single friendly face. I just needed someone to sit with, just for today. Sadly, this was the moment I realized I really had no other friends. There was nobody else I could sit with. I finally made my way to an empty, dirty table in the back of the cafeteria.

I wished desperately that someone would join me, and I angrily wondered why my friends couldn't have simply sat at this empty table.

Halfway through lunch, a teacher walked over to my table. I wondered frantically if I had done something wrong to draw his attention. I didn't want to get in trouble.

"Hey, Brianna," Mr. Hickey said to me kindly. His voice was soft and comforting, but that didn't stop my anxiety. "Did you and your friends have a fight or something?"

I shook my head vigorously, "No, we're fine."

"Then why are you sitting all alone?" he seemed concerned, and a small part of me was thankful that somebody was taking notice, but I didn't dare say anything about my friends.

"I just felt like sitting here for a change, I guess. I don't really know." I shrugged and bit into my sandwich like it was no big deal.

He nodded slowly, and started turning away. "Okay, well, if that's all. Enjoy your lunch." He looked back at me over his shoulder, but only for a moment, before a group of boys shooting milk out of their noses drew his attention and he was gone.

The next three days followed a similar pattern, only it soon became a race not to be the last to the table. I was desperate, but somehow, I was always last. For three days I sat by myself at the dirty table in the corner. Mr. Hickey didn't approach me after that first day, but I never missed his glances in my direction.

One day this pattern was broken. I was sitting alone at my table, like always, when a small voice asked, "Can I sit here?"

Startled, I looked up to see a girl named Stephanie who I only vaguely knew. She had ridden the same bus as me the year before, but other than that I had never really had much contact with her.

"Yeah, sure," I said, eagerly making room for her.

Suddenly, lunch didn't seem so miserable. We talked all period, and my heart felt like it was going to burst. Stephanie's act of kindness was hugely important to me, and I have never stopped feeling entirely grateful to her. I also didn't miss Mr. Hickey's quick smile as he watched us from over his shoulder.

The next day, it wasn't just Stephanie who joined me for lunch. Emily came over, as well as three other girls who were friends with Stephanie. A few short days later, my entire table, once empty, was almost completely filled.

Finally, there was only one person missing.

"Can I sit here?" Vicki asked softly.

I looked at her for a long moment, and Stephanie opened her mouth to deny her.

"Yeah, there's a seat next to Michelle." I cut in.

Vicki scurried over to the indicated seat, and Stephanie turned to me, asking why I had let Vicki join us.

I had no answer other than sometimes a little kindness can go a long way. I had learned a lot over those few days, and finally I saw who my real friends were. Stephanie, who was practically a stranger, had seen me when I needed help, and she was the only one to come to my rescue when my "friends" abandoned me. Now I want to reach out to others, to spread kindness and love, just as Stephanie did for me.

~Brianna Abbott

Care Bags

You give but little when you give of your possessions.
It is when you give of yourself that you truly give.
~Kahlil Gibran

Annie loves going to the mall with her mom and bringing home big boxes full of teddy bears, games, coloring books and crayons. But she is no spoiled child. On the contrary, the fourteen-year-old is one of the most generous, kind-hearted kids you'll ever hope to meet.

Annie's mom, Cathy, is a child-abuse prevention educator. Every day she talked to schoolchildren, teaching them how to protect themselves and report abuse. At a conference she attended, a social worker asked Cathy and other adults at the meeting to save tiny shampoos and soaps whenever they stayed in hotels.

"Usually children who need emergency shelter come with nothing but the clothes on their backs," Cathy told her daughter that night. Annie knew she wanted to help somehow.

Later, lying on her bed surrounded by her collection of Beanie Babies, books and toys, Annie thought about how safe and loved she felt. And then she had an inspiration.

"I'll collect shampoos and soaps because the kids need them," she told her mom, "but I'll also collect toys and games and other fun stuff to make them feel happy, too."

Annie contacted Children's Services, which loved her idea. She and her mom composed a letter describing her idea, and she hand-delivered the letter to local merchants.

Many businesses were happy to help. They gave Annie gift cards to buy toys, stuffed animals and books. Area pharmacies, grocery stores, hotels and dentists donated toothpaste, shampoo, packets of tissue and other toiletry items. Women's groups and schools volunteered to sew beautiful fabric drawstring and handled bags. Annie filled each bag with new items she had collected and named them "Care Bags."

She pinned this poem to the outside of each bag:

This little bag was made especially for you,
To say I think you're special, and I care about you, too.
Inside you'll find a bunch of things like toothpaste, soap or a toy,
I collected all this stuff for you to fill your heart with joy.
I hope this makes you happy, today and every day,
And remember someone loves you in a very special way.

After only a few weeks, Annie delivered thirty Care Bags, which were distributed to needy foster children and crisis-care kids throughout the city. Annie was told the children loved the care bags, and they carried them everywhere. One little boy even slept with his.

As word of Annie's Care Bags spread, other merchants began donating diapers, pacifiers, night-lights and gift certificates. Complete strangers, Girl Scout troops, 4-H clubs, schools and church groups from all over the United States began sending boxes of stuffed animals, receiving blankets, school supplies, journals and decks of playing cards. The town even gave her space in a local senior center, where donations are stored and volunteers help Annie fill the bags. A computer expert helped Annie create a Web site: www.carebags4kids.org, which has encouraged many others to get involved.

Over the past three years, Annie has assembled over four thousand Care Bags. Annie has never met any of the Care Bag recipients, but she knows she's making a real difference.

"It was so nice to receive something when everything was falling apart," one little girl wrote to thank Annie. "It's nice to know someone really cares."

~Heather Black

The Note

Kind words do not cost much. Yet they accomplish much.
~Blaise Pascal

W hen I was in the fifth grade, I fell in love—real love—for the very first time. It only took about a week into the school year for it to happen, and I was completely, head-over-heels crushing on Mike Daniels. No one ever called him just Mike; it was always one word—MikeDaniels. Blond hair that stuck up in every direction and blue eyes that crinkled in the corners when he laughed—visions of Mike Daniels occupied my every dream.

To say I wasn't the most popular or prettiest girl in our class would be an understatement. In fact, I think I must have been the original geek. I was so skinny that I still had to wear days-of-the-week panties and dorky undershirts when most of my friends were starting to wear bras and more grown-up undergarments. My mom made me wear brown orthopedic lace-up shoes to school every day, because I had a foot that turned in and my parents wanted to "correct it before it was too late." Right smack dab in the middle of my two front teeth was this giant space that even gum surgery the year before hadn't fixed, and the two teeth on either side of my front teeth overlapped, making me look like I had fangs. Add a pair of thick glasses, thin baby-fine hair (with a home permanent from my mom—help!), knobby skinned-up knees and elbows—and what do you get? A kid that only a parent could love.

I wouldn't—couldn't—tell my friends that I was in love with Mike Daniels. It was my secret to write about in my journal. In my dreams, Mike Daniels would all of a sudden grasp what a beautiful soul was hiding inside of my gawky body and realize that he loved me for who I *really* was. I spent hours writing poetry for him and stories about him, until one day I got up the nerve to actually write to him about how I felt.

Our teacher, Miss Finkelor, was really awesome about most things, but the one thing she was majorly serious about was not writing notes to each other during class. Everyone did it anyway. Except me. My only shot at self-esteem was being teacher's pet, and I excelled at it. I loved it so much it didn't even bother me when kids teased me about being the teacher's favorite.

It was a huge decision for me to go against the one thing that Miss Finkelor detested—note passing. But I knew that there was no other way to tell Mike Daniels about how I felt—and I also knew that if I never told him, I was going to burst... or maybe even freak out. I vowed to do it on Monday morning.

So, first thing Monday morning, in my very best printing, I wrote, "I love you." That was it. Nothing else—no flowers, no poetry—just, "I love you." I passed it to Dianne, who sat between me and Mike Daniels, and whispered, "Give this to Mike Daniels," trying to look really casual, like it was a request to borrow a book from him or something. I held my breath as I watched him open and read it—then read it again. Then he folded it up and put it into his pocket. *Oh my God, what have I done? What if he shows it to his buds at recess? They'll all laugh their heads off. I'm a fool. An idiot. Why did I tell him?* I felt like I was going to throw up.

I was so involved in feeling like I was going to hurl, that I didn't even feel Dianne punching me in the arm. Then she shoved a note in my hand. Slowly, I opened it. It was my own note. *Great, he thought it was so stupid that he sent it back to me,* I thought. Then it dawned on me—he had written something on the back of it. "I like you, too. I'm glad we're friends."

I didn't know whether to laugh or cry. I was so relieved that he didn't trash me—that could have easily happened if Mike Daniels hadn't been a really nice guy. With that one little gesture of kindness, Mike Daniels made me feel special—and, not only that, but I felt that somehow, he *had* seen the real me hidden in the body of a fifth-grade geek.

I kept that note for years—all the way through the eighth grade. Whenever I felt bad about myself, I would reread Mike Daniels' note and remember that act of kindness. It didn't matter to me what inspired him—if it was pity, or the recognition of things to come—that note gave me strength to go through the challenges of the tough years that followed fifth grade.

~Patty Hansen

Mikey's Goal

The greatest test of courage on earth is to bear defeat without losing heart.
~Robert Green Ingersoll

Last night was the last game for my eight-year-old son's soccer team. It was the final quarter. The score was two to one, my son's team in the lead. Parents encircled the field, offering encouragement. With less than ten seconds remaining, the ball rolled in front of my son's teammate, one Mikey O'Donnel. With shouts of "Kick it!" echoing across the field, Mikey reared back and gave it everything he had. All round me the crowd erupted. O'Donnel had scored!

Then there was silence. Mikey had scored all right, but in the wrong goal, ending the game in a tie. For a moment there was total hush. You see, Mikey has Down's syndrome and for him there is no such thing as a wrong goal. All goals were celebrated by a joyous hug from Mikey. He had even been known to hug the opposing players when they scored.

The silence was finally broken when Mikey, his face filled with joy, grabbed my son, hugged him and yelled, "I scored! I scored. Everybody won! Everybody won!" For a moment I held my breath, not sure how my son would react. I need not have worried. I watched, through tears, as my son threw up his hand in the classic high-five salute and started chanting, "Way to go Mikey! Way to go Mikey!" Within moments both teams surrounded Mikey, joining in the chant and congratulating him on his goal. Later that night, when my daughter asked who had won, I smiled as I replied, "It was a tie. Everybody won."

~Kim Kane

Conversation Starters

1. The story on page 301 is called "Goals and Dreams—A Winning Team." It tells the story of Jodi, the teacher of a fifth grade class in Atlanta, Georgia. In the beginning of the school year, the students were not kind toward each other. What topic brought the class together as a team?

2. On page 308, "The Eleventh Box" is a short story to enjoy. Pastor Bill Simpson asks us, the reader, a question relating to his passage. What is your most memorable Thanksgiving?

3. Page 322 tells the story of "Mikey's Goal." How does Mikey's teammate show kindness to him when he makes a goal during the soccer game?

Chapter
11

Be the Best You Can Be

Being Grateful

The Boy Who Had Everything

Gratitude is an art of painting an adversity into a lovely picture.
~Kak Sri

When I was a baby, my parents gave me anything I wanted. We would walk into a store, and anything that I wanted was mine; all that I had to do was to ask. I would play with a toy for a while, get bored, and ask my parents for a new toy. Then my dad died when I was two and a half, and I got even more stuff as my mom, friends and family gave me more and more stuff to try to make me feel better. My mom continued to treat me to whatever I wanted until I was seven and my world changed.

That was when the real estate market crashed. My mom had thought that buying houses was a good idea as a way to invest her money to take care of us. After the crash, I went from the kid who got an iPod when his tooth fell out and who had the coolest house to hang out in, to literally having nowhere to stay. My mom's best friend, my Auntie Loren, took us in until my mom could figure out what to do.

After the real estate crash, when I would ask for a new toy, or bike, or even to see a movie my mom would say "maybe for your birthday" or "I'm sorry honey, but we can't really afford that right now." I didn't know it then, but my mom had grown up in a family where money was never a problem, so this change was as big for her as it was for me. My constant requests for toys and video games were not helping my mom, who was already a widow, deal with her feelings about our new crisis—our financial situation. But I wasn't used to hearing "no" so for a year or two I kept asking.

Then something happened that would change my way of thinking forever. My mom had been working really hard all year, just to pay for the necessities, like our water and power bills. When she asked me what I wanted for my birthday I said that I wanted a new video gaming system. I didn't know that it was expensive. All I knew was that my friends had them and that I wanted one too.

On my birthday, I started opening my presents, believing that I would get what I asked for. As I opened the last gift, I found two or three T-shirts and a pair of jeans. When my mom asked me what I thought, I said that I loved them, but she could tell how disappointed I was and she started crying. I hugged her harder than I had ever hugged anyone before. I realized how hard she was working and that she couldn't afford to give me anything I didn't need and that most of the money that my mom made went to paying for rent and food.

From then on I didn't expect to get everything that I asked for. When I did, I was so excited and grateful. I think I learned the difference between what I wanted and what I needed. I learned to appreciate the toys or games I did have and to take good care of them. When I wanted a new iPod, I had to work to buy it. I got a job folding clothes at our local laundromat, and after working there for just over a month every day after school, I had enough saved up to buy that iPod.

The feeling of having truly earned something is one of the best feelings in the world. I also am lucky to have wonderful people in my life. They have made me appreciate that it doesn't matter what I have or don't have. What matters more is who I am and who I get to spend time with.

It may have been hard going through that experience, but I was able to learn some really important lessons. Now I am grateful for everything I have and I understand the feeling you get from working to earn something for yourself. People used to think I was "spoiled" because I always had everything and didn't understand how fortunate I was. Recently, my godfather Ty told my mom that he loved to give me things because I never ask for anything and am always so grateful. I guess I've really changed.

~Jackson Jarvis

My New Friend

*How wonderful it is that nobody need wait a single moment
before starting to improve the world.*
~Anne Frank

When I used to think of Christmas, I thought of presents, cookies, decorations, and a huge tree. Now I think of Christmas as a time to spend with your family and appreciate what you have. My vision of this holiday changed one remarkable night.

My parents had told my brother and me that we were working at the homeless shelter on Christmas Eve to help with the dinner. Honestly, I could not believe what my parents wanted to do and I threw a fit. I was only nine years old, but still, looking back on that behavior shocks me. As I walked into the homeless shelter and saw about thirty homeless men and women gathered around their tables singing holiday carols with smiles spread across their cheerful faces, my heart melted. Just this sight changed my whole attitude about not being home on Christmas Eve.

I headed to the kitchen and started making plates of turkey and mashed potatoes. As I piled the mashed potatoes on each plate I looked outside the window to see each and every person's eyes sparkle and their mouths move to the words of "Jingle Bells." I remember just wanting to go out there and sing along with them. I looked past all the differences I had with them and just felt like they were family. As the carols died down, we started to bring out the food that was on plastic plates with a Santa in the middle. Every single person would smile and thank me once I put their food down and wish me a Merry Christmas.

One specific man really touched me. As I set down his plate he said, "Thank you sweetie." Now this was not unusual—basically everyone there said it, but then he said to me, "You know, this is very kind what you are doing for us. Not many people would help us out, or even want to get close to us. You're a real angel for doing this. I remember when I was your age I would keep my distance from homeless people, but it's reassuring for me to see a young girl like you help us out. Thank you and Merry Christmas."

I was at a loss for words but I managed to say, "Thank you very much. Merry Christmas to you too."

When we left to go home I turned back to look for that nice man. I saw him in the corner bundled up with one thin blanket and a two-inch pillow. Tears blurred my vision; all I wanted to do was stay with him, bring him my big comforter I sleep with at night that I usually push to the side of my bed, and give him someone to talk to. But I had to keep walking out to our car. Now I never wanted to leave, and I couldn't believe I had complained that I didn't want to come.

I got home and as I sat down to eat a pizza with my family for Christmas Eve dinner I started crying my eyes out just thinking about the night I had, the smiles on the people's faces, and most of all the friend I had made. The man who I will never forget, who said the words I will carry with me forever.

I snuck downstairs that night, not to check for Santa, but to take away the letter I wrote him and write a new one. It said:

Dear Santa,

I wrote you a letter earlier, but I am writing a new one now. Please take care of the man I met earlier and give him some of my gifts that you were bringing me. Please keep him safe from the outdoors and make sure he is happy. That's all I want this year. You can still bring me presents, but the one thing I want is for you to look out for my new friend.

Love,
Erin

My vision of everything had changed that night. Christmas is now the time I think about my friend, and how lucky I am to have what I have. It's not the time to worry about the new bike I want anymore; it's time to worry about how my friend is and if he realizes how he changed my life.

~Erin McCormack, 13

My Abilities

Always be a first-rate version of yourself,
instead of a second-rate version of somebody else.
~Judy Garland

I once had a blind friend in elementary school named Easton. I remember one day when I asked him, "Easton, if they came up with a way to cure blindness, would you want to get your blindness cured?" To my surprise, he said no. He said that this blindness was a way of life for him. It was what he was used to. It was what he had known all his life. I was confused. I mean, if I were blind, I surely would want to see. Then, when I was in middle school, I was diagnosed with a nonverbal learning disability and Asperger's syndrome. It was because of these that my social, organizational, and handwriting skills (among other things) were less than up to par.

Several years after I was diagnosed, I started thinking about that day when I had asked Easton if he wanted to have his blindness cured. It was then that I was able to see what he meant. I realized that I was thankful for my disabilities, and that I wouldn't want them to be cured. Like Easton, my disabilities have become a way of life for me. Sure they inhibit my social skills, so I tend to be the kid who sits there quietly and reads while everyone else talks with their friends. And sure my social mannerisms can be awkward at times. But I do have a few very close friends who mean the world to me. And you know what? Sometimes it's nice to be alone. I can't really explain it; it just is.

Sure I tend to be somewhat uncoordinated and not very good at sports. But I'm pretty good at acting. I've been in several school productions: I've been Daddy Warbucks in *Annie*, Ike Skidmore in *Oklahoma!*, Francis in *The Tempest*, Charles in *My Fair Lady*, and even Grandpa in *You Can't Take It With You*, and I have also gotten inducted into the International Thespian Society. Acting is something for which I have a passion.

Sure my handwriting tends to be sloppy sometimes, and sometimes it hurts to write, but because of that I get to type my notes—except in math, where someone takes notes for me. Sure my disabilities have inhibited my math skills, but they have also helped me to become pretty good at English. Statistics say that most kids with the disabilities similar to what I have struggle in math but are pretty good in English.

I don't expect you to understand why I am thankful for my learning disabilities instead of wishing they could be taken away. It wasn't until years after I was diagnosed with my disabilities that I could fully understand Easton's reasons for accepting his blindness. I don't think you can understand it unless you've experienced it. When it comes down to it, my learning disabilities are just my way of life. They are a part of me. It is the way God made me, and I cannot wait to see how He uses these disabilities in the future. Sure my disabilities have taken things away from me, but they have given me so much more. That is why I am thankful for my learning disabilities.

~Ben Jaeger

Where I Belong

We should not be asking who this child belongs to,
but who belongs to this child.
~Jim Gritter

"Why didn't your parents want you? How does that make you feel?" "Is your real family dead?" "Will you have to go back someday?"

It wasn't easy being adopted—especially being a brown girl from Central America, with two white parents. Until seventh grade, it hadn't been too much of an issue for me. I'd gone to a small church school with the same people I pretty much saw seven days a week. We all knew each other as well as if we were related, and we'd grown up together from babyhood. Everyone knew I was adopted, and it was no big deal.

But when I was twelve, I left my safe cocoon for a bigger, public middle school. Like my elementary school, the new school was mostly white. I was used to that. What I wasn't used to were all the questions.

Now, I know—from the statistics—that there were probably as many as three or four other adopted kids in my class. But they were the same color as their parents, so nobody had to know their private business. I, on the other hand, couldn't hide.

It wasn't so bad when my mom came alone to help out at school or attend a meeting. When kids saw her, they just assumed I had a Latino dad. There were other mixed-race students in my class and, just like I'd grown up with the same group of kids at my elementary school, these kids had all grown up together, too. They were used to mixed marriages.

At first, I didn't want anybody to know. I just hoped and prayed only one parent would show up to things. Then, for all anyone knew, I could just be another biracial kid. But, all too soon, people found out, and I had to start answering questions.

Of course, a lot of people didn't care either way. But when you're twelve and you feel very different, it really seems like everybody is staring and whispering—when in actuality, they aren't even paying any attention to you at all.

Some kids were just innocently curious. Others were downright mean about it. They were the kind of kids that tell their younger brother or sister, "You're adopted"—like it's a bad thing—even when they aren't.

At first, it felt as if I was defending myself. Maybe it was none of their business, but brushing them off would only have made things worse. I had to admit I was adopted. I had to explain why I was adopted, and what that meant.

It was frustrating a lot of the time. People just didn't get it. They couldn't understand why somebody wouldn't be living with their "real" parents. They couldn't imagine what it would be like, living with "strangers."

It drove me crazy. What did "real" mean, anyway? My adoptive parents were as real as anybody else's. I was their "real" kid. We sure weren't artificial. And after twelve years together, we were anything but strangers.

As time went by, I made true friends. They came over to our house and hung out. My mom or dad drove us to the mall or the movies. My friends were soon as comfortable with my family as the kids I'd grown up with.

But some of the other kids still didn't get it. It was as if they thought adoption was wrong or scary. I guess I could have kept trying to get through to them, but finally I realized they would probably never understand—and that was not my problem.

Adopted kids are just like any other kids. When we get in trouble, we get grounded. Our parents clean up our messes and stay with us when we're sick. They yell at us when they get mad. They're proud when we do well. Sometimes, they hurt our feelings or don't understand us, or they let us down. And sometimes they stand up for us, or they sit and listen when we are sad or worried. Adoptive families are forever, and we are just like anyone else.

It wasn't till I got a little older that I realized how lucky I really was, and that adoption was something that made our family even more special. I had friends with parents who were in jail or had just disappeared. One girl lived in a group foster home. Some kids were failing out or school or doing drugs, and their parents didn't even seem to care.

I am blessed to have a home and a family that cares about me. I know, too, that I'm blessed to have a birth family that loved me enough to let me be adopted when they weren't able to provide for me. A lot of people aren't so lucky. I am where I belong.

~Marcela Dario Fuentes

The Flower

"I have many flowers," he said,
"but the children are the most beautiful flowers of all."
~Oscar Wilde

For some time I have had a person provide me with a rose boutonniere to pin on the lapel of my suit every Sunday. Because I always got a flower on Sunday morning, I really did not think much of it. It was a nice gesture that I appreciated, but it became routine. One Sunday, however, what I considered ordinary became very special.

As I was leaving the Sunday service a young man approached me. He walked right up to me and said, "Sir, what are you going to do with your flower?" At first I did not know what he was talking about, but then I understood.

I said, "Do you mean this?" as I pointed to the rose pinned to my coat.

He said, "Yes sir. I would like it if you are just going to throw it away." At this point I smiled and gladly told him that he could have my flower, casually asking him what he was going to do with it. The little boy, who was probably less than 10 years old, looked up at me and said, "Sir, I'm going to give it to my granny. My mother and father got divorced last year. I was living with my mother, but when she married again, she wanted me to live with my father. I lived with him for a while, but he said I could not stay, so he sent me to live with my grandmother. She is so good to me. She cooks for me and takes care of me. She has been so good to me that I want to give that pretty flower to her for loving me."

When the little boy finished I could hardly speak. My eyes filled with tears and I knew I had been touched in the depths of my soul. I reached up and unpinned my flower. With the flower in my hand, I looked at the boy and said, "Son, that is the nicest thing I have ever heard, but you can't have this flower because it's not enough. If you'll look in front of the pulpit, you'll see a big bouquet of flowers. Different families buy them for the church each week. Please take those flowers to your granny because she deserves the very best."

If I hadn't been touched enough already, he made one last statement and I will always cherish it. He said, "What a wonderful day! I asked for one flower but got a beautiful bouquet."

~Pastor John R. Ramsey

The Color of Gratitude

Green is the prime color of the world,
and that from which its loveliness arises.
~Pedro Calderón de la Barca

Seeing the world differently than everyone else is an experience all its own, especially when you don't even know that you are seeing things differently. I didn't know I was colorblind until I started school. I had been excited to start school and I loved everything about it — the playground, circle time, snack time, making new friends. Everything except coloring. I hated picking out crayons and staying in the lines. I never asked for a coloring book at restaurants. I just did not get what all the excitement was about.

My parents didn't question it. They just assumed it was not something I enjoyed and often joked about the fact that I was very smart but was failing coloring in preschool. That is, until the day I came home full of news about my new friend, Devon, who was tall, funny and... green. My mom laughed it off at the time, assuming Devon must have been wearing a green shirt.

A few days later I attended my first flag football practice. My mom sat on the sideline watching as I learned for the first time the rules of football. I played with all my heart. At the end of the practice my new coach came up to my mom and me and told me what a good job I had done. When my dad called from work later that day to hear about my first football experience, I told him how the green coach had praised me.

The following day my mom accompanied me into the classroom to meet my "Martian" of a friend. When I pointed him out my mom began to chuckle. She told me that he was brown, not green. Within a few days I was sitting in a doctor's office taking a colorblindness exam and sure enough I tested positive. I was officially brown/green colorblind.

Since then I have learned how to deal with colorblindness by reading the names on the crayons or colored pencils. My mom has had to draw charts and label them if I need to see shades for a school assignment. But most importantly I have learned that color doesn't matter as long as I wake up each day and experience the wonders of brown grass and green tree trunks.

~Bailey Corona

Tears in the Bathroom Stall

The only real mistake is the one from which we learn nothing.
~John Powell

A s a sixth-grader, I began noticing how other kids were separating into cliques. There were the geeks, the jocks and the popular cool kids. I wasn't sure where I belonged. And I think that was the problem.

Our teacher had assigned "secret buddies" for the coming week. The purpose of this assignment was to do nice things for your buddy without letting them know who was doing it. We could leave encouraging notes on their desk or mysteriously leave a card in their backpack or book. Our teacher wrote each kid's name on a piece of paper and threw them into a bucket, then we each closed our eyes and drew the name of the classmate who we were to secretly befriend and support over the next five school days.

By the middle of the week, everyone, including me, had turned this assignment into a contest to see whose secret buddy could leave the best gift. Instead of encouraging notes, we left stationery sets on our buddy's desk. Instead of giving compliments, we were giving bubble gum, lollipops and even money. It seemed that everyone was getting cool presents from their buddy. Everyone except me, that is.

My buddy followed our teacher's directions without a fault. I received handmade cards, notes with nice thoughts and countless smiley-face pictures proclaiming that I was one of the nicest girls in the class. My buddy seemed to think highly of me from the notes that were left, but the lack of gifts made me wonder what was up with whoever had pulled my name.

On the last morning of our assignment, I walked into my classroom and noticed that there was a package on my desk. At last, my buddy had grasped the idea that everyone else had! I ripped open the tissue paper and just stared down at my desk. There sat a canister of perfumed powder. The girls sitting near me giggled and went off about the "old lady" gift I had received. And to make matters worse, the powder had already been opened. I felt my face turn red as I shoved it into my desk.

I tried to forget about the embarrassing gift, but when I was in the bathroom before recess, the same girls who had seen me open the powder started talking trash about my secret buddy for giving it to me. I quickly joined in. "How lame," I heard myself saying. "What could my buddy be thinking by giving me such a stupid gift? My grandmother wouldn't even want it."

The girls laughed at my remarks and filed out of the bathroom. I stayed to wash my hands and let the water run through my fingers as I thought about what I had just said. It wasn't normally like me to say mean things like that about someone.

As I turned off the water, I heard a creak. I turned around to see one of the bathroom stall doors open. A girl from my class took two steps out of the stall and looked up at me. There were tears streaming down her face.

"I'm your secret buddy," she whispered to me. "I'm sorry about the gift." Then she ran out of the bathroom. Her sobs stayed with me long after the door had closed.

My secret buddy was a girl named Rochelle, a girl who came from a poor family. She and her siblings were targets at school for those who felt they were better just because their parents had money. Yet through all the teasing and harassment, Rochelle never had a bad word to say back to anyone. She just took the horrible treatment silently.

I was sick to my stomach as my cruel words ran through my mind. She had heard every single thing that had been said. And, once again, she silently took it in. How could I have been so mean?

It took me a few days, but I finally found the courage to face up to Rochelle and apologize. She told me that she had felt bad all week about not being able to leave any cool gifts for me. Her family could not afford it. So finally, her mother had given up the one thing that was a luxury to her so that Rochelle would have something to give. Her mother had assured her that the nice girl Rochelle had talked about would like the powder. Rochelle couldn't wait to get to school that morning and put it on my desk.

And I had ruined everything for her.

What could I say to Rochelle? How could she ever forgive me for making fun of her? Along with my apologies, I told her the truth. I admitted that I had only said those things to be cool, to try to fit in. I didn't know where I belonged, I explained.

Rochelle looked me in the eyes and said that she understood. She had been trying to fit in, too. "We aren't that different from each other, are we?" she smiled. Her simple words, spoken from her heart, found their way straight into mine.

Up until then, like everyone else, I had avoided the "Rochelles" of the world. But after that day, I gained respect and admiration for people like Rochelle — people who give from the heart.

~Cheryl Kremer

Conversation Starters

1. "The Boy Who Had Everything" on page 329 teaches a lesson about being grateful. What is the difference between a want and a need?

2. "My Abilities" is the title of the story on page 335. Why is Ben grateful for his learning disabilities?

3. The story on page 342 is called "The Color of Gratitude." Why do you think Bailey chose this title for the story?

Chapter
12

Be the Best You Can Be

Getting Through Tough Times

Perfectly Normal

Never, never, never give up.
~Winston Churchill

The year was 1963.

That's when I was born... to "perfectly normal" parents at a "perfectly normal" Cleveland hospital.

I would like to say that I was a "perfectly normal," healthy baby, ready to take on the world. But instead, I was born with multiple deformities. My eyes were almost on the sides of my head, and I only had holes where my nose was supposed to be. I had a club foot and was missing all but one toe, if it could be called that. Also, three of my fingers were missing on my right hand. A cleft palate had an opening in my top lip and extended all the way to the right eye. Unfortunately, even one leg was shorter than the other.

The hospital staff, I was told, thought I had too many problems to survive. The doctors, in fact, refused to show me to my parents and, incredulously, even gave my parents forms to sign to "give me up for science."

I can only thank God that my parents had other plans for my life. I belonged to them and to God. They intended to love and accept me just as I was, despite acknowledging that it would be a long, hard road ahead.

At the age of seven months, I began to undergo a very long series of operations. However, the first seven were deemed failures. The surgeons, it seemed were trying to do too much at once. I, on the other hand, was like a puzzle that needed to be "put together" one piece at a time.

While successive surgeries were a little more successful, my appearance was still far from normal. In fact, very few people knew that I had already had sixteen operations by the time I was ready for third grade.

When I began kindergarten, I was placed in a special-education classroom because my appearance and imperfect speech were not accepted. Aside from being labeled a "special-ed" kid, I endured constant ridicule from other students who called me "stupid," "ugly" and "retarded" because of my looks. I also walked with a limp and had to wear special shoes and braces on my legs. I spent almost every school holiday in the hospital having operations and also missed a lot of school. I wondered if I would ever get out of special classes. My desire to become a "normal" child prompted my parents to pursue tests that would place me back in regular education classrooms. My parents and I worked very hard that summer to get ready for the big test. Finally, I was tested.

I'll never forget the day I waited outside the principal's office while my parents received my test results. The brown door between them and me seemed to loom bigger and bigger as time went by. Time passed in slow motion. I longed to put my ear to the door to hear what was being said.

After an hour passed, my mother finally emerged with a tear streaming down her cheek. I thought, *Oh, no, another year in special-ed.* But much to my relief, the principal put his hand on my shoulder and said, "Welcome to 3B, young man!" My mom gave me a big hug.

Another milestone in fourth grade was the "miracle" that my parents and I had longed for. I was selected to undergo a very experimental surgery that would resculpt my entire face with bone grafts. The surgery was life-threatening and lasted ten hours. I survived this operation, my eighteenth, which really changed my life. At last, my nose had a shape, my lip was "fixed" and my eyes were very close to being in their normal position.

While I now faced a new chapter in my life from a physical perspective, I hadn't seen the end of my trials.

Within the next few years, my mother developed cancer and died, but not before instilling in me a sense of worth and the determination never to give up.

When other kids called me names, she had prompted, "Don't let those names bother you. Feel sorry for those kids who were not brought up right."

In addition, my parents taught me to be thankful for my blessings, pointing out that other people might have even greater challenges.

Their words eventually impacted my life when I did see people with greater challenges—in hospitals and whenever I did volunteer work with children who were mentally challenged.

As a teenager, I came to realize that my purpose in life was to help others become successful with whatever gifts they were blessed with, despite the things that society might point out as handicaps or shortcomings. In fact, my father advised, "Mike, you would make a great special-ed teacher." I knew what it was like to be a special-ed child.

However, I simply wasn't ready to make teaching my career choice at that point. Instead, I earned a degree in business and went on to become a very successful salesman, spending seven years in retail management. Then, I went on to become a very successful bank employee, spending five years as a loan officer. Still, something in my life was missing.

Despite the fact that I had met and married a special-ed teacher, it took me twelve years to realize that was my calling also and that my dad had been right.

Continuing my college education, pursuing a master's degree in education, I now teach in the same school district as my wife.

My classroom is a kaleidoscope of children with special needs—emotional, physical and mental. My newest career choice is my most challenging yet. I love to see my students' smiling faces when they learn something new, when a few words are spoken and when an award is won in the Special Olympics.

I've now gone through twenty-nine surgeries. While many have brought a lot of pain to my life, the fact that I have survived them all only seems to reiterate to me that God has a purpose for my life, as well as for every other life. I see my purpose being fulfilled one child at a time.

I may not have been a "perfectly normal" healthy baby, but I am ready to take on the world—thanks to God and to people like my mom. The motto she gave me will always be the motto I use in my own classroom: Never give up.

~Michael Biasini

Annie Wiggle-Do

To live with fear and not be afraid is the final test of maturity.
~Edward Weeks

"Look who's here to see you, Brenda," the nurse said.

She led a tired-looking woman to the girl's bedside.

Brenda huddled on her side, facing the wall. When her mother touched her shoulder, she pulled her head closer to her chest, as if making her body smaller would help her disappear altogether.

The nurse patted the mother's shoulder.

"Brenda's still not talking to us," she said in a low voice.

Brenda's mother bit her lip to keep from crying. She remembered exactly how bubbly and happy Brenda had been before the car accident that led to the amputation of her leg. She'd been one of the most popular girls in her sixth-grade class.

When Brenda first awakened from her surgery, she had raged at her mother. *Why had this happened?* Now, she felt like a freak. No one would ever want to be her friend. She would never date, never have a boyfriend. Then, Brenda had just stopped talking.

"I wish I could bring her friends to visit her," said Brenda's mother. "It's just too long a bus trip, though, about three hours each way."

The nurse smiled. "Don't worry. We have a plan."

Shortly after Brenda's mother left, two nurses wheeled in a stretcher.

"Moving day, Brenda!" one said cheerily. "We need this bed for someone who's really sick. We've picked out the best roommate in the hospital for you."

Before Brenda could protest, the nurses had rolled her onto the stretcher and whisked her down the hall. The room was awash with light, posters and music.

"Here's your new roomie, Annie Wiggle-Do," one nurse told a dark-haired teenager in the other bed. "She's just beginning to get better, so please don't kill her with your corny jokes."

Fourteen-year-old Annie grinned. As soon as the nurses left, she hopped out of her bed and sat on the end of Brenda's.

"I lost my leg from bone cancer," she announced. "What happened to yours?"

Brenda was so astounded she couldn't even form a word.

"You're lucky," Annie continued. "You've still got your knee. They had to take mine, hip and all, see?"

But Brenda's eyes had already found the raw scar and empty hip socket. Her gaze seemed frozen, like a magnet held it there.

Annie scooted back to her bed. "I'd like to socialize, but my boyfriend's due any time now, so I have to get ready."

As Brenda watched transfixed, Annie reached up and took off her hair! Her head was completely bald.

Annie giggled. "Oh, I forgot to warn you, the stuff they gave me to kill the cancer also killed my hair. But check this out! My parents, my grandma, my boyfriend and some kids from school all brought me wigs!"

From her bedside stand, Annie removed a tangle of wigs. Brown wigs and blond wigs, short-haired and longhaired wigs, curly wigs and straight wigs.

"That's when I thought up 'Annie Wiggle-Do,' Annie said. "Get it? 'Any wig will do.' Annie Wiggle-Do?"

Laughing at her own joke, Annie chose a curly blond wig and arranged it on her head. She just managed to dab on some pink lipgloss and powder before a group of boisterous teens burst into the room. Annie introduced Brenda to them all. Her boyfriend, Donald, winked at Brenda and asked her to keep Annie out of trouble.

Before long, Brenda began chatting with Annie and her friends. They didn't make her feel like a freak at all! One girl even shared with Brenda that her cousin wore an artificial leg, played basketball and rode a motorcycle. By the time the nurses shooed all the visitors from the room, Brenda felt more like the old Brenda.

The girls talked into the night. Annie shared her dream of becoming a comedy writer. Brenda told Annie about her secret desire to act in live theater.

"Ladies!"

A night nurse came in and shined her flashlight on Annie and Brenda. "It's after midnight," the nurse scolded. "What do you have to say for yourselves?"

"Nothing, your honor," Annie said. "We don't have a leg to stand on!"

They all laughed, but Brenda laughed hardest of all.

As the nurse's footsteps faded down the hallway, Brenda snuggled under her blanket. "'Night, Annie Wiggle-Do," she whispered. "I can hardly wait 'til morning."

~Kathleen M. Muldoon

Then and Now

You cannot dream up confidence. You cannot fabricate it.
You cannot wish it. You have to accomplish it.
~Bill Parcells

At the age of ten, I began to suffer from an autoimmune skin condition called alopecia areata. I had no idea what it was. It started out with a small patch of hair loss on the back of my head. I literally woke up one morning and a patch of my hair was gone. The patch was about the size of a quarter. I told my mom right away. She was clueless as to the reason for the hair loss, but more worried about the harm it might cause.

When we went to visit my local doctor, I felt like I was improperly diagnosed. I was told the condition was related to stress and in a short period of time the hair would grow back after I took some prescribed antibiotics. I continued to see many different doctors, tried all sorts of different remedies, but still had no answers or clue as to the cause.

At the age of twelve, during the summer, absolutely everything fell off. The skin disease spread throughout my body and I was officially diagnosed with alopecia universalis, which results in rapid loss of all hair, including eyebrows, eyelashes, and everywhere else on my body. The only good information I was told about the condition was that it is not life threatening, harmful or contagious.

I found out that this skin disease also affects over five million

Americans. It is currently believed to be an autoimmune disorder, and there is no standard treatment for alopecia universalis. It was heartbreaking for me, at that age, to receive such news. At the time, I didn't even know how to begin to face the facts. I was scared, embarrassed, confused, upset, and disappointed.

At that point in my life, it was bad enough dealing with the poor living conditions of the ghetto, but now I had a skin condition to add to everything else. There were some tough times. The biggest thing I feared was not what the world would think of me, but what my fellow students would say. The New York City public school system can be pretty hostile and I was afraid to face my peers.

I remember that first day of school back in September so clearly. I tried to do everything I could to hide my new look, but it turned out to be in vain. The other kids noticed my alopecia right away. For the majority of the school year, I constantly wore hooded sweaters, fitted sport caps, just about anything I could find to cover my head and eyebrows, which stood out the most when you would look at me. It was difficult to gain peer acceptance.

I got in trouble many times because in public school they would make you take your hat off in class—no exceptions. I would always put up a fight about taking my hat off and would be sent to the principal's office on a weekly basis. It was awful. The faculty in my school wouldn't give me a break. My mom would have to come to school about every other month just to talk to my teachers about being a bit more compassionate with me.

The worst part about the whole ordeal was the reaction of other kids. Teens can be so hurtful to one another. Even my own friends would tease me. I heard it all from "egg head" to "bald eagle" to "cone head." I also used to get compared to that albino boy from the hit 1995 movie *Powder*. The whole ordeal was rather shameful. Just imagine a daily occurrence of jokes and teasing all throughout my school years and in my own neighborhood, just because I lost my hair.

I was the same Charlie, yet I was treated differently because of hair loss. It actually came to the point where I didn't even want to step out of my house. I would pretend to be sick to avoid going to school. It not only affected my education, but my self-esteem was destroyed.

As hard of a challenge as it was for me as an adolescent, my solution came to me via a recreational outlet—the game of basketball.

All of the hardness that I'd developed over time was still bundled up inside me. As a kid, basketball allowed me to express myself in a way that created value and purpose for me. It became my exercise of the body and mind, the development of my character and leadership on and off the court.

What I appreciated most was that we were equals on the basketball court and the only way to distinguish one from another was through our performance, not our looks. The game helped me understand what fairness and equality were all about. I was treated just like one of the guys on the court. I was accepted for who I was, not what I looked like. The fact that I was a gifted basketball player gave me the opportunity to build my confidence more than anything else.

Self-confidence is at the root of self-fulfilling prophecies. If you want to become a great basketball player or just be great at anything, believing in your abilities is a must. You need to believe and be determined to achieve your goals. The things that separate you from the rest of the pack are your mental approach, fearlessness, and self-belief. It doesn't really matter who you are or what you've gone through in life. For me, when it comes to basketball, an aggressive, attacking attitude puts fear in the opposition and creates openings to score. I have this saying I stick by: "I have alopecia; alopecia doesn't have me." I'm the one in control of myself.

I never lost hope for a better living, a better way. My childhood experiences have now led me to provide other youths with motivation and to assist them in making positive changes in their lives, communities, and emphasizing belief in their goals. I have grown to have a great compassion for children all across America who lose hope due to the destruction caused by bullying.

Through my foundation, programs are implemented to address the ongoing problem of bullying in our society in hope that unhealthy, social interactions move towards more positive interactions that will build better relationships. I created the Charlie Villanueva Foundation with a mission to support, through education, motivation, and recreational guidance, projects that enhance awareness about bullying, and to provide assessment and intervention tools. I firmly believe that a childhood should have a foundation of hope and belief. Being able to bring a smile to a child's face and show them that those who are different, for whatever reason, can succeed and overcome brings joy to my life. I'm living proof of it.

When life gets to the point where you no longer look forward to tomorrow, there is a lack of belief. Basketball was my escape and it has given me a sense of belonging. Now the taunts of my early childhood drama have turned into admiring cheers as I have found success in becoming an NBA player.

~Charlie Villanueva, Milwaukee Bucks Power Forward

The Joy of Giving

Neither fire nor wind, birth nor death can erase our good deeds.
~Buddha

I was eleven when my grandparents and I fled our country, Hungary, with only the clothes on our backs. We ended up in a refugee camp, also called a displaced persons camp, where we joined throngs of other refugees who had arrived before us.

Our new home was made up of old army barracks that were lined up like soldiers as far as the eye could see. Although the camp was cramped, it was an improvement over the life we had known in our war-torn country for several years.

Soon after our arrival, we were taken to one of the barracks that would serve as our new home. They had small rooms with sleeping cots, a blanket covering the entrance, and not much more. But I was grateful for the "safe" roof over my head, and the warm soup they served us.

Soon, a girl with long, curly black hair came over and introduced herself.

"Hi, my name is Piri, and I sleep on the other side of the cardboard wall, so we're neighbors," she said, smiling at me. I liked her instantly.

"Nice to meet you," I said. "My name is Renie, and I'm eleven. How old are you?"

"I'm nine and a half," Piri replied, "and I can show you around the camp. We've been here over a year now."

So Piri and I became friends, and although I soon made friends my own age, I let her hang around with us. It was nice to have someone look up to me and admire me just because I was older. And it was comforting to have her on the other side of the cardboard wall at night so I could tell my problems to her.

Because most of us in the camp had no money, we looked forward to the donated clothes they gave to us each spring and fall. And if the clothes came from America, we fingered them in awe, for that is where most of us hoped to go.

Of course, the clothes weren't new, but they were clean and good, and we were grateful to get them. This also meant that no one looked better than anyone else at camp.

One winter morning, we had lined up to receive our winter clothes when the man in charge made an announcement.

"This year, a rich lady in America donated this beautiful fur coat in a young girl's size." He held up the coat for everyone to see. *Oohs* and *aahs* rang out through the crowd.

"Since we only have one coat and many young girls, we have decided to have a drawing for it. Girls will come up and try it on, and if the coat fits, they will write their name on a piece of paper and drop it in this box. Then we will draw the name of the winner."

"That coat looks like it will fit you perfectly," my grandmother said. "Go try it on, and put your name in the box."

"It looks too big for me," Piri said. "But I will keep my fingers crossed that you win the coat. It would look beautiful on you."

So I went and felt the coat. It was soft, plush, and lovely to the touch, and I wanted it very badly. So did many of the other girls. And after what seemed like forever, a small girl was asked to reach into the box and draw a name.

"Renie Szilak," the man shouted, waving a piece of paper in the air. "Come on up here, young lady, and get your coat."

I stood there in a daze, not quite believing it was true until Piri nudged me on. I walked up, feeling the hundreds of eyes watching me. And when I walked back, wearing that beautiful coat, I heard a voice in the crowd call out, "You look just like a real princess in that coat!" It was the cutest boy in our school. I blushed, but I hoped I was walking the way a real princess would.

"I can't believe some girl in America gave up this coat," I told Piri as we walked back to our barrack.

"Maybe it no longer fit her," Piri said.

"But it is so beautiful. I won't give it up even after it no longer fits. It will be mine forever!" I vowed.

By this time, Piri had become the closest thing to a sister I would ever have. Since her father was sick and needed her mother at his side most of the time, she spent much of her time with my family and me. And since both of our families had applied for immigration to the United States, a lot of that time was taken up with dreaming about our future lives there.

"I hope we'll be neighbors in America and always be friends," Piri would often say.

"I hope so, too," I would add.

That winter, I felt like a refugee-camp princess. Everywhere I went in my new coat, admiring glances followed, and when I walked to school, boys who usually threw snowballs at the girls let me walk by untouched.

Then spring arrived, and I put the coat in a box and shoved it under my sleeping cot. But I knew it would be there for me next winter.

Not long after, we received the news we had been awaiting. Our papers had been approved, and in September we would board the ship taking us to our new country: the United States of America. I rushed out to find Piri and tell her the good news, thinking their papers had come through, too. I found her outside the barrack, her eyes red from crying.

"What's wrong?" I asked.

"We haven't been approved. They say my dad is sick. Only healthy people can go to America," she replied quietly, turning my world upside-down.

"Oh, I am sorry," I said, putting my arms around her, wishing I could do something more to help her. We spent the remaining few months practically glued to each other, but soon the day we had to part arrived.

Piri and I were about to say our last farewell before my family and I boarded the truck that would take us to the ship.

"Don't forget me. Write to me," Piri said, hugging me as tears rolled down her cheeks. Suddenly, it hit me hard that not only would we never see each other again, but Piri would not be going on to a new life in a new country. I had to somehow ease her sadness. I broke away from the crowd and ran after my grandfather, who was just boarding the truck with a large box in his hand. I yanked the box from him without an explanation and raced back to Piri's side.

"I want you to have the coat. I love you, little sister, and I'll write as soon as we have an address," I said tearfully, shoving the box into her hands.

"But... but you said you would never give up this coat," Piri stammered.

"I'm not giving it up. I'm passing it on to my little sister. Think of me whenever you wear it."

Then I raced to climb aboard the truck, which was about to depart without me. I will never forget the expression on Piri's face as she stood there clutching the box, teetering between sadness and gladness. That was the moment that I, a mostly selfish girl, discovered how much joy there is in giving.

It was mid-November by the time I could send my address to Piri. I received her happy reply just a few days before Christmas. There was a photo enclosed in the letter, too. It showed a girl with curly black hair and a beaming smile. She wore a beautiful fur coat, and she looked just like a real princess it.

And that made my heart happy.

~Renie Burghardt

Forgiving My Dad

*In this world it is not what we take up,
but what we give up, that makes us rich.*
~Henry Ward Beecher

I was seven years old and my little brother was only four on the day my parents told us they were going to get a divorce. I couldn't believe it. I remember every detail of that day. They had taken us to a park by a little stream for a picnic. It was a nice, sunny day, and the spot was really beautiful. We were sitting under a big oak tree when they told us. My parents must have thought that if they took us somewhere nice, maybe the bad news wouldn't be so hard for us to accept. *Yeah, right.*

When they told us they wouldn't be living together anymore, I cried. So did my brother, but I don't think he really knew why. I remember thinking, *How could they do this to us? What is going to happen to us? Was it our fault? They said it wasn't our fault, and they both still loved us very much. If they did, why were they doing this?* Dad told us we would live with him. I found it very hard to understand.

We moved away from the town that we used to live in as a family—just me, my brother, and our dad. I know it was just as hard for our dad to accept as it was for us. Sometimes, I would walk into the bedroom of our small place and find Dad crying. I hated to see him like that. He tried to hide it from us as much as he could, but you could tell he'd been crying because his eyes were red. I pretended not to notice.

My brother missed Mom a lot, and he cried a lot, too. I did my best to be there for him, and I tried to help Dad by cooking things for dinner—simple things like beans on toast. I don't know if it helped much, but I didn't know what else I could do. I would also get my brother ready for school and clean up our bedroom in the morning, so Dad wouldn't have to.

After a few months, Dad told us we would have to go and live with our grandparents for a while. He said he had to go back to college to get his degree so he could get a better-paying job in order to take care of us. At the time, I was so upset and angry. *How could he leave us after we had already lost our mom? He had told us we would live with him!*

We had to take a plane to where our grandparents lived because it was so far away. Our grandparents were pleased to see us, as always, but this time they were especially welcoming. This was going to be our home for a while. It came time for Dad to leave, but I didn't want him to go. He told us he wouldn't be able to visit as often as he would like because he would be very busy at the university. As I watched him walk away, I couldn't believe he was leaving us. *It was bad enough that Mom was gone, but now Dad, too?*

He visited us every couple of months for a few days at a time. It was always hard when he had to leave because we weren't sure when we were going to see him again. Sometimes we would take a flight, just my brother and me, to spend a few days with him. The flight attendants were always really nice to us. But it seemed that by the time we got to Dad's, we had to turn around and go back to our grandparents' house. The visits were never long enough.

Finally, after three years of living with my grandparents, Dad came to visit for the last time. He had finished school, and found a good job and a nice place for us to live. I had missed him for so long that I cried when he told us we'd be living together again and that he was finally taking us home!

When we are kids, we don't really understand why our parents do some of the things they do. I didn't really understand why my dad had to leave us for so long or why we couldn't just stay with him. But he made the difficult choice of having his parents look after us so he could get a better education and find a better job. It was very hard for him, too, but he did the right thing.

Now I understand that what he did, he did for us.

~Sarah McIver

White Water

Life loves to be taken by the lapel and told: "I'm with you kid. Let's go."
~Maya Angelou

The "For Whites Only" signs over the water fountains in H. L. Green's Store really bothered me. I'd seen the signs before, because I spent more time in Green's than any other place. They had cloth in the back, stacked as high as possible on tables, and more came in boxes each week. Momma loved picking through the piles, and when she got off work some evenings we headed to Broad Street. If there was a new shipment of fabric, I knew how to amuse myself while Momma searched for hidden treasures.

I knew where everything was in the store, and I liked walking up and down the aisles pretending I was the boss and I pretended it was up to me to keep the merchandise looking neat. It was also up to me to count all the money at the end of the day. I pretended I had a big box of money and got someone to carry it to the bank for me. Sometimes I even looked through the cloth myself with an eye for something that would look good on my Barbie doll. Grandma had been helping me make clothes for her.

On late weekday afternoons, there weren't many people in the stores downtown. One day, Momma and I got off the bus in front of Green's. A clerk had told her there was going to be a new shipment of cloth coming in that morning, and Momma wanted to get into it before it was all picked over. I knew she was going to be busy for a while, so I decided to walk around the store. I walked up and down the aisles, but nothing looked special to me.

Then I saw the water fountains. All three of them sat there looking back at me. A shiny large one with a big "White Only" sign over it. Next to it was a smaller fountain with a wooden step in front. And, a few feet away, a broken-down, sad fountain with the water running all the time. The handle on the faucet was broken, and the sign above it looked just as bad. A black sign with white letters read, "Colored." The whole thing was dingy, and somebody would have to be very thirsty to take a drink from it.

I'd seen the fountains many times, but this was the first time I'd been around them when no one was watching. No clerks or shoppers were anywhere near. It was a perfect time to finally see exactly what the white folks were hiding. I would finally get to drink some water from the "White Only" fountain. My knees shook. I knew I was taking a big step. Would white people's water kill me? Worst of all, maybe I'd turn white and colored people wouldn't like me anymore. I had to take the chance anyway. If anyone saw me, I would just say I was thirsty and made a mistake. Most of the clerks knew my face from being in the store so much. They would go to the cloth department and get Momma. She would probably just tell me not to try that again, I reasoned.

I quickly ran to the smaller fountain, climbed onto the wooden step and looked behind me to make sure I was still alone. The beige knob on the spigot turned easily. The water ran into the basin. It looked like regular water.

My heart was pounding fast, and my hands were so sweaty I could hardly hold onto the knob. I took a deep breath and waited for my life to flash before my eyes. I knew the water could kill me, but the only thing I saw in my mind was me sitting at my piano recital, trying to remember my piece, "Turkey in the Straw." Maybe I hadn't been alive long enough and what should have been a flash was just a drop. I closed my eyes, leaned down and took a big mouthful. I hopped off the step and raced to the end of one of the aisles. My mouth was filled with water, but my throat wasn't working at all. Try as hard as I could, I couldn't swallow!

My cheeks puffed out, filled with water, and I figured I'd better go and get help. Momma was busy digging in a box of cloth pieces. I pulled at her skirt, and without turning around, she told me we would get a hot dog before we left the store. I couldn't talk with the water in my mouth, so I tugged again. I moaned through the mouthful of water. Thinking I was playing some kind of game, Momma turned away from the cloth long enough to place both hands on my face, smile and squeeze my cheeks. I fought the urge to spit because it would have sprayed all over Momma. I wouldn't have had to worry about the white people's water killing me because she would have finished me off, right on the spot! I gave one big gulp and felt the water go down my throat all at once. Momma went back to her cloth box, and I headed toward my favorite aisle in the toy department to die or turn white, whichever came first.

I carefully looked at my hands to see if I was changing color. I stopped and stared in a mirror on the cosmetics aisle. My eyes were as brown as ever. I felt the same as always, just a bit scared. Finally, Momma came to the toy department and said it was time to get a hot dog. I was happy she still recognized me.

The lunch counter at H. L. Green's was my favorite of all places downtown — the one in the back, of course, the one up front was for white people. The stools were uncomfortable, but the hot dogs, fries and drinks made up for everything.

I was afraid to tell Momma I'd taken a drink from the white fountain because I didn't want her to worry in case I didn't make it. I decided it was best not to say anything.

After we got home, I checked in the bathroom mirror all evening to see if I'd changed. My heart didn't feel weak, but I wasn't sure how a dying person was supposed to feel. No one had to argue with me to go to bed that night.

I put on my best nightgown and took my favorite pink teddy bear to bed with me. I thought maybe I would fall asleep and wake up the next morning white as snow. Granddad would wonder where the little white girl in my bed had come from. Grandma would fall down on her knees in prayer, and I didn't know what Momma would do. Maybe dying in my sleep would make things easier for everyone. I lay there waiting for something to happen. I was afraid to close my eyes.

The next morning, I was happy to hear the rooster crowing! I had all my parts and was still breathing. I rushed into the bathroom to look at myself. I was the same color as always and everything was in the right places. Colored people who drank from forbidden fountains didn't turn white or die!

The next time I went into H. L. Green's Store and saw the drinking fountains with the "For Whites Only" signs, I giggled, *That's what you think!*

~Jayme Washington Smalley

The Bionic Woman
Is Black

*I feel that the most important requirement in success is
learning to overcome failure. You must learn to tolerate it,
but never accept it.*
~Reggie Jackson

can still remember my mother and father sitting my brother
and me down one summer day and explaining the Educational
Integration Program that was to be instituted in the fall. The
program was designed to take inner-city kids—like us—and
provide them the opportunity for a better education in the tradition-
ally white suburban communities. I was not sure what "better education" meant, but I trusted my mom and dad when they said that this
was something they had never had—a chance at receiving an equal
and fair education.

On the first day of school, riding on the bus an eerie silence and
thick tension in the air confirmed that the other kids on the bus were
just as anxious, hopeful and frightened as me. When our bus arrived
on the school grounds, I expected a big "Welcome" sign greeting us
as the first class of integration students. After all, this was 1979 and
we were in Los Angeles—right?

To my surprise, however, we were greeted with eggs, tomatoes
and rocks thrown at our bus. Fear and confusion overwhelmed me. I

had seen this type of thing on TV. Tears of pain and anger stung my eyes when I witnessed water hoses hurting the people marching for equality, and I got chills when I heard Dr. King say, "… one day little black kids and little white kids can play together and go to school together… free at last, free at last." I realized that I was that little black girl he was talking about, and maybe staying in this scary school with these mean people was my way of contributing to what Dr. King had died for. If I ran back to safety, then we really weren't "free at last." So I convinced my parents to let me stay.

An athlete since the age of eight, I had just begun to run track when tryouts were announced for both a Charlie's Angels and a Bionic Woman competition. I was thrilled and sure I could win. At ten years old I ran the fastest in the entire school. I had mastered my roll… stop… point… and "Freeze, sucker!" to sheer perfection. In the days leading up to the big competition, which included over forty hopeful little girls and over seventy-five curious onlookers, I sharpened every skill to ensure my placement. I knew all the key lines of both the Angels and the Bionic Woman.

On the day of the big competition I was calm and assured.

"Ready. Set. Go!"

I was out in front instantly! When I finished the one-hundred-yard race, many of the girls were just approaching the seventy-five-yard mark. This gave me the additional boost of confidence I needed as the only African American in the competition. The judges were five very popular girls and a boy I guessed represented Charlie.

Only the first six of us who placed in the race advanced to the "Roll, Freeze and Pose" competition. I waited to be the last candidate, and my competitors did just as I thought: They giggled, fumbled and foiled the freeze. I, however, froze right on the mark—hot asphalt and all. My performance was so impressive that the audience gave a gasping "WOW." You would have thought I had been an Angel for years—at least since I had been six!

Finally, it was time to decide who would be Charlie's Angels and the Bionic Woman for the entire school year. I stood there as the judges huddled, periodically looking over their shoulders before their final selection. With six girls left, three would be Angels, one would be the Bionic Woman, and one would be alternate. This would leave only one person who would not be selected at all.

I looked to both sides to see who that could be. Maybe Cindy—she came in last in the race, or Kim—she couldn't coordinate herself enough to roll and freeze. Maybe it would be Michelle, who made a habit of calling everyone ugly names and just did not come across as an Angel. I felt sorry for whoever was not going to be chosen.

"The decision is made!" exclaimed Charlie's agent.

"The official Charlie's Angels will be Diane, Tiffany…," I felt my heart sink, "and Cindy."

"The official Bionic Woman…," the young judge went on to say.

My mind was racing, partly in disbelief and partly in hopefulness. *One chance, I know I will be chosen for this,* I thought, as I could feel my palms sweating and my chest getting tight to hold back the tears.

"Bionic Woman will be Michelle." He went on to announce, "Kim was chosen as the alternate."

Boos began to fly from the audience.

As each person approached me to protest the decision, I could see nothing but blur between my tears. My head spun, and my anger rose. I had been cheated and I didn't know why. I stood frozen on my mark. I replayed the entire chain of events in my head to see what I could have done better or should have done with more passion. After five horrifically long minutes of scanning my brain for answers, I concluded that I could not have produced better results. I had outperformed every other girl.

I deserved an answer, so I walked directly over to the judges, "Why was I not selected if I outperformed everyone in each competition?"

Suddenly, as if waiting for me to ask that question, the school ground fell silent. Everyone stopped and stared, and I wondered then if I had made a big mistake. *Nothing could embarrass me more than what just happened,* or so I thought.

The judges just looked at me with no sense of care or concern for my feelings and asked the question that would change my life forever, "What hero have you ever seen that was black?"

Another girl taunted, "We did not choose you, Lisa, because you don't look like any Angel or the Bionic Woman, but you can try out again next year if you happen to begin to look more like them in the future."

I walked away crying, as they laughed hysterically.

That day in September 1979, I became acquainted with some of the pain and hurt my grandparents and great ancestors endured. Since that year in fifth grade, I committed myself to being a hero for other little girls who needed one, and so I became a motivational speaker.

Twenty years later, during my keynote at a church in Los Angeles, I shared my commitment to change and the importance of empowerment. I emphasized that the cost of living this dream can never exceed the cost of throwing it away. I received a standing ovation from the audience and was elated and overjoyed.

As I made my way through the crowd stopping to acknowledge admiring guests, a hand touched my shoulder and the most familiar voice said, "You are so inspiring; you are a true heroine."

I turned and nearly fainted. I stood amidst three thousand people and hugged Lindsay Wagner (television's Bionic Woman), scrambling to explain that she was my longtime favorite.

She said clearly and with conviction, "Today, you became my favorite and the true Bionic Woman."

On that day, I forgave each of those judges from my childhood for judging my outside—and not seeing my inside. I also forgave myself for being angry for the dark skin I was born in and the pain that it brought. I knew in that moment that it didn't matter which heroine I looked like, because I now knew exactly which heroine I resembled: me.

~Lisa Nichols

Before
and After

There is no education like adversity.
~Benjamin Disraeli

The sound of gunshots woke me up in the middle of the night. I turned to my alarm clock. The red numbers read 2:00 A.M., blurring my vision. "Ah man," I said, realizing that I had to wake up for school in five hours. Now I wouldn't be able to sleep. I wondered who was shooting the gun outside, and if this had something to do with the day my cousin brought a silver pistol to the room we shared. Looking down to his bed, I heard our black iron bunk bed screech. I screamed, "Ricky did you hear that?" When he didn't reply, I worried that he was dead. I jumped down to the freezing cold floor and my feet felt as if I were standing on a bag of spikes. "Ricky!" I yelled frantically, but he still did not budge. I put my hands on his shoulders, moving him over. Finally, after what seemed like an hour, he awoke.

"What the hell are you doing?" he said. I started to say that I was worried, but I didn't want him to think I was "soft," so instead I said I needed to ask him a question.

"It's two in the morning; wait until tomorrow," he yelled. I went back up to bed, with the boulder of my cousin's death off my shoulders. I closed my eyes, which felt like they had been open for decades.

I awoke to the sound of my clock. It was 7:00 A.M. My bed felt like it was made of bricks, but my body wouldn't move. I knew I had to get to school.

I washed my face, brushed my teeth, and then put on the blue slacks and white button-down shirt that we were required to wear. Walking out of the living room, I realized that I was the only one awake in the whole five-bedroom apartment. Twelve of us lived there, and out of the ten that attended school, I was the only one ready. My aunt and uncle were the two exceptions who didn't have to get up.

As I opened the big, metal door, the wind rushed into my face, giving me chills. I walked to school quickly, trying to avoid my friends who refused to go.

My best friend, Kenneth, spotted me. "Darren!" he yelled through the morning sky. Running up, he said, "Where are you going?"

"To school. Can't you see the book bag, stupid?"

"Why are you going?" he yelled. "Your aunt doesn't care if you do or don't."

Annoyed, I just walked away from him, not giving him an answer. It was true; I could do anything I wanted and not get into trouble, at least not with my aunt and uncle. "Why am I going?" I asked myself, as I walked up the school steps. It was simple — I needed school. School was my way to get out of the ghetto. It was what would give me a better future.

I walked into my class and sat at my designated desk. Everyone was quiet and their eyes were red. My teacher, one of the toughest people in the world, stood up in front of the class with tears flowing down his face. I looked at the desk next to mine and realized my friend Jose, who usually sat there, wasn't at his desk. Jose always had my back in everything.

"Where is he?" I whispered to Ashley, to the right of me. She started to cry, and I suddenly realized that my friend would not be in school that day — or ever again.

"He was shot and killed last night," she sobbed. I felt my eyes start to water. One of my closest friends was dead, and memories of death in my own family started to run through my head like a movie I couldn't forget. Anger filled my body and I became tense. I walked out of the class, through the frigid streets and up to Jose's apartment. I found his mother weeping in her room. I could not look in her eyes. She hugged me and told me that he was gone and we sat there together, crying.

In the funeral parlor, it was quiet and smelled like old people. Tears were in everyone's eyes. My friends were there, anxious to get the people who did this. I, on the other hand, only wanted to make my life better before something like this happened to me. I stood up in front of everyone and gave a testimonial. "Jose was always there for me. I love him and know he is going to a better place, to heaven. Many people want to get the people back who did this to him, but we have to let it go. If we don't, it will be a constant revenge circle and life will end for all of us. It's time we actually started to work and go to school. Higher education is the key for us to live in a more civil society. There is a struggle of poverty and violence in the African-American society as a whole, and we need to change that."

As I walked back to my seat, I got stares of disbelief. I looked at Jose's mother, and she looked at me with agreement. I knew she was proud of me, and I knew life had to change. "Rest in peace, Jose," I said as I walked out of the church.

That was all in eighth grade.

I wake up to the sounds of raccoons bashing through the metal garbage can and birds chirping. Looking across at my roommate, Ramin, I realize that I'm late. I quickly rummage through my clothing to find something suitable for school. Now I live in Swarthmore, a sleepy suburb of Philadelphia. I put on a wrinkled shirt and blue jeans so I can run down the street to catch the yellow school bus with all the other teens in the neighborhood. I attend Strath Haven High School, where I am an ABC scholar. The ABC program takes academically inclined inner city students and brings them to live in a better school district. The brakes of the bus screech as we stop in front of the main entrance. I slowly walk into the school and down the stairs to my English class. My new school is difficult, but it assures me that my hard work will soon lead to college, a great job, and hope for the future. I am one step closer to my goals.

~Dan Haze Barten

Conversation Starters

1. In "Annie Wiggle-Do" on page 355, Brenda is going through a tough time. How does Annie help her get through it?

2. In the story "White Water" on page 369, Jayme tells us a story from a time in history when she grew up. What does she think the store sign means?

3. "Before and After" begins on page 377. In this story, Dan's circumstances change from the beginning to the end. How is his life different before and after the death of his friend Jose?

Meet Amy Newmark

Amy Newmark was a writer, speaker, Wall Street analyst and business executive in the worlds of finance and telecommunications for more than thirty years. Today she is publisher, editor-in-chief and coauthor of the Chicken Soup for the Soul book series. By curating and editing inspirational true stories from ordinary people who have had extraordinary experiences, Amy has kept the twenty-one-year-old Chicken Soup for the Soul brand fresh and relevant, and still part of the social zeitgeist.

Amy graduated *magna cum laude* from Harvard University where she majored in Portuguese and minored in French. She wrote her thesis about popular, spoken-word poetry in Brazil, which involved traveling throughout Brazil and meeting with poets and writers to collect their stories. She is delighted to have come full circle in her writing career — from collecting poetry "from the people" in Brazil as a twenty-year-old to, three decades later, collecting stories and poems "from the people" for Chicken Soup for the Soul.

Amy has a national syndicated newspaper column and is a frequent radio and TV guest, passing along the real-life lessons and useful tips she has picked up from reading and editing thousands of Chicken Soup for the Soul stories.

She and her husband are the proud parents of four grown children and in her limited spare time, Amy enjoys visiting them, hiking, and reading books that she did not have to edit.

Meet Dr. Milton Boniuk

Dr. Milton Boniuk has practiced ophthalmology for nearly sixty years, and is The Caroline F. Elles Chair of Ophthalmology and Professor of Ophthalmology at Baylor College of Medicine in Houston, Texas. A native of Nova Scotia, Dr. Boniuk attended medical school at Dalhousie University in Halifax, Nova Scotia before moving to the United States for his residency at Jefferson Medical College in Philadelphia, followed by a fellowship at the Armed Forces Institute of Pathology in Washington, D.C.

Dr. Boniuk and his wife Laurie live near their children and grand-children in Houston. The Boniuk family has a strong commitment to philanthropy and a vision for change. Their belief that the world can be made a better place guides the work of The Boniuk Foundation, which sponsored this collection of Chicken Soup for the Soul stories. The Foundation believes that all religions, cultures, and ethnicities have a unique contribution to share with the world, and that differences among individuals are to be celebrated and not feared. Thus, the values of compassion, tolerance, and respect must be instilled in our young people, and this volume is designed to do that in an entertaining and accessible way.

Dr. Boniuk and his wife Laurie have also funded The Boniuk Institute for the Study and Advancement of Religious Tolerance at Rice University, with the mission of promoting research, education, outreach, and better parenting to foster religious tolerance by using innovative methods to reach young people, their parents, and their grandparents. The Institute's logo is seen on the cover of this book, with its three key words—Tolerance, Respect, and Compassion—surrounded by the symbols of many of the world's major religions.

Sharing Happiness, Inspiration, and Wellness

Real people sharing real stories, every day, all over the world. In 2007, *USA Today* named *Chicken Soup for the Soul* one of the five most memorable books in the last quarter-century. With over 100 million books sold to date in the U.S. and Canada alone, more than 200 titles in print, and translations into more than forty languages, "chicken soup for the soul" is one of the world's best-known phrases.

Today, twenty-two years after we first began sharing happiness, inspiration and wellness through our books, we continue to delight our readers with new titles, but have also evolved beyond the bookstore, with wholesome and balanced pet food, delicious nutritious comfort food, and a major motion picture in development. As a socially conscious company, we use the sales of our products to give back, supporting numerous non-profits in the U.S. and across the globe. Whatever you're doing, wherever you are, Chicken Soup for the Soul is "always there for you™." Thanks for reading!